A Practitioner's Guide to Adapting the NIST Cybersecurity Framework

Volume 2 of the
**Create, Protect, and Deliver
Digital Business Value** series

a Williams Lea company

Published by TSO (The Stationery Office), part of Williams Lea,
www.tsoshop.co.uk

Mail, Telephone, Fax & Email
TSO
PO Box 29, Norwich, NR3 1GN
Telephone orders/General enquiries: 0333 202 5070
Fax orders: 0333 202 5080
Email: customer.services@tso.co.uk
Textphone 0333 202 5077
www.tsoshop.co.uk

DVMS Institute LLC
742 Mink Ave., #135
Murrells Inlet, SC 29576
Phone (401) 764-0721
www.dvmsinstitute.com

If you have any feedback that you would like to record in our change control log, please send this to
commissioning@williamslea.com

First edition (2022)
ISBN 9780117093959

J003938305

Contents

Foreword

"Did you hear about the security breach over the weekend?" is a common Monday morning greeting amongst IT professionals. It's become so common, in fact, that we aren't even shocked by it any more. But regardless of how common it is, the impact of cybersecurity incidents on organizations can be catastrophic. The average cost per data breach incident is $4.4 million according to the 2022 report from IBM Security.* This is enough to get the attention of senior management and the boards of directors of any organization – indeed, it is enough to threaten the very survival of many of them.

As if that weren't enough, a cybersecurity incident also causes an interruption of business value creation and damage to reputation. As bad as that sounds, of greater concern, perhaps, is the increase in cyber warfare between and against governments. Here, the compromise of highly sensitive information presents an all-too-real threat to people, governments, the environment, and beyond.

While there's been much progress in improving the general state of cybersecurity, the scope, severity, and frequency of compromises continue to rise. It seems like the bad guys are winning. But there is hope. In *A Practitioner's Guide to Adapting the NIST Cybersecurity Framework*, authors David Moskowitz and David Nichols get to the core of what I believe is the underlying challenge we face: that cybersecurity, by and large, is treated as a standalone function; a department tasked with the impossible job of singlehandedly securing the organization and its data from those who would do it harm.

The NIST Cybersecurity Framework (NIST-CSF) has become the gold standard in cybersecurity practice, but it leaves a gaping hole in the how-to department. Until now, the practitioner was left to their own devices to "implement" the NIST-CSF in their organization. The very phrase "implement NIST-CSF" sets the stage to attempt to apply foreign controls to existing "how we do things" practices. This unnatural forcing of one upon the other with limited connection to organizational strategy and business risk is set to fail.

The authors advocate a systems approach where organizational strategy embraces the concept of strategy-risk as a single unit: not "strategy here, risk there" nor "strategy informed by risk" (or even "strategy to address risk"). But strategy-risk – the recognition that creating value separate from how that value is secured from risk – is problematic. What they have created is a practical, start-where-you-are overlay that provides a holistic approach to create, protect, and deliver digital value. It offers practical, adaptive guidance that can be applied immediately, regardless of how an organization is currently structured and functioning.

At its heart is the Digital Value Management System™ (DVMS), which is "… not one-size-fits-all, but a systems model applicable to all, regardless of size." The overlay concept is important as it allows an organization to identify the minimum viable capabilities necessary to achieve the desired ability to create, protect, and deliver digital value. The overlay acknowledges existing capabilities and identifies where capabilities are either missing or require additional improvement. What emerges is an "improvement roadmap to deliver adequately created and protected digital value." And with it, a plan and a governance and execution system to ensure that the organization's strategy-risk is baked into the organization's DNA.

The only time I put *A Practitioner's Guide to Adapting the NIST Cybersecurity Framework* down was to pause to let the concepts soak in. I found myself constantly saying "yes!" as if the authors have walked the journey I've been on for the last several decades in IT leadership and operations. The approach presented here addresses the challenges I've seen throughout my career, from support technician to CIO and consulting; from Fortune 10 to government agencies, to small and growing companies.

I sincerely hope you find this book to be as insightful and practical as I have.

Greg Sanker
Former CIO, senior IT leader, author, speaker

*Bree Fowler (2022), reporting for CNET (US media website).

Preface

When we started on our journey to write a three-volume series about how to create, protect, and deliver digital business value, we originally intended this book to be a "how to guide." And we succeeded, but the scope of the "how to" aspect grew considerably.

Our thoughts mimic Wayne Dyer's quote in Chapter 3: "If you change the way you look at things, the things you look at change." As we looked at things from multiple perspectives, the scope of what we were looking at exploded. The more questions we asked, the more we learned, and the more we realized how much more is discoverable. Our journey through this book is as much about our maturing understanding of value and what it takes to protect it, as it is about "grokking"* – taking a systems view of digital business risk management.

This book is about understanding the role of cybersecurity, not as a technical endeavor but as an aspect of managing digital business risk that results in treating value creation and value protection as two sides of the same coin. We focus on the practitioner's journey of understanding and what it means for an organization to change how it looks at the stakeholder value it creates. It prepares the practitioner to take a systems view of value and its protection, and to look at cybersecurity as an aspect of quality and value – not as a technical undertaking.

We take the practitioner on a deep dive into the CPD Model and describe how it operationalizes the organizational capability to create, protect, and deliver digital business value. In doing so, the practitioner learns how the organization can become highly adaptive and achieve cyber resilience as an outcome of managing digital business risk.

Our intention is to change how the reader looks at things and to develop a different perspective and mental model of cybersecurity that encompasses the entirety of digital business risk management. This approach prepares the reader for *Living on the Edge of Chaos*, Volume 3 in this series.

David Moskowitz
Executive Director for Content Development, DVMS Institute LLC

David Nichols
Executive Director, DVMS Institute LLC

---

*The root word "grok" was coined by Robert Heinlein (1961) in his book, *Stranger in a Strange Land*. It's become part of the English language, meaning "to understand profoundly and intuitively." https://www.merriam-webster.com/dictionary/grok.

About the authors

David Moskowitz

David is the content architect of the DVMS Institute. In this role, he actively looks for and works with subject matter experts to develop relevant content for the institute.

David started his formal career as an operating systems programmer and systems architect, before going on to look at different forms of systems and complexity while serving in the US Army. After his military service, he continued to apply a systems approach to his job, working on an anti-submarine warfare program for the US Department of Defense. By applying a whole-systems perspective, he addressed organizational and inter-personal issues and created a high-performing team.

The team stumbled into an approach that today many people would recognize as parts of IT service management and Kanban. It included a formalized approach to managing change, combined with incremental development performed in short iterations that received constant feedback. Later, as a consultant, he assisted organizations in adopting what they considered to be technical disruptions, applying a critical lesson learned from experience: "Every problem was, at its core, a people problem, not a technology problem." Technology was either an enabler or an inhibitor. The recurring mantra of these efforts was, "Solve the problem; don't treat the symptom."

David first met Dave Nichols in 2008, and since then they have worked together to develop a systems approach to accelerate the creation and delivery of business value. David views cybersecurity as a critical aspect of quality and value.

David thanks his wife Rosemary for her patience, tolerance and encouragement, without whom this book would not have been possible. He can be contacted at david.moskowitz@dvmsinstitute.com; for more information, visit www.dvmsinstitute.com.

David Nichols

Dave is the executive director of the DVMS Institute. The institute's mission is to enable organizations to create, protect, and deliver digital business value through a curated portfolio of content and programs that bring value to its member stakeholders. Dave's role is to work with the industry's leading practitioners in risk management, service management, cybersecurity, assurance, and business leadership to produce industry-leading guidance and programs that will enable organizations to survive and thrive in a digital business world.

Dave spent his formative years on US Navy submarines, where he gained his knowledge of complex systems and how to function in high-performance teams. He took these skills into civilian life, where he built a successful career in software development and service delivery.

In 2000, Dave formed itSM Solutions with his partners, Janet Kuhn and Rick Lemieux, to create and deliver service management certification training and consulting programs to Fortune 500 companies. In 2015, his team created the award-winning APMG-accredited NIST Cybersecurity Professional (NCSP®) training scheme, which teaches organizations how to rapidly engineer and operationalize a cybersecurity risk management program. Dave also oversaw the certification of the NCSP program by the National Cyber Security Centre in the UK and its listing as a qualified training scheme by the US Department of Homeland Security's CISA organization.

Dave would like to thank Zelda, his wife of more than 50 years, for her support and inspiration when it was needed most. He can be contacted at david.nichols@dvmsinstitute.com; for more information, visit www.dvmsinstitute.com.

Acknowledgments

DVMS Institute and TSO kindly thank those who participated in the review process:

Roy Atkinson, CEO, Clifton Butterfield LLC

Michael Battistella, President and FSO, Solutions³ LLC

Patti Blackstaffe, CEO of the Strategic Sense group of companies: GlobalSway, Small Biz Creative, and In The Lead Seat

Ian W. Daykin, entrepreneur and business consultant

Russell Herrell

Bradley Laatsch, North America delivery manager for HPE Education Services, Hewlett Packard Enterprise

Rick Lemieux, Executive Director and Chief Product Officer, DVMS Institute

Ed Moses, Director, Specialist Industries Ltd

Anthony Orr, Solutions Director for SDI Presence, ITIL author, ITSM thought leader

Greg Sanker, former CIO, senior IT leader, author, speaker

Patrick von Schlag, President, Deep Creek Center Inc.

Dedicated to Rick Lemieux and Lori Perrault – they are responsible for the latitude we have in what we do and provide the support necessary to get it done.

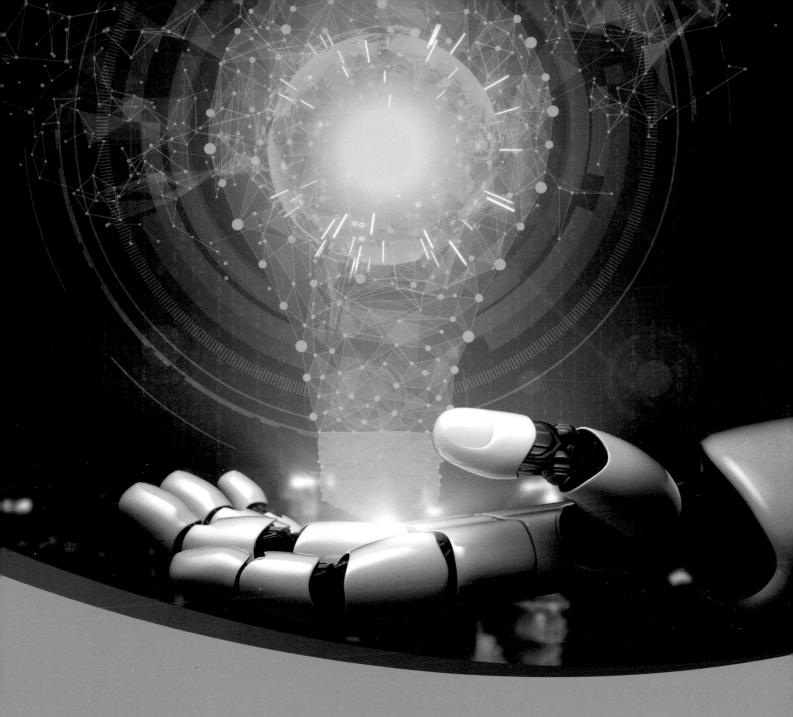

CHAPTER 1
The journey

1 The journey

"The journey of a thousand miles begins with a single step."
Lao Tzu

Lao Tzu's statement is incomplete. Yes, the journey begins with a single step. However, if your starting point is the New Jersey shore (the beaches of the Atlantic Ocean), and your objective is to get to the Pacific Ocean, your first step should be to the west: walking east will only serve to get you wet. Consequently, we extend Lao Tzu's quote to read, "The journey of a thousand miles begins with a single step *in the right direction.*"

Starting a cybersecurity journey in the right direction requires maturing existing organizational capabilities first. Why? Consider that there are cybersecurity control requirements for cybersecurity incidents and configuration management. Instead of adding and supporting these requirements separately, integrate them into existing organizational capabilities. This approach is consistent with the idea that cybersecurity is an organizational responsibility, not something to be siloed in a single department.

This last idea, organizational responsibility, is essential because the actual destination isn't cybersecurity, it's the management of digital business risk. The destination applies a strategy-risk-based approach[1] that creates and protects digital business value, achieving cyber resilience as a by-product.

This book covers this idea in the context of the Digital Value Management System™ (DVMS), which combines a principle-based enterprise risk management framework with a holistic view of the organization in the form of systems thinking. In other words, the cybersecurity journey starts by improving or adding organizational capabilities; the journey addresses expanding existing capabilities rather than adding distinct requirements for cybersecurity segregated from what we might label "business as usual." The initial goal is to be proactive and stabilize existing capabilities before tackling cybersecurity issues. The goal is cyber resilience, not cybersecurity.

As part of stabilizing the environment, understand and document how work flows within the organization: not how it's "supposed" to flow, but the reality. Also, pay attention to how communication, innovation, and improvement flow. Sometimes this will follow an organization (org) chart, but many times it won't. It is essential to understand reality versus assuming. This approach is the only way to leverage the system to make meaningful and long-lasting (i.e., "sticky") changes.

What do we mean by the phrase "leverage the system"? The answer to this question lies in one of our first principles (covered in detail in Chapter 5): "Adopt and apply systems thinking." The principle potentially requires learning to see and perceive the organization differently – see the organization as dynamic and interconnected elements contributing to the value it delivers to stakeholders.

---

1 We formulated the idea of a single entity "strategy-risk" based on the authors' experience that treating strategy and risk as separate concepts wasn't working. Then a study by North Carolina State University (2022) formally confirmed our approach. Strategy-risk treats the two as inseparable: two faces of the same coin.

The DVMS is neither framework nor method: it is a scalable overlay that applies to any organization. It is composed of three layers:

- The top layer is what the organization already does. It's a black box to the outside world. It could use existing frameworks and methods. These are the organizational capabilities to stabilize
- The middle layer, which we call the *Z-X Model*,[2] provides the seven minimal viable capabilities any organization needs: the capabilities to govern, assure, plan, design, change, execute, and innovate.[3] Every framework or methodology, practice, or process is subsumed by one or more of these minimum viable capabilities
- The bottom layer of a model supports the creation, protection, and delivery (including support) of digital business value. We call the model the *CPD Model*™ (CPD being an abbreviation for "creating, protecting, and delivering" digital business value). It represents an approach to linking strategy and governance with governance and execution to create and protect digital business value.

Cybersecurity is a single aspect of digital business risk management. The overall goal should be cyber resilience that enables the organization to create, and appropriately support and protect, the delivery of digital business value.

There are only two possibilities for adopting and adapting a cybersecurity informative reference. You treat cybersecurity as an organizational responsibility with accountability starting at the top, or you don't. It's a binary choice. If you want to start your cybersecurity journey in the right direction, take the first step to learn to see the whole, not a hole.

One of the themes repeated throughout this book is that value creation and value protection are two sides of the same coin. It's essential to do both: value must be protected appropriately for the organization, understanding that value changes over time. Cybersecurity is an intrinsic aspect of business value.

The idea of a shift in perception is associated with another theme: the need to apply systems thinking, which views cybersecurity as an enterprise responsibility, and not that of a single department (or similar internal organizational unit).

1.1 Using the book

Chapter 2 introduces the key to taking a proactive stance to protect created digital value: anticipating what threat actors will do, requiring asking different questions that have their basis in systems thinking. The purpose of asking questions is twofold:

- The initial questions provide the basis to identify the business systems (and everything that underpins, supports, or enables them), which is essential to the mission to create and protect digital business value
- Additional questions help determine the system weaknesses, allowing probing and proactively determining where and how to direct remediation efforts.

Chapter 3 provides an approach to systems thinking and explains how it differs from traditional thinking. Systems thinking, or thinking in systems, is not something you *do*: it's something you *learn* and *practice*. Systems thinking is similar to agile in that the organization doesn't *do* agile: the organization *becomes* agile. The people in the organization must learn to see the whole (the organization as a whole), not a hole (i.e., the organization viewed as siloed departments). It's critical for everyone in the organization, whether a single-person company or a million-people multinational enterprise, to understand that value created and not appropriately protected has little to no value for stakeholders.

---

2   The name is derived from the internal solid lines (the Z) and the dotted line (making an X).
3   We apply the term "innovate" to the capability as a superset of "improve." There are four aspects to "innovate" (incremental, sustaining, adaptive, and disruptive) that are covered in more detail later in this book.

The chapter reviews a simple supply chain simulation game and looks at the lessons from gameplay. This discussion provides a basis for understanding how to apply leverage (and at what points) to modify the system. Knowledge management is a critical aspect of human systems. You'll also find this topic covered. Finally, the chapter decomposes the CPD Model, explaining how it supports digital business risk management by creating, protecting, and delivering digital business value.

Chapter 4 provides a detailed link between cybersecurity and the DVMS, starting with an in-depth examination of the Z-X Model capabilities. The chapter introduces the Digital Value Capability Maturity Model (DVCMM) to gauge the organizational ability to use the Z-X Model to create and deliver appropriately protected digital business value. The chapter builds on the systems thinking material in Chapter 3 in the context of the CPD Model.

Chapter 5 covers an adaptive way of working. This is a strategy-risk-informed approach to using cybersecurity to manage digital business risk and create and protect digital business value. It incorporates a principle-based approach to enterprise risk management – the very core of what it takes to manage digital business risk. Why an adaptive approach? It's the best way for the organization to keep pace with the dynamics of the changing environment, including internal and external factors and the constantly evolving threat landscape. The chapter covers organizing to create and protect digital business value – and this isn't an org-chart-based approach. The chapter also covers a generic approach to agile as an essential aspect of an adaptive way of working. The final discussion in the chapter addresses the relationship between agility, resilience, the CPD Model, and managing digital business risk to improve the cybersecurity posture.

Chapter 6 provides detailed information on integrating cybersecurity into the Z-X Model capabilities and resulting practice areas, as distinct from an approach that consigns cybersecurity to technical departments. It details the dependence of cybersecurity on organizational capabilities represented by the Z-X Model – doing so by taking a phased approach that uses the DVMS FastTrack™ model.

Chapter 7 provides a deep dive into strategy-risk in the context of the CPD Model. It highlights the need to consider the material covered previously in this book – specifically regarding the importance of adopting new or different mental models that facilitates asking different questions. The chapter also covers the goal, question, metric (GQM) approach and Question Outcome–Question Metric (QO–QM) to learn to ask better systems-thinking-based questions.

We briefly introduced the idea of the DVMS as a scalable overlay to address the digital business risk management critical to creating and protecting the delivery of digital business value in the first book in the series, *Fundamentals of Adopting the NIST Cybersecurity Framework* (Moskowitz and Nichols, 2022). **Chapter 8** covers how this works, with suggestions that apply to any organization, regardless of size or geography.

1.2   For NIST Cybersecurity Professional students

The material in this book provides the rubric for the NIST Cybersecurity Professional (NCSP) Practitioner and Specialist courses. It presents the narrative that accompanies your course material. The book contains more information than will fit into the course. Consequently, we recommend that you read the whole book rather than focusing on just the material in the syllabus.

The tuition for NCSP students includes the book. For the non-student, because the information in this book is more in-depth, you do not need the *Fundamentals* book to understand the application to an organization.

If you understand the flow of the story in this book, it will be easier to pass the course examination.

1.3   The rest of the story

This book continues the story regarding a practical approach to adopting the NIST Framework for Improving Critical Infrastructure Cybersecurity (NIST-CSF) that is covered in the *Fundamentals* book – this time at the practitioner and specialist level. There are several concepts and models introduced in that volume covered in more detail in this volume, including:

- Systems thinking
- The DVMS, and the DVMS as a scalable overlay
- The CPD Model
- The Z-X Model
- Strategy-risk
- The COSO[4] principles.

The *Fundamentals* book is a good place to start if you want guidance in adopting the NIST Cybersecurity Framework.

This book and the rest of the series support the journey in the right direction to build a resilient organization that manages digital business risk. Enjoy the journey.

---

4   We recommend the Committee of Sponsoring Organizations of the Treadway Commission (COSO) approach because of its principle-based approach to risk management. What is important are the principles, not the specific COSO approach. The source for the COSO principles is the COSO Internal Control Integrated Framework (2013) and is used with permission of AICPA. On the COSO website, you can find the executive summary (COSO, 2017) and a summary of the COSO principles and approach (COSO, 2019).

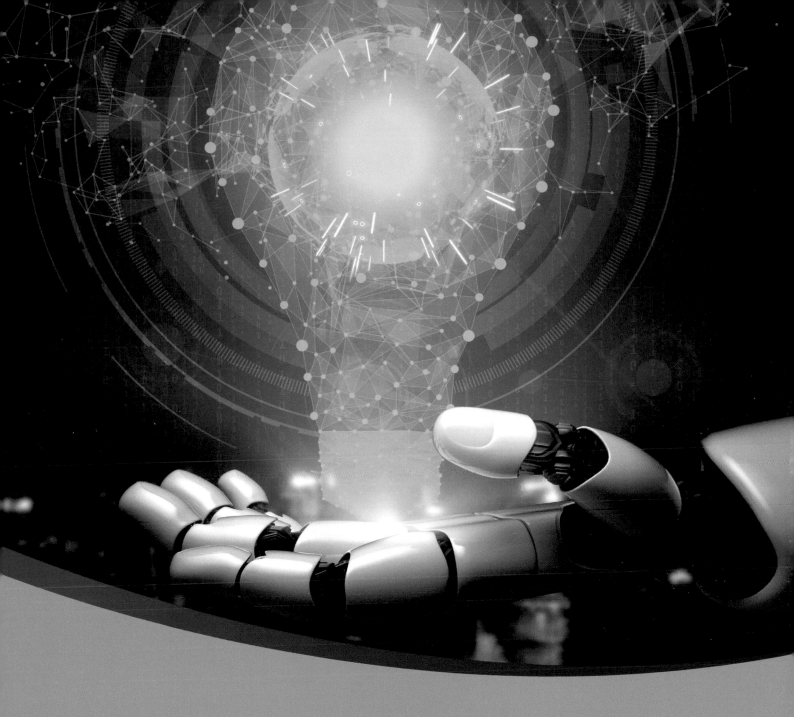

CHAPTER 2
Be the menace within – a proactive approach

2 Be the menace within – a proactive approach

"When you have exhausted all possibilities, remember this – you haven't."
Thomas Edison

Deliberately being the menace within, what many call *white-hat hacking*, applies insider knowledge to the process of exposing risks to digital assets. Being the menace differs from traditional penetration testing in that it is broader than just trying to get in. It also considers insiders who have intimate knowledge of your systems and deliberately or accidentally expose or threaten what the organization would rather keep private and safe.

Cyber resilience depends on four primary factors:

- Identifying your digital assets (including data, systems, applications, and more)
- Knowing the relative value of each asset
- Ensuring appropriate governance and resulting policies to protect the assets
- Planning for the inevitable cyber incident.[5]

Digital assets represent a target for threat actors. The organization must accept the likelihood of a cybersecurity breach. Organizational governance must provide appropriate planning and consideration for this eventuality, define reasonable precautions to attempt to prevent it, and respond to a penetration when prevention isn't sufficient. It is equally essential for the organization to assume that no amount of protection will prevent the occurrence.

Even though the discussion is about digital assets, which might sound like a technical issue, it's not. Identifying digital assets starts with the business systems that use them.

2.1 Identify and prioritize business systems

Once you have identified the business systems, the next step is to identify the layers of technical systems and resources that support each of them. This activity serves two purposes. First, it lets you map the relationships between business and digital assets. Second, this information is required to implement appropriate security controls for configuration management. This approach is consistent with the NIST-CSF's five core functions: Identify, Protect, Detect, Respond, and Recover (NIST, 2018).

This methodology is essential because it sets up the effort to prioritize cybersecurity efforts. Different digital assets require different levels of protection. The correct approach to strategy-risk requires that the most significant contributors to the organizational strategic intent are given higher protection and monitoring levels than others – and this is where digital asset governance comes into play.

The core idea is to take a holistic view of the organization, starting with the business systems combined with a potentially different perspective regarding the "system" represented by the organization. This leads to the idea of systems thinking and a related question: "What is systems thinking?"

---

5   The organization must accept the likelihood of a cybersecurity breach. Organizational governance defines the risk appetite (expressed as part of strategy-risk) and establishes approaches to a response.

8

The Learning for Sustainability website defines systems thinking this way:

"Systems thinking in practice encourages us to explore inter-relationships (context and connections), perspectives (each actor has their own unique perception of the situation) and boundaries (agreeing on scope, scale and what might constitute an improvement). Systems thinking is particularly useful in addressing complex or wicked problem situations. These problems cannot be solved by any one actor, any more than a complex system can be fully understood from only one perspective. Moreover, because complex adaptive systems are continually evolving, systems thinking is oriented towards organizational and social learning – and adaptive management."
Learning for Sustainability (n.d.)

It's important to notice the bold text in the quotation: interrelationships, perspectives, and boundaries. When we talk about "business systems," it's in the broader context of systems thinking. This makes it imperative not to turn the exercise suggested in the first paragraph of this section into a session about configuration management. That is not the intent. The idea is to understand the layers of systems, starting with the business systems and adding more detail. The goal for the exercise suggested by this section is simple: identify and quantify the organizational risk if any of these systems are compromised.

Don't assume you know the systems involved. Think differently; start by asking questions.

2.1.1   The role of questions

"The ability to ask the right question is more than half the battle of finding the answer."
Thomas J. Watson

Everyone knows how to ask a question. So why have a section about it in this book? The answer is relatively simple and may elicit a "Duh?" from some. You only get answers to the questions you ask.

There is a point to this.[6] The better the question, the better the answer. Questions open doors to learning, growing, getting an idea, or improving ideas; they also enable us to develop a different perspective – an aspect of systems thinking. Questions help us interact and connect with others. Questions help us understand interrelationships and boundaries – two more aspects of systems thinking.

There are many different types of questions, with the following a short sample:

- **Evaluative questions** seek a conclusion or opinion ("What would happen if …?")
- **Explanation questions** seek clarity and understanding ("Why is this the best way to accomplish …?")
- **Factual questions** are simple and easy ("Is this correct?")
- **Reflexive questions** address self-reflection ("What can I do to improve …?").

---

6   Questions are a critical aspect of the CPD Model as represented by the Question Outcome–Question Metric (QO–QM) approach covered in more detail in Chapter 7.

We ask questions for different purposes, such as:

- Opening doors
- Connecting and engaging with others
- Generating or improving ideas
- Seeking to understand or develop a different point of view, a different perspective, and get out of a rut.

For our purposes, it is better to ask open-ended questions, i.e., questions that cannot be answered by a simple "yes" or "no."

The authors used this approach (asking different questions) to address everything in this book series. We started with this simple question root based on the assumption that the picture of cybersecurity as a technical issue was incomplete: "What's missing?" This question led to other "Wh" questions, such as "Why ...?", "What else ...?", and "Who should ...?" Exploring this thought chain led to developing the models and approaches presented in this book series. Specifically, we focused on the last two purposes listed above: improving ideas and developing a different perspective.

It's critical to consider how to ask a question. Consider this simple example:

Can we do this?

This question addresses capability. The typical answer is a simple choice of three possibilities (and variants): "yes," "no," or "maybe."

If we change the question slightly by adding a single word, we alter the intent radically:

How can we do this?

This question addresses the development of a method. The assumption in this question is different: we assume we can do something, and seek a way to accomplish it.

Avoid asking accusatory questions as part of the approach to asking different questions. For example, "Why did you do this?" accuses; "Can you help me understand why you did this?" does not – it collaborates.

You've probably heard the adage about repeating the same steps expecting a different result as a definition of insanity. If you want different results, you must approach the questions with a new perspective. This idea is part of what is included in systems thinking: thinking differently.

The following sections explore the questions introduced in the *Fundamentals* book:

- What are the critical business systems? Which of these systems are mission-critical?
- What underlying IT systems, data, and services directly enable, support, or deliver these business services?
- What IT systems underpin these systems and are typically invisible to users?
- What is the appropriate level of protection for these systems and data to mitigate the business risk?
- Where are the associated data and applications stored for each business system? Does the data have appropriate assured protection? (E.g., third-party cloud data protection meets organizational requirements specified in a contract, not assumed)
- What is the risk to the business if any of these systems or data is compromised? (This question also addresses priority – the most risk to the business should get first attention)
- Are suppliers or partners involved with storing, transmitting (including transit through), or processing the associated business data applying appropriate protections?
- How do we know? Are we sure? (Ask these last two questions in response to the answers above. They also establish the predicate for assurance.)

The last question, "Are we sure?", is less about the answer to the question and more about the delivery of the answer. More work is needed if there is any hesitancy or the voicing isn't convincing. The purpose of this last pair of questions is less about rote or quick answers than it is challenging assumptions. Acceptance of the answers expresses a risk-informed approach.

Before examining these questions, it's essential to understand why this approach is necessary.

2.1.2 Develop a three-dimensional view of the business

What do we mean by "a three-dimensional view of the business"? It's analogous to a holographic view of the business. From any observation point, you "see" a view that connects the lowest-level technical system to the highest-level business system. If the perspective is technical, a view of this business hologram reveals how every system connects, directly or indirectly, to other systems, including technical or supporting systems and the business systems that use the technology. Similarly, if the perspective is business, the view shows every system (business or technical) that "touches" the business system under observation.

This type of view enables anyone in the organization to appreciate the interconnectedness of all systems. In Chapter 6 we'll demonstrate that this approach is critical to supporting an organized phased approach to adapting cybersecurity controls from the informative references, and to improving configuration management.

2.1.3 Identify business systems

How do you identify the business systems? The simple answer to this question is, don't assume. Start with a table-top exercise.[7] Ask the question, "What are our business systems?" Don't limit the answer to in-house systems: include cloud services or anything else from a third party. This exercise does not address priority – it's about discovery and enumeration; priority determination comes later.

Start with a formal exercise either in person, virtually, or using a form or questionnaire. The object is to avoid assumptions that include reliance on automated discovery. Identify the various stakeholder constituencies to accomplish this objective by ensuring every stakeholder cohort is represented on the team. For example, someone with a very technical responsibility (e.g., network monitoring) will probably also use systems for human resources.

The first question addressed to everyone in the organization is: "What business systems do you use?" It's likely that many people will not know the formal names for these systems or may know only a nickname for them. Note that there are several ways to ask questions to elicit the desired response:

- What business systems do you depend on to do your job?
- What job-related capabilities are supported by digital assets?

This second question might not provide system-specific names, but it might be possible to determine the systems if you know the digital assets. In other words, don't stop the effort if you get, "I don't know."

Don't forget to include applications, such as Microsoft Office.

Before moving on to the next question (in section 2.1.4), ask three more questions:

- Have we identified every business system?
- How do we know? How can we verify this is true?
- Are we positive?

---

7   A table-top exercise is a team activity conducted around a table with participants from multiple knowledge domains within the organization. Even a one-person company can still conduct this exercise by involving stakeholders to help.

You can't protect what you don't know exists

While this statement might seem obvious, it doesn't mean it's consistently applied. Consider the case of a Tier 1 research university in the US. The university terminated (downsized) an employee. The now disgruntled former employee, who had been part of the configuration management team, installed illegal software on a system that was not part of the university configuration database.

The former employee called the Software Publishing Association (SPA) and reported the "offense." Shortly after, law enforcement searched all university assets and found more illegal software than the software the disgruntled employee had installed. If the various systems had been part of the configuration records, regular and automatic scanning might have discovered the illegally installed software before the police did.

Note: There was no malicious intent behind the exclusion of the systems in question. They were not directly connected to the university network, and therefore were overlooked and omitted when a tool scan created the configuration database. Additional scans were performed only midway through each academic semester. The impact on the university was costly, with fines for discovery plus an additional expense of $30 million over five years to conduct mandatory audits and reporting.

Ask these questions and then collate the answers to ensure you do not overlook a single business system. An automatic scan will find hardware and software, not necessarily business systems. The essence of strategy-risk requires a different approach: identify the business and related systems at risk, not hardware and software.

2.1.4   Identify the directly related IT systems

After identifying the business systems, it's appropriate to ask questions about the IT systems that support, enable, or directly underpin each of them. This effort does not involve an extensive drill-down into every IT system – it just includes the most obvious ones.

For example, many business systems likely depend on a local area network – yes, pure hardware may be considered a system for this and subsequent questions. This question raises the need to consider hardware- and software-enabling systems, which pay dividends when examining specific cybersecurity requirements.[8]

This endeavor will likely require teams with a different composition than the previous exercise.

Business systems are the face of the organization to stakeholders – how you interact with the business, not its technology. Do not limit this activity to just the surface or obvious systems. Are there separate user interfaces (or other frontends)? What about systems authenticating, authorizing, and providing access to these business systems? If so, include them in the list. Are specific applications (or a combination of applications) that support the business system or service identified in the question in section 2.1.3? If so, include them as well.

---

8   We recommend thinking about cybersecurity "controls" as requirements to produce an outcome versus a switch or similar device. There's more about this topic in Chapters 6 and 7.

2.1.5 Identify the underlying IT systems [9]

Once you've identified the first layer of IT systems that support the business systems, you can drill down on the technical systems. This step documents the systems no one outside of IT sees (including the business systems maintained by either the business side or a third party acting on behalf of the business). It includes databases, monitoring hardware and software, real and virtual machines, and the rest of the hardware and software infrastructure used to run the business. It also includes everything provided and maintained by third parties (e.g., cloud services). As noted above, in the story about the university: *You can't protect what you don't know exists.*

2.1.6 Identify each business system's associated data and applications

It's not enough to identify the business systems: it's also essential to identify the related data. There are a series of questions that might help:

- Where is the data stored? The answers to this question should include where the data lives (at rest), any data caches or temporary stores, and its backups. Is any of that data maintained in the cloud?
- How is it accessed? Is the data accessed directly by the user or indirectly by another system?
- How does the data move through the infrastructure? Through what systems or networks does the data move or transit?

For each of the previous questions (in sections 2.1.2–2.1.5), validate the discovery of systems and data by asking variants of the following:

- Have we identified everything in this category? Don't limit or filter this question by adding or thinking the term *relevant*
- How do we know?
- How can we be sure?

Note: Ask similar questions to the six above for business and IT applications. For example:

- Where do the applications live?
- Who has access?
- How does the application interact with other applications?

If any hesitancy or doubt emerges answering the last set of questions, it's essential to keep digging. That's one of the reasons why this is a team exercise.[10] At this point, paranoia could be helpful: "What if I/we have missed something?"

Yes, it's possible. The list might be incomplete – specifically, the underlying systems provided by partners and suppliers: see section 2.1.9. Before we address what's missing from the list, we must understand the risk to the organization.

---

9   For a small organization with a well-understood infrastructure, the previous step might be sufficient, allowing this step to be skipped. If the underlying systems are not totally and completely understood, use the two steps suggested here. If you aren't certain, err on the side of following both steps.

10   Even a one-person organization might need help with IT infrastructure discovery. Don't assume you know: ask yourself the three questions noted above, starting with "Where do the applications live?", and then add one more, "What if I've missed something?"

2.1.7 Identify the organizational risk if a system is compromised

Once the business infrastructure is understood and documented, it's essential to ask cybersecurity risk-related questions. First, to ensure we have a common language, we define cybersecurity risk as the potential for harm or loss related to any digital business system and supporting infrastructure resulting from a cyberattack or data breach.

These are related terms: threat, vulnerability, risk, and impact.

> *"A **threat** is anything that can cause harm. A **vulnerability** is an exploitable weakness that results in the realization of a threat to achieving business objectives (i.e., impacting the ability to create, protect, and deliver value). A **risk** is the presence of a threat, combined with a vulnerability and the likelihood of occurrence. The **impact** is the effect of the risk if it occurs (i.e., a breach)."*
> Freund and Jones (2015)

Assess every business system, including the underlying IT components of each one.

What is the potential harm and impact when a particular threat occurs? What is impacted (strategic intent, reputation, or anything else)? How far-reaching is the damage caused by the realization of a threat? The answer to the questions regarding harm and impact supports prioritizing the threat (and the need for associated protections).

How do you identify vulnerabilities in your existing business systems and supporting infrastructure? You could start by ensuring that patch levels are current. While that might reduce or eliminate some vulnerabilities, it's not enough. The ability to determine business system vulnerabilities might need outside resources. We recommend using MITRE ATT&CK®. Why? Consider the following from the website:

> *"MITRE ATT&CK® is a globally-accessible knowledge base of adversary tactics and techniques based on real-world observations. The ATT&CK knowledge base is used as a foundation for the development of specific threat models and methodologies in the private sector, in government, and in the cybersecurity product and service community."*
> MITRE ATT&CK (n.d.-b)

ATT&CK presents a matrix of bad actor tactics, techniques, mitigations, and so on. One of the common use cases (MITRE ATT&CK, n.d.-a) for ATT&CK is "assessment and engineering," which is an excellent starting point to determine system vulnerabilities.

The MITRE ATT&CK database contains information about different types of attacks. This includes how an attacker gains access and progresses through the business system, and what an attacker does to escalate privilege, avoid detection, or attempt to map or discover more resources available on your network. Use this information to help identify known vulnerabilities present in your systems.

Use this information to assess cybersecurity organizational risk with information about threat and harm combined with vulnerabilities, risks, and impact. The assumption that a breach can't happen is misguided; it potentially leads to a failure to mitigate digital business risk adequately.

Some systems might have several documented vulnerabilities while others might have only a few. The MITRE ATT&CK database provides "lagging" information. Even if there are no recorded weaknesses, this does not mean that these systems are free from vulnerabilities.

Search the ATT&CK database based on different types of systems and capabilities. For example, you may be able to skip the related entries if your organization prohibits products from a vendor (including software) – however, don't assume: instead, check and verify. You need to ask questions if you find references to the organizational hardware and software:

- Is this vulnerability found in our systems?
- Has it been fixed or patched?
- How do we know?
  - How can we be sure?
  - Is there tangible evidence to support the claim?

Failure to address these vulnerabilities raises the possibility of cyber exploitation with corresponding elevated organizational risk. Does the organization plan to address business continuity if a business system is compromised? Take note of the potential assumptions made in every set of questions. Ensure the context is "when" not "if" – apply the same approach to the third-party (vendor and partner) systems; don't assume, ask.

Tools to mitigate risk

The US Cybersecurity and Infrastructure Security Agency (CISA) has a web page that lists free cybersecurity services and tools (CISA, n.d.). While tools and technology do not replace the vulnerability and risk assessment suggested here, the CISA information still might prove useful.

The web page lists five foundational measures that we also recommend. They are briefly listed here for your information; if you want to find out more, consult the CISA web page for specifics and more broadly the CISA website to stay abreast of the changing dynamics.

- **Fix the known security flaws and software** Check the regularly updated CISA Known Exploited Vulnerabilities (KEV) Catalog
- **Implement multifactor authentication (MFA)** I.e., a layered approach to secure accounts
- **Halt bad practices** E.g., replace end-of-life software
- **Sign up for CISA cyber hygiene vulnerability scanning** Register via email to vulnerability@cisa.dhs.gov
- **Get your stuff off search (engines)** Know what the organization exposes to search engines, and clean it up to reduce the attack surface (as discussed in the *Fundamentals* book, threat actors used a white paper on the Microsoft website for information to attack the retailer Target).

And that's the point. The questions are important: they keep you from making assumptions that expose the organization to significant damage resulting from a cybersecurity breach.

Assign priority to apply vulnerability mitigation based on its impact on your organization. The higher the impact, the higher the priority. Another circumstance that may be a factor in assigning priority is the amount of time recovery of business activities will take when each business system is compromised. Modified by the value and urgency to recover a business system, time may be a factor; all other things being equal, the more time and effort required potentially mitigates in favor of higher priority.

This step takes a lot of effort: don't shortchange it; don't assume you know.

2.1.8   Identify each business system's current state of protection

Once you've identified the systems the organization uses to deliver value and categorized the risk to the organization if any of these systems are compromised, the next step is to determine the state of existing protections for those systems. The business systems with higher impact and urgency earn a higher priority for the associated mitigation effort.

> **Business impact analysis**
>
> Suppose the organization maintains a business impact analysis (BIA) as a regular part of business continuity planning. In that case, some information necessary to prioritize the approach for each system might be readily available. However, it's essential that the organization does not rely exclusively on its continuity planning unless cybersecurity is or was an integral part of the development of the BIA.

The MITRE ATT&CK database contains information about mitigations for each noted attack and vulnerability. Use this information to assess the current degree of protection (or state). As noted in section 2.1.7, it is essential to ensure that approved and potentially tested vendor patches are appropriately applied.

Again, it's essential to ask questions when you find documented vulnerabilities:

- For each documented vulnerability, does the mitigation apply to our systems?
- Has the mitigation been applied? If not, is it something we can do locally, or do we need vendor intervention?

Don't forget to include in-house developed systems, or systems developed or customized explicitly for the organization. This approach may present a challenge: in-house developers might not be the best judge of their security practices, requiring either internal auditors or a third-party evaluation.

This effort is a difficult undertaking. No amount of testing can prove the absence of bugs or vulnerabilities. Furthermore, the MITRE ATT&CK database, no matter how frequently it's updated, always lags the potential range of exposures and vulnerabilities. Ask more questions, particularly about any in-house or customized hardware or software:

- Was the software designed to be tested?
- How extensive is the test database? What is the extent of test coverage?
- Is the test database updated concurrently with incremental improvements, new features, or new versions? Is there evidence demonstrating the performance of the updated tests after each software update or change?

Even when the architecture and design for each business system include the imperative for cybersecurity, old-fashioned code reviews and code walk-throughs will be necessary to accurately determine the system state of cybersecurity protections. This step is an essential aspect of the strategy-risk assessment.

2.1.9   Determine the state of protection provided by partners and suppliers

Don't stop with your in-house systems. Every system supplied by a third party must be subject to the same level of scrutiny. Your organization may not be able to directly examine third-party systems, which will require contracts that stress partner and vendor cybersecurity requirements at an appropriate level to reduce organizational risk and exposure.

Don't assume. Ask!

- What provisions does the third party have in place to protect your organization?
- What provisions does it have to support your organizational requirements for business continuity in the event of a breach?
- What tangible evidence or proof can it offer to support the answers to the two questions above?

2.1.10   Develop an approach to integrated assurance

We touched on this briefly in section 2.1.8: was the system designed to be testable? This idea highlights the need to engage two different perspectives in evaluating the development of any business system: the perspective of the *implementor* and the perspective of the *auditor*.

The implementor's perspective focuses on *creating* value; the auditor focuses on *protecting* value. It is essential to engage both views during the development of any business system, which requires development teams to be composed of separate members for each point of view.

Treat this as a learning opportunity for both the implementor and the auditor. The implementor needs to ask, "How do I protect this?" The auditor needs to ask questions about testability, verification, and validation. The auditor's questions focus on cybersecurity in the broader context regarding system quality assurance.

This approach may represent a significant change for the organizations that bifurcate development and quality assurance/testing. We recommend that the development teams include the implementor and auditor perspectives, enabling their related activities to be concurrent rather than serial. We'll have more to say about this in subsequent chapters.

Including both perspectives (implementor and auditor) as part of each activity does not suggest self-assessment is acceptable. Seek outside help if the organization does not have sufficient resources to have different people in each role. You know this to be a good idea if you've ever asked someone to proofread something you've written – you see what you intended, and a third party sees what is on the page.

2.2   Being the menace

What does it mean to be the menace? It puts you in a proactive role to find and address vulnerabilities before the bad actors exploit them. Examine everything discovered in section 2.1. Use that information as the source of potential exploits to "attack" your organization. You know the internal weaknesses; figure out how to exploit them. In other words, your job is to pretend to be a threat actor. The insider already has access; use that to probe for weaknesses. Don't ignore attempting to simulate what an external threat actor might do, including attempts at social engineering (e.g., getting people to click on a nefarious link).

2.2.1   More than penetration testing

Penetration testing simulates attacks on your computer systems. The object of this effort is threefold:

- Test digital system security
- Discover potential vulnerabilities in those systems
- Assess current detection and response.

In addition, penetration testing can help an organization learn to handle cybersecurity breaches.

Because of the work performed in response to section 2.1, we already have a list of potential vulnerabilities and established business impacts when any business system is compromised. By thinking like a bad actor attempting to exploit known vulnerabilities, you adopt a proactive approach to maintain organizational cyber resilience, which requires ongoing due diligence to treat using tools like the MITRE ATT&CK® as a continuous exercise, not "once and done."

2.2.2   Goal, question, metric approach overview

The goal, question, metric approach (GQM)[11] supports the effort to be the menace and, as we'll see in Chapter 7, to improve overall cyber resilience.

As its name suggests, there are three parts to the GQM approach:

- **Goal** The conceptual level from a specific point of view
- **Question** The operational level to achieve the goal
- **Metrics** The quantitative level associated with each question (the actual values for metrics can be quantitative or qualitative).

Define **goals** for products, practices, processes, resources, and other areas. Anything that requires useful metrics is a candidate for GQM. Goals represent targets for achievement and define a gap. The best way to create goals for GQM is in a team, not individually. Why?

The team members' relevant and distinct points of view are essential in creating the goals. Cross-domain knowledge makes it more likely to represent the gaps subject to measurement. The overall purpose of GQM is to ensure that you have the appropriate metrics to answer the questions that support the achievement of the goal.

Questions address the operational level of GQM. Goals are not cast in concrete; questions may lead to goal revision. Questions should have a quantifiable basis – you will create metrics to answer them. Questions also serve to support buy-in for the goal, if appropriate. Questions may support qualitative evaluation (e.g., from the project manager's perspective, is "x" acceptable?)

Metrics answer quantitative or qualitative questions that will support your understanding of how you will know whether you've achieved an aspect of the goal. Approach metrics creation from the systems thinking perspective (introduced in Chapter 3). Avoid local optimizations that focus on tasks instead of the product or outcomes. The metric is not the goal: metrics help determine the achievement of the desired goal or outcome.

There are two types of metrics: quantitative/objective and qualitative/subjective. Objective metrics have a measurable value (e.g., hours spent on task X, or whether documentation exists to support a specific aspect of the goal [true/false]). Subjective metrics require a point of view (expressed in the goal, e.g., X is sufficient from the project manager's perspective). In the same way that questions may lead to refining the goal, analyzing the questions could lead to refining or clarifying the question to ensure the development of appropriate metrics. Any given metric may apply to multiple questions without needing to be rewritten.

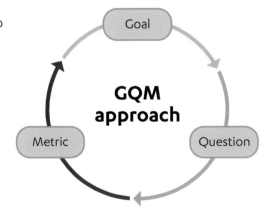

If you get the idea that the process of working with GQM can occasionally be circular, you'll be correct (see Figure 2.1).

Figure 2.1 The circular nature of the GQM approach

---

11   Used with permission of Professor Victor R. Basili (Basili et al., n.d.-b).

The overall GQM flow starts with assembling the right people for the team, with appropriate cross-domain knowledge. The next step requires the team to create and agree on the goals. With the goals in hand, write the appropriate qualitative and quantitative questions. From each question, derive the metrics. Review the whole set and revise it as needed. Then wash, rinse, and repeat for the next goal.

With the recording of the metrics, the next step is establishing an infrastructure to support the measurement program. It is essential to treat measurement as an integral part of project activities. As measurement data arrives, analyze it, focusing on the goals.

Recall that goals should have a point of view. The point of view establishes the roles that interpret the result – this is essential for qualitative questions.

We use GQM to develop metrics for the implementation of cybersecurity controls and the attacks on those controls from "the menace."

While the discussion here is about "being the menace," the application of GQM, as we'll see in Chapter 7, is much broader. GQM is extraordinarily useful for developing metrics.

2.2.3   Use cases and misuse cases

Use cases help support the implementation of cybersecurity controls by documenting the requirements for each control in the context of the organizational adaptation. A class of use cases called *misuse cases*[12] addresses "being the menace."

Note: Use GQM to improve and provide metrics for use cases and misuse cases, for example, coverage of outcomes for use cases and vulnerabilities for misuse cases.

2.2.3.1   Use cases

While many people think use cases[13] are for software development, they originated in the telecommunications industry (Wikipedia, 2022r). Use cases apply to anything with interactions between entities (called *actors*).

Use cases help support the implementation of cybersecurity controls by documenting the requirements for each control in the context of the organizational adaptation. Creating a use case is typically an exercise that requires understanding requirements and writing prose, which produces a twofold challenge: knowing what and how much to write, and doing it repeatedly.

So what is a use case? It's a document that describes the behavior of a system as determined by interactions with that system. While use cases can be expressed in multiple forms, including graphical and programming, prose is better for our purposes. You should not require special training to understand the use case. While learning to read them takes only a few minutes, learning to write them takes longer.

A use case answers the general question, "How do I, how do we, how does it do something?" It answers the question in the form analogous to one or more scripts. There are multiple uses for use cases, such as:

- Describe a process
- Document a system's functional requirements

---

12   The term *misuse case* is derived from and is the inverse of *use case*. It describes the process of executing a deliberately malicious act against a system (Wikipedia, 2021b).

13   The seminal work in this field is a book by Alistair Cockburn, *Writing Effective Use Cases* (Cockburn, 2001). One of the authors has purchased this book multiple times, lending it to others who asked if they could keep it. What follows is only an overview of use cases, based on this highly recommended book.

- Document a system's design specifications
- Focus discussions about a set of requirements for future software or a future system.

Each of these takes a slightly different writing style. There isn't a single template suitable for writing all use cases. The way you structure a use case depends upon many factors, including:

- Casual or formal
- Team and project size
- Whether or not the project is mission-critical and has liability or risk issues.

The more mission-critical or the higher the liability or risk, the longer and more detailed the specific use case template is required. Teams writing these mission-critical use cases must include members with appropriate cross-domain knowledge. These use cases also require stricter reviews and more scrutiny.

Consider each use case as a source of material to develop goals, questions, and metrics in the following way:

- List the goals or objectives from the use case to establish appropriate goals for GQM
- Develop questions for each goal
- Develop metrics that answer each of the questions.

Use cases don't cover all requirements. For example, they don't cover data formats, external interfaces, business rules, imposed rules, and regulations. Use cases may cover only about one-third of all requirements. Even so, all requirements link or connect to use cases, making use cases an excellent place to develop GQM matrixes for cybersecurity initiatives. Use cases also add significant value when brainstorming system failure conditions,[14] leading to the discussion of misuse cases.

2.2.3.2 Misuse cases

Misuse cases cover different conditions from examining failure conditions. Failure conditions explore the responses to the "what if" (unexpected) behaviors that result from a specific use case action. Where the use case describes actions taken *by a system*, a misuse case describes a deliberately *malicious attack on a system*.

Use the information in the MITRE ATT&CK database as a source of information to create misuse cases to attack your systems. Depending on the sophistication of your infrastructure and the organizational risk identified as a result of following the guidance in section 2.1.7, consider combining relevant attacks in your misuse case – not to create a weapon, but to probe for vulnerabilities.

The approach to creating a misuse case is similar to that for producing a use case; the difference is in the applied mindset. Use cases map a set of interactions between actors and systems: the attitude needed to create a misuse case addresses attacking those systems.

2.2.4 Exploiting vulnerabilities as an insider

One of the reasons to use the MITRE ATT&CK database is to understand what the threat actors know about vulnerabilities. The insider with malicious intent doesn't need the MITRE ATT&CK database to discover vulnerabilities. They already know them. The database is a source of information for the good guys to develop malicious insider attacks.

---

14 A system failure condition occurs when the system behaves unexpectedly, not due to an attack or other malicious behavior. The best example of a system failure condition is the Microsoft Windows "blue screen of death" (BSOD).

It is possible that an insider might not have malicious intent and accidentally trip, find, or create a vulnerability. To address this scenario, perform actions outside the prescribed behaviors in the use case and then update the use case to show the response to these behaviors as a use case extension.

2.2.5 Think like a bad external actor

Suppose you've spent your life living on the good side. In that case, it might be challenging to get inside the mind of a threat actor[15] and think like one, which is one of the reasons why we suggested the use of cross-functional teams and the role of questions in this section. The same approach is valuable to attempt to think like a bad actor. Spend some time exploring the MITRE ATT&CK database from the perspective of bad actor creativity.

No amount of security will prevent an attack. Thinking like a bad actor, both internal and external, will help identify vulnerabilities to address in risk-based priority order.

Why go through this exercise? The goal is to change the thinking about cybersecurity so that it encompasses cyber resilience. Part of this new thinking is what helped the authors develop the concept of *strategy-risk*.

2.3 Understanding strategy-risk

This section addresses what we call *strategy-risk*, why it's critical to an organization seeking cyber resilience, and how it's fundamental to the organizational ability to create, protect, and deliver digital business value.

At many companies, the focus on strategic risk has broadened; it is no longer limited to traditional areas such as operational, financial, and compliance risk. Emerging trends suggest that companies take a broader view of strategic risk, integrating strategic risk analysis into their overall business strategy and planning processes (Deloitte, 2013).

Using strategy-risk as an approach to strategic risk supports the idea that digital business value *creation* requires *protection*. Anything of value that is not appropriately protected has no value to the stakeholders because it is open to theft, misuse, or denied or degraded legitimate use. This link between value creation and value protection is another reason why we treat strategy-risk as a single entity.

Strategy-risk concepts that link digital value creation with digital value protection require different thinking. Why? How we think about a problem or challenge affects the questions we ask to address it. How does strategic risk differ from strategy-risk? How does the concept of value factor into strategy-risk and impact organizations' decisions about creating, protecting, and delivering digital business value? How does strategy-risk in the context of the CPD Model enable cyber resilience?

---

15   We use the terms "bad actor" and "threat actor" interchangeably.

The CPD Model and business value

The CPD Model (covered in detail in Chapter 4) represents a mental model that supports the realization of the NIST Cybersecurity Framework guidance – in other words, how to think about the organizational capabilities needed to operationalize the Framework by implementing the cybersecurity controls of the selected informative references. The CPD Model enables an organization to create, protect, and deliver digital business value.

Value is subjective; the point of view or perspective defines the limits of value for each individual. All value has one or more stakeholders. The CPD Model subsumes stakeholders and their points of view as part of strategic and operational intent. The mantra is simple: *protect value* – unprotected value has no value. In the context of cybersecurity, unprotected value opens the organization to unlimited and unmitigated risks. The organization assumes the consequences when (not if) an unprotected asset that supposedly provides value is compromised, stolen, or made inaccessible. *Protecting value is not "once and done" – maintain it or lose it*. Value exists in a dynamic environment and is subject to changes to internal needs, external requirements, and a dynamic threat landscape.

An organization adopting the NIST Cybersecurity Framework and using the CPD Model must seek clarity and focus on what matters when creating, protecting, and delivering digital business value. The CPD Model ensures the organization can identify and close performance gaps.

Using strategy-risk in the CPD Model creates an adaptive system that enables the organization to create, protect, and deliver digital value. It also enables the organization to internalize continual innovation as a critical core capability, making it cyber-resilient by adapting to its changing internal and external requirements and the dynamic threat landscape.

2.3.1 Strategy-risk and being the menace

The Deloitte report on "Exploring strategic risk" contains the following (emphasis added):

---

*"Traditional approaches for managing risk tend to focus on monitoring leading financial indicators as well as the evolving regulatory environment. However, because they are generally grounded in audited financial statements, the resulting risk strategies and hedges are largely driven by prior performance and past negative events – and do not necessarily serve to detect future strategic risks or predict future performance. As such, **they are more focused on protecting value than creating it.**"*
Deloitte (2013)

In broad terms, strategic risk looks at four types of risk:

- **Strategic** Risks created by or affecting organizational business strategy and strategic objectives
- **Operational** Major risks that affect the organizational ability to execute its strategic plan
- **Financial** Includes financial reporting, valuation, market liquidity, and credit risks
- **Compliance** Major legal and regulatory compliance risks that affect the organizational ability to execute its strategic plan.

Organizations typically treat strategy and risk separately. Some organizations split the two functions across two or more groups. Today cybersecurity changes the dynamics of risk. Risk must play an integral role in developing every strategy, requiring organizations to think differently. Instead of thinking about strategy *and* risk, consider a single entity: strategy-risk. We chose this construct because strategy and risk are inherently inseparable, like space-time. Strategy-risk supports the idea that digital business value *creation* requires *protection*. Simply put: any value that is not appropriately protected has no value to the stakeholder.

Take note of the last sentence in the quote from the Deloitte report: "… more focused on protecting value than creating it." Looking backward is not an approach that can recognize future strategic risk in the context of future performance. Looking backward like generals preparing to fight the last war blinds the organization to the highly dynamic threat landscape. The essence of treating strategy and risk as a single entity, strategy-risk, combines the necessary looking backward with a forward-looking consideration that enables the organization to create and protect value.

One of the reasons why we suggest proactively "being the menace" results from combining strategy and risk into strategy-risk and the inseparable nature of value creation and its protection. A few forward-looking indicators are part of mainstream IT thinking (e.g., critical success factors [CSF] are usually poorly understood). The essence of the DVMS is linking strategy and risk to form strategy-risk combined with creating and protecting digital business value. These two concepts form the basis of the CPD Model, which seeks to balance backward- and forward-looking metrics. Being the menace is a proactive approach to ensure that the value created is protected appropriately.

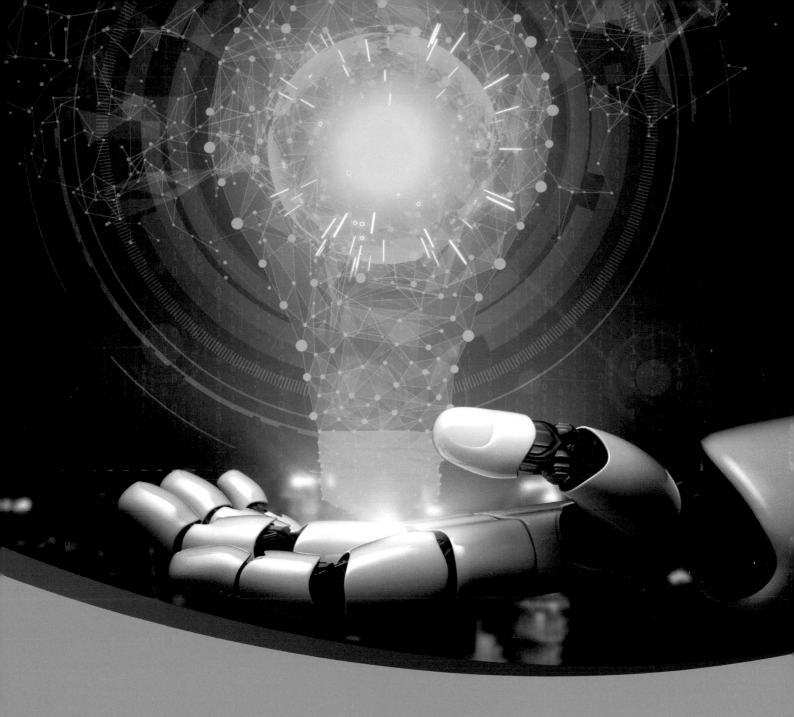

CHAPTER 3
Systems: simple, complex, complicated, and resilient

3 Systems: simple, complex, complicated, and resilient

"If you're not confused, you're not paying attention."
Tom Peters (1988)

Tension metrics create inherent competition or conflict – good, fast, or cheap: pick two. The challenge is that by picking two of the three, we elevate the two selected to be more important than the one. Tension metrics seek to find the appropriate balance – in this case, good, fast, *and* cheap – while maintaining the relative importance of all three. Finding the right balance is a potential problem of complexity. Add more variables, and the complexity increases exponentially.

Systems are composed of interacting parts. It's not the number of the parts (or elements) that makes a system complex – it's the number and scope of the connections and interactions between the elements.

Complexity is not bad: it has the potential to increase the resilience of a system when it is properly designed and managed (e.g., the internet is a complex, highly resilient system). A level of redundancy and duplication characterizes resilient systems. The small organization that relies on a limited number of resources, including staff with similar backgrounds and perspectives, may lack the capability to respond to threats or capitalize on opportunities. As the organization grows and adds diversity – of people, processes, and technology – it increases organizational complexity and potentially contributes to organizational resilience.

What makes something simple? We define a task as simple when all (or most) conditions and information for the task require little to no additional research (or the information needed is readily available with no dependencies or gating factors from third parties). We define a change as simple if and only if it has zero to minimal impact on other components (i.e., there are zero unintended consequences). The hallmark of "simple" is precise predictability with clear and direct links between cause and effect combined with no unintended consequences.

As the need for further research to understand the effort for a task increases, we conclude that it is more complicated than a simple one – it requires many more steps (including the research effort). In addition, things get more complicated as the scope of effect expands to multiple system elements. Provided the scope and the full impact are understood, the effort becomes complicated without necessarily being complex.[16]

When a change or leverage point requires more work to understand the potential far-reaching implications for the rest of the system, things get complex. Dealing with the interactions between system elements is part of coping with complexity; something is complicated when it requires more steps, care, and diligence to achieve an outcome. Something becomes complex as the number of interactions between the elements increases, which increases both the risk and likelihood of unintended consequences. The hallmark of complexity is thoroughly blurred lines between cause and effect.

Systems can be complicated and complex; thinking in systems requires understanding the difference; leveraging a system to improve its performance requires knowing where to target your energies and the type of results achievable from the effort. Managing complexity requires understanding the system and its subsystem exchanges and interactions, including the effectiveness and efficiency of the system as a whole.

---

16   Simple is making a sunny-side-up egg; complicated is making eggs Benedict.

3.1 Speaking in systems

Systems thinking, or thinking in systems, is not something you do; it's something you learn and practice. Systems thinking is similar to agile in that the organization doesn't *do* agile; the organization *becomes* agile.

The essence of creating, protecting, and delivering digital business value requires a holistic look at everything the enterprise does. Creating and protecting value are parallel efforts, not serial. This perspective is at the core of the CPD Model. Once this perspective is adopted, it's impossible to treat cybersecurity as a bolt-on. But this raises the question: why is it currently treated as a bolt-on?

There are many technical reasons for the current approach to treating cybersecurity. The straightforward answer is that that's the way many people think about it. Want different results? You have to think differently, requiring a different mental model – and different questions. To be clear and ensure we're on the same page when we talk about a "mental model": we're talking about a way of thinking about something.

What does it take to learn systems thinking – to think in systems terms? A partial answer to this question requires keeping an open mind and learning to think differently, shift perspective, and develop a different mindset.

3.1.1 Traditional thinking versus systems thinking

Think about the language we use when we set about solving a problem. We *analyze* the problem. Consider this definition of the word "analysis": "the process of breaking a complex topic or substance into smaller parts in order to gain a better understanding of it" (Wikipedia, 2022b). Breaking this complex topic or entity into smaller parts attempts to determine only the things that matter while ignoring the rest. Analysis isolates the small parts of the system under study. It examines elements, not the whole. For example, consider the ideas behind root cause analysis. The wording *root cause* suggests a single-point cause. There is rarely a single point of failure in complex systems.

An occasional analysis result is the "fix" that exposes other errors or vulnerabilities. Sometimes, despite detailed and extensive analysis, there is no apparent solution.

On the other hand, systems thinking recognizes that parts contribute to the whole: a system is not the sum of its parts – it's the product of their interactions. Parts of the system are interdependent with the whole of the system. When a part of the system impacts the system as a whole, it depends on another part for its effect.

No part of the system, or any subset of its parts, has an independent effect. Take a system apart, and it loses its essential properties. You cannot improve the elements of a system separately. System performance depends on how the parts interact, not how they operate separately. Systems thinking requires expanding our view beyond parts or components to include interactions between or among them.

Treat these interactions within a system as behaviors: actions that respond to signals, i.e., messages to or from people or other systems (including interaction within "this" system). These behaviors occur within a structure – the structure of the system – this is called working *in* the system. System behavior and structure are linked: you can't change one without impacting the other. When you work to change system behavior and structure, you're working *on* the system.

Systems thinking, or thinking in systems, requires a break from analyzing parts to see the whole. It requires the internalization of a different type of thinking that includes:

- Evaluating behaviors over time
- Learning to see the whole
- Asking different questions
- Multidimensional rather than linear thinking
- The soft variables that are hard to measure (e.g., learning, asking, thinking, evaluating).

"But to tear down a factory or to tear down a government or to avoid repair of a motorcycle because it is a system, is to attack effects rather than causes; as long as the attack is upon effects only, no change is possible. The true system, the real system, is our present construction of systematic thought itself, rationality itself, and if a factory is torn down but the rationality which produced it is left standing, then that rationality will simply produce another factory. If a revolution destroys a government, but the systematic patterns of thought that produced the government are left intact, then those patterns will repeat themselves in the succeeding government. There is so much talk about the system. And so little understanding."

Robert M. Pirsig (1974)

3.1.2 The beer game or learning to love systems thinking

In 1960, Jay Forrester invented the beer game at the MIT Sloan School of Management (Wikipedia, 2021a), resulting from his work on system dynamics (Wikipedia, 2022o). The game focuses on the supply chain dynamics, specifically the bullwhip effect (Wikipedia, 2022c) – a phenomenon resulting from the interaction of demand forecasts and supply chain inefficiencies. It provides an excellent example of some of the concepts we've already discussed: a system of systems and the relationship between system structure and system behavior.

While there are several versions of the game, we'll focus on a précis drawn from the explanation in Peter Senge's *The Fifth Discipline* (Senge, 1990).

This drama has three characters: the retailer, the wholesaler, and the brewery. The retailer maintains an inventory of a brand of beer called "Lover's Beer" that sells four cases per week. The cases are delivered once a week, and the retailer gives the delivery truck driver an order to restock the number of cases sold the previous week. Once the retailer has given the order to the driver, it takes four weeks to deliver the order.

The truck driver collects all the orders from the retailers on his route and gives them to the wholesaler. The wholesaler maintains an inventory and aggregates the retailer orders to place a single order with the brewery to maintain his inventory. The brewery uses the orders from multiple wholesalers[17] to determine the amount of beer to brew to maintain its inventory.

The retailer typically sells four cases of Lover's Beer per week. Time passes, and in one week he sells eight cases of the beer. He gives the truck driver the order to replenish his stock (eight cases). He has enough of the Lover's Beer in stock, so the sales that are double the usual amount do not cause immediate concern. The following week, the retailer sells another eight cases of Lover's Beer and orders eight more. The following week, the same thing happens again; this time, the retailer decides to play it safe and order 12 cases.

At this point, the retailer is more than a little bit concerned. In week four, he discovers that a popular music video mentions the beer. The Lover's Beer inventory is almost completely depleted, so he orders 16 cases.

In this fourth week of increased orders for the beer, there's evidence of trouble in paradise: only five of the eight cases ordered four weeks ago are delivered. As several cases appear on back order, things keep going from bad to worse with the subsequent weekly orders. By week eight, the retailer focuses more on Lover's Beer than any other product. Now totally frustrated, the retailer calls the wholesaler to try to determine what's happening.

---

17   For the game we're only concerned about the three main characters in the story: a single retailer, a single wholesaler, and the brewery. You can find another explanation of the beer game on Readingraphics (n.d.).

By week eight, the wholesaler is almost as frustrated as the retailer. In week six, the wholesaler had heard about an article in an industry publication about the music video. The wholesaler had raised orders to the brewery to stay ahead of the increase in orders for Lover's Beer. After reading the article, he increased orders to the brewery even further. The wholesaler is in the same position as his retailers: he's got back orders with the brewery.

Consequently, he delivers partial orders to the retailers. This goes on for a while. By week 16, the wholesaler gets almost all the beer ordered and waits expectantly for orders from the retailers that don't arrive. The pattern continues, and the wholesaler believes it's a retailer problem, or the music video that sparked the run on Lover's Beer is no longer in favor. Either way, it's not the wholesaler's fault.

The brewery has a slightly different problem. It makes beer in response to orders; it takes two weeks to brew a batch of beer. It takes a few days to bottle the beer once brewed, and more time to ship it to the wholesalers. The elapsed time from bottling to wholesaler delivery is one week. It takes one week to ship the beer from the wholesaler to the retailers. The brewery is conscious of the delay caused by the brewing process, which is why it maintains an inventory as a buffer for the brew cycle.

The brewery ramped up production in response to the wholesaler orders. Even so, it couldn't fully supply the wholesalers, and Lover's Beer was on back order. When the brewery caught up with the apparent demand, the number of orders for Lover's Beer crashed. The brewery blamed the wholesaler; the wholesaler blamed the retailer; and you can see where this is going.

The retailer never sold more than eight cases in any one week. The retailer increased the order size to support his inventory, not because there was an increase in the sales over the eight cases per week. The orders stopped flowing up the chain because the retailer's back orders arrived; given the constant sales of eight cases per week, the retailer didn't need to order more immediately.

The following sections explore lessons from the beer game and other systems thinking aspects.

3.1.2.1   Lessons from the beer game

Each of the three protagonists in the game had a system; combined, these made up a system of systems. The structure of the system of systems contributed to the bullwhip effect. Each of the three people operated within this larger context and acted similarly. The three systems combined added complexity to the whole. The problem experienced by each actor was inherent in the system – system structure impacts or controls how people make decisions.

There was no communication between the principal actors at the beginning of the game other than the transmission of orders. When personal contact finally occurs, it's in the context of "What did you do?" A real or perceived blame game is the antithesis of systems thinking.

3.1.2.2   Learning to see the whole

None of the protagonists in the beer game saw anything other than their small contained system. They didn't, or couldn't, see the whole, which contributed to their actions. The beer game establishes a perfect example of the classic maxim "Can't see the forest for the trees." The thinking of each party revolved around their situation, not the whole system of systems – they looked at a single tree, not the forest. Another more practical label applies to this type of thinking: *siloed thinking*. Thinking in silos precludes seeing the whole.

Systems thinking requires a view of the whole. We said earlier that a system is not the sum of its parts: it's the product of the interactions of the parts. Looking at the interactions between the parts is an aspect of seeing the whole. It's about asking how each part interacts with, impacts, or depends on other parts for its effect. In this case, the protagonists didn't look at the interactions; they only looked at their "part" of the system.

There are several ways to address this challenge. One of the most obvious is transparency and communication; this approach helps break down silos. While it might not be possible to change the inherent latency in the system, as a thought exercise, consider what would happen if the latency was one week instead of four – examine this with and without associated transparency and communication.

3.1.2.3   Recognize that systems are dynamic – though sometimes slow

The problem for each actor in the beer game is the result of linear thinking. It also results from an isolated set of behaviors that looks at each occurrence of an event: in the retailer's case, the increase in orders for Lover's Beer. Each party operated within system constraints. They knew it took four weeks from when the retailer placed an order until fulfillment through the supply chain: the retailer to the wholesaler, the wholesaler to the brewery, back to the wholesaler, and finally to the retailer. Even though they "knew," they didn't consider this when taking their actions.

In system-speak terms, neither the retailer, the wholesaler, nor the brewery considered system behavior over time, leading to a brief discussion of system archetypes[18] as a visual language for systems thinking. Sometimes it's easier to understand something by looking at a picture instead of reading prose.

Consider the simple thermostat that controls your heating (or cooling) where you live. Set the thermostat temperature to 68°F (20°C), and the room appears to stay at that temperature; the tendency is to believe the behavior is relatively static. We know the heater periodically cycles on and then off, but the room temperature displayed on the thermostat stays constant at 68°F.

Figure 3.1 represents a simple behavior-over-time graph of room temperature versus time.[19] The light grey line represents the thermostat set temperature; the curved line that oscillates above and below it represents the actual room temperature. The graph shows what's actually happening versus what we perceive by being in the room.

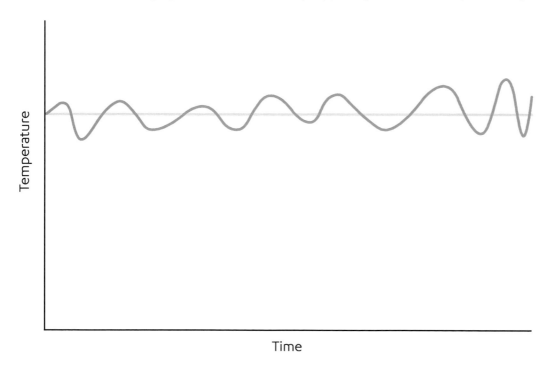

Figure 3.1 Temperature behavior over time

---

18   It's beyond the scope of this book to delve into the subject in detail. For more information, see Braun (2002) and Kim (1992).
19   More information about behavior-over-time graphs can be found in Kim (n.d.).

The X-axis of a behavior-over-time graph is always time, in whatever increments are relevant for the occasion; the Y-axis is always the behavior (or event) you want to measure; the increments are quantitative or qualitative.

The behavior-over-time graph reveals the system behavior over some period, which can be more revealing than an instant snapshot. This view is priceless when there is a latency between the actions associated with a cause and the effect – the graph may help you identify a reason for a change in trend that was invisible (or not obvious) when it occurred.

The behavior-over-time graph reveals critical information. It shows the delay in negative feedback; this delay causes oscillation and potentially impacts its amplitude. When you attempt to align a system to its goals, it's difficult, if not impossible, if you only receive delayed system state information. The graph also shows what happens if the feedback is timely and the response is not. In the case of the beer game, the system didn't allow the protagonists to respond to short-term changes because the delays were long term. [20]

3.1.2.4   The system as a cause – ask different questions

Because the protagonists in the beer game were looking only at their actions, it was easy to blame somebody else for the problems they experienced. They didn't have a systems view, and therefore didn't or couldn't perceive the inherent problems in the system. One of the challenges they faced was the opaqueness of the system: there was very little transparency or communication until it was too late.

Our external review and analysis can identify something the protagonists couldn't. We can recognize the system as a cause and work to change the system rather than casting blame. Think about this for a few minutes. How can we recognize a problem with the system if we're *in* the system? This approach is akin to asking how well we can perceive the forest if we look at only a single tree.

The capability to recognize a systemic problem starts with realizing that the system can be a problem. The beer game actors did this by focusing on inventory. They didn't notice that the sales spike was static at eight cases (i.e., four additional cases) per week; they knew about the delay, which should have been factored into their thinking but wasn't (recall the discussion about the behavior-over-time graphs).

The rules of the system of systems portrayed by the beer game are mostly implicit: the only explicit rules involved ordering and the four-week delay before receiving delivery. It was the rules in the system that governed the behavior of the protagonists. If you want to change the behaviors, you must change the rules, which is the province of most senior management.

None of the actors in the beer game asked questions about the behaviors or the conditions of any other player. They did not demonstrate an understanding of how the system structure influenced their behaviors within the system. What they needed to do was ask different questions. The implied question from the retailer and the wholesaler was, "Where's my stuff?" The brewery asked, "Where are my orders?"

The wrong questions demonstrate a lack of systems thinking. What's needed is a different approach, which requires asking other questions. For the beer game, the questions start with, "What is the nature of (the delay or the orders, etc.)?"

"Where's my ..." represents system-independent thinking; "What is the nature of ..." represents system-as-a-cause thinking. This idea of asking different questions is something that we pointed out in the *Fundamentals* book; it's a critical skill for the practitioner. Questions about "the nature of ..." might allow discovery of the relationship between system structure and system behavior. The same approach might also preclude the blame game that manifested in the later cycles of the beer game.

---

20   The idea of system stocks and flows is also relevant. You can find more information on Wikipedia (2022m) and in section 3.3.

3.1.2.5   Multidimensional versus linear thinking

Section 3.1.2.2 suggested that each beer game protagonist saw only their isolated view of the whole. They saw their actions as a cause and blamed others for the results. Let's take a step back from the beer game for a moment. Consider an organization with a toxic culture.

In this type of organization, it's not unusual for employees to be unhappy or disgruntled. The company might view these employees as a threat and perceive the need for a disciplinary response. On the other hand, the employees view the company as unfair and potentially worse and not caring about its employees. These unhappy or disgruntled employees might convince others of their point of view. Figure 3.2 shows these points of view graphically.

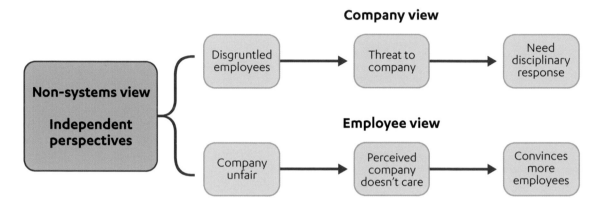

Figure 3.2 Independent, non-systems view of independent perspectives

Each perspective represents a linear form of thinking – a form of closed-mindedness to another point of view. Neither independent outlook reflects the impact that one has on the other. Figure 3.3 shows what happens when we connect the two perspectives. What we see is the impact the behaviors have on the whole system. It shows the reinforcing and potentially downward spiraling nature of the interactions. This type of diagram is called a causal loop diagram (Wikipedia, 2022d; Learning for Sustainability, n.d.) in the visual representation of systems thinking.

Take the idea of the reinforcing feedback shown in Figure 3.3 and apply it to the beer game. You can see how the latency inherent in the system contributed to increased negative views combined with increased "panic" of the game participants – using this form of graphical representation surfaces the idea of "system as a cause," discussed in section 3.1.2.4.

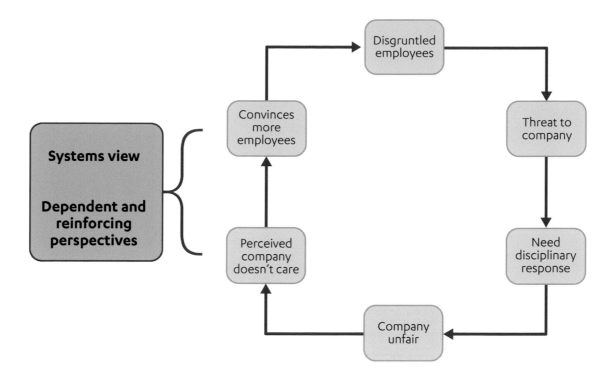

Figure 3.3 Systems view of dependent and reinforcing perspectives

This graphical view also highlights something that we quoted in section 2.1 from the Learning for Sustainability website about systems thinking. It's essential to consider point of view and the relationships between the perspectives.

Specifically, it highlights what happens when we connect the linear (isolated or siloed) perspectives in Figure 3.2 to show that they relate nonlinearly. The behaviors that one set of actors initiate impact the behaviors of others. The siloed view presented in Figure 3.2 provides little basis for understanding the system dynamics – how one group of actors' behaviors influence other behaviors.

3.1.3   Other aspects of systems thinking

The issue of perspectives is an essential aspect of systems thinking. We must apply quantitative measurement to qualitative value when considering this idea. In other words, some elements of improvement-related innovation will directly result from quantitative measurement, for example, the number of cybersecurity incidents or the number of attempted breaches. These are directly observable, measurable, and countable.

For other types of measurement, capturing perspectives or expectations requires something different. We recommend using Likert scales[21] or similar tools to quantify the qualitative. This approach allows us to collect and analyze things that are difficult or impossible to measure accurately. For example, we can get an absolute count of the number of cybersecurity incidents; we can't collect data about the satisfaction with how well the organization responded to those incidents with the same level of precision.

There is still another way to approach understanding the beer game. The protagonists addressed their respective problems at the event level: sales and orders. The underlying causes inherent in the system aren't obvious: they're

---

21   Wikipedia (2022h): e.g., on a scale of 1 to 5, do you agree or disagree with X?

hidden from their point of view. They needed to establish a different perspective to look at the whole, not just their events.

The iceberg model tool (Figure 3.4) allows us to grasp system dynamics better. The beer game protagonists saw only the events, the tip of the iceberg – there's much more. The iceberg model looks at four levels:

- **Events** A perceived snapshot of immediate occurrences; potential symptoms of underlying issues
  - · What just happened?
- **Patterns** Trend or behavior over time
  - · What is the behavior over time?
- **Structures** What influences the patterns; pattern/trend connections
  - · What influenced the patterns?
- **Mental models** Beliefs, attitudes, or assumptions
  - · What beliefs, attitudes, and assumptions exist about the system?
  - · What beliefs, attitudes, and assumptions keep the system in place (static)?

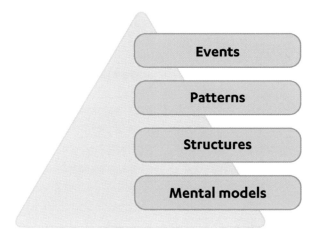

Figure 3.4 The iceberg model

Start by asking questions, a theme that we've repeated throughout the books in the series:

- What happened? What are the events that occurred?
- Either continue with questions about the behavior over time, or plot them in a behavior-over-time graph if the visualization would help
- How does the system structure influence or contribute to the pattern of events?
- What are the assumptions about the system? What are the beliefs and attitudes that form the basis of the assumptions?
- Is there anything missing? What did we miss?

This last pair of questions relate to an idea we've raised: How do we know? How can we be sure?

Questions originate from our mental models. To change a mental model, we must (a) recognize it and (b) ask different questions that explore different options. This concept is part of the guidance provided by using the iceberg model.

3.1.4   The relationship between system structure and behavior

At a simplistic level, we can identify system structure by identifying its parts, the connections between the parts at various interaction points, and the specification for interactions between them. While this is only part of the story, it provides a starting point for mapping and understanding system structure.

We model a system from a particular perspective. This perspective establishes the boundaries or scope regarding what is in or out of consideration for the model. Because the model considers perspective, it's likely incomplete, consistent with George Box's oft-quoted aphorism from statistics: "All models are wrong, but some are useful."

A model of the beer game would start with the events based on sales and orders. But, as previously noted, this represents the tip of the iceberg. While the game rules documented the latency inherent in the beer game system, the protagonists did not fully factor that into their behavior. If they had done so, the retailer might have sought to discover why the sales of Lover's Beer increased earlier in game play.

The failure to consider the latency part of the system structure gives us a clue regarding the protagonists' behaviors. The structure *of* the system constrains the behaviors *within* the system. Interactions occur at defined, potentially fixed points and intervals, with little or no interaction between the parties. They didn't share what they knew until it was too late. This lack of information sharing demonstrates a critical point: knowledge management isn't just for internal use.

3.2   Leverage, change, and adaptive resilience

To understand how to change a system, you must first recognize and understand the system. It is essential to understand not just the potential system leverage points; you must accept latency (behavior over time, and potentially stocks and flows), different perspectives, and how they impact each other (causal loop diagrams). It's not complicated – there are a limited number of leverage points; practical application of the leverage points might be complex.

3.2.1   Complicated is not complex

To understand complex systems, you must understand why they aren't complicated; and, similarly, why complex systems aren't simple.

Paraphrasing Albert Einstein, there exists a compelling and simple solution for every complex problem that is wrong. It's not because complex problems are unsolvable: it's human nature to seek the simplest solution because solving hard problems is hard. Perhaps it's more of an issue of not understanding the difference between complicated and complex.

Let's start with a simple problem and get that out of the way. Assume that you don't know how to cook, but you have a someone coming over tonight for dinner, and you want to prepare a great meal. You recall that "there is an app for that." You install the app and follow the recipe without confusing baking powder with baking soda, or tomato paste with tomato sauce. Similarly, you don't overcook or undercook the pasta, and so on. Following a recipe is a way to solve a simple problem. This approach assumes minimal experience and the ability to read and understand the directions. If this assumption isn't valid, the problem isn't simple. Even so, with practice and experience, an aspiring cook can generally be assured that the resultant meal is not only edible but enjoyable. This approach applies to any process consisting of documented activities.

It gets a bit trickier when things get complicated. Complicated problems differ from simple ones because they require more coordination or specialized knowledge. In addition, some problems are complicated because of their scale. Consider the example above about cooking pasta. It becomes complicated when we must prepare and serve a pasta dinner for a large catered affair with the condition that it be served hot and al dente. Part of the goal is to ensure everyone gets their food within a short period so that the first person served doesn't finish their meal before the last person gets theirs – a complicated problem.

Here is another example that addresses a complicated challenge. After World War II, Wernher von Braun led the Saturn V rocket development, forming the basis for the NASA moon missions. The effort required solving different and related problems by coordinating multidisciplinary specialists to bring together a complicated system of components that sent astronauts to the moon and brought them back alive.

In his article "Complicated or complex – knowing the difference is important" (Allen, 2016), Will Allen points out that it's essential for management teams to understand the difference between complex and complicated. He described the following aspects of how to manage in a complicated environment.

How do you manage in a complicated environment?

- *Role defining – setting job and task descriptions*
- *Decision-making – find the 'best' choice*
- *Tight structuring – use the chain of command and prioritize or limit simple actions*
- *Knowing – decide and tell others what to do*
- *Staying the course – align and maintain focus*

Will Allen (2016)

Okay, so what makes complex problems, well, complex?

Complex systems are a bit more "squishy." Solving a complex problem requires understanding the system's components and their relationships, how they interact with each other (and other systems), their properties for self-organization, and how they adapt and evolve within the environment in which they exist. It's this adaptive nature of the system that contributes to its complexity.

"Research into complex systems demonstrates that they cannot be understood solely by simple or complicated approaches to evidence, policy, planning, and management" (Allen, 2016). Decomposing a complex system and acting on its parts doesn't work because once isolated from the whole, complex system components behave differently than when connected. Everything we learned in "systems analysis class" works well for understanding complicated systems but doesn't translate to understanding complex systems. Predicting the weather is complicated; understanding the climate is complex.

Complex systems are adaptive – complex adaptive systems (CAS) exhibit a dynamic network of interactions (Wikipedia, 2022e). This pesky aspect of CAS allows them to defy engineering efforts. Another is that *all* CAS components adapt *all* of the time. However, if we study the "whole" system and its operation, we might influence its behaviors by implementing well-thought-out and constructive interventions.

The bottom line is that a CAS requires organizational leadership and management to take a different approach. Specifically, Will Allen's article suggests:

- *Relationship building – working with patterns of interaction*
- *Sensemaking – collective interpretation*
- *Loose coupling – support communities of practice and add more degrees of freedom*
- *Learning – act/learn/plan at the same time*
- *Notice emergent directions – building on what works*

Will Allen (2016)

The difference between a technician and an engineer is that a technician may bend something to make it work, whereas the engineer will reform it. Perhaps an analogy for complex systems is that a leader won't try to fix it but will seek to understand it and provide a good reason to change its behaviors (and/or structure).

The "Ah-ha" moment in understanding a complex system occurs when you understand that it's trying to adapt to its environment based on the established rules and the goals for the system. Like Hal's behavior in the book and movie *2001: A Space Odyssey*, rules and goals must align, or you must accept the ensuing chaos.

3.2.2   The day your universe changed

"If you change the way you look at things, the things you look at change."
Wayne Dyer

In his sequel to his popular TV series *Connections*, James Burke, a British science historian, introduced *The Day the Universe Changed* (Wikipedia, 2022p). The series revolved around the philosophical idea that the universe essentially only exists as one perceives it through what one knows; therefore, if and when perception changes, this new insight means that the universe has changed (new perception means new reality). We are talking about this because changing the behavior of a complex system is easy; getting the desired behaviors and outcomes is exponentially more difficult.

You don't fix complex adaptive systems, but you coax them into changing their behaviors through a well-thought-out application of leverage. The use of the term "coax" is deliberate: it applies to the context of the organization as a complex adaptive system, not as a method or approach. Getting the necessary buy-in to apply leverage may require organizational change management.

In her paper "Places to intervene in a system," Donella H. Meadows wrote:

"Folks who do systems analysis have a great belief in 'leverage points.' These are places within a complex system (a corporation, an economy, a living body, a city, an ecosystem) where a small shift in one thing can produce big changes in everything."
Donella H. Meadows (1997)

The paper identified nine leverage points used to intervene in system behavior. We cover these leverage points only briefly. We strongly recommend reading the paper in its entirety.

3.2.2.1   Overview of system leverage points

The list of leverage points is sequenced from least to most impactful.

9   Numbers (subsidies, taxes, standards)

8   Material stocks and flows

7   Regulating negative feedback loops

6   Driving positive feedback loops

5   Information flows

4   The rules of the system (incentives, punishment, constraints)

3   The power of self-organization

2   The goals of the system

1   The mindset or paradigm from which the goals, rules, and feedback structure arise.

3.2.2.2   Leverage point 9: Numbers

Numbers are lowest on the list for a reason. Recall the adage, "What gets measured gets done." This approach focuses energy and effort on the part of the system, not the whole. Working to impact the numbers might provide short-term success, but think about what happens when an organization focuses on short-term costs (a number); in the long term, costs go up, not down.

3.2.2.3   Leverage point 8: Material stocks and flows[22]

This looks at how resources flow through the system and are consumed or stored as a buffer to mitigate spikes in demand (i.e., they act to stabilize a system).

Stocks and flows represent how resources are stored (stock) and the rate of change to the "store" (flow). They represent the physical aspect of a system and have an enormous impact on the behavior of a complex system. Two parameters govern the impact stocks and flows have on a system:

● The size of the stock (the accumulator)
● The flow rate in or out of the stock.

A large stock can provide a stabilizing effect on the system. If the stock is too large, the system might react too slowly.

Similarly, the system can become chaotic if the stock is too small. There is a similar reaction to rates of flow (in-flow or out-flow too fast or slow for the stock). The challenge is to find the right balance. Organizations can impact complex system behaviors by focusing on a single part without understanding how that change will ripple throughout the system. A small change in a stock or flow parameter could drive the system into chaotic behavior, resulting in wild swings in its behavioral outcomes.

---

22   Aronson and Angelakis, n.d.

> **Stocks and flows**
>
> Stocks and flows form the foundation of a system dynamics model. Stocks represent things that can accumulate or drain (e.g., a bathtub that can be filled from a faucet or drained). Flows represent things that can increase or decrease stocks (e.g., open a faucet to fill the tub, and open the drain to let water out of the tub). Flows represent actions; stocks represent accumulations (or buffers).

3.2.2.4   Leverage point 7: Regulating negative feedback loops

Complex systems comprise positive and negative feedback loops. Negative feedback loops act as a throttle or governor for associated positive feedback loops and keep the system operating within established tolerances. The performance impact is proportional to the influence on the system they regulate. The US Federal Reserve uses interest rates and money supply to control the inflation rate.

Leverage can safely be applied to change behaviors only within system tolerances. Negative feedback keeps complex systems within defined tolerances. Combined with positive feedback, it creates a self-correcting system. Weakening or eliminating negative feedback increases the risk of driving a complex system into chaos.

> **Understand system tolerance**
>
> Review Figure 3.1: the perceived comfort of the room depends upon the thermostat tolerances. If the device tolerance is ±1°F, the space will likely feel more comfortable, with less perceived heating and cooling, than with the tolerance set at ±5°F.

3.2.2.5   Leverage point 6: Driving positive feedback loops

A positive feedback loop is self-reinforcing. The more it works, the more it works: examples include unchecked population growth and an infectious disease.

Consider a nuclear reactor that's used to generate electricity. The first step to "turn the reactor on" is to withdraw the control rods from the reactor, which allows the radioactive fuel to produce fission.

- Fission occurs when a neutron strikes an atom, causing it to split into two smaller atoms and release additional neutrons and energy in the form of heat
- These additional neutrons hit other atoms; this process continues until the chain reaction becomes self-sustaining or critical[23]
- This steady state of the reactor produces enough heat to generate steam
- The steam drives turbines to produce electricity (a positive feedback loop).

Control rods dampen the fission process and control the power produced by the reactor (the negative feedback loop). Remove the control rods too quickly, and the fission reaction runs away. It produces more heat than can be removed to produce power (stocks and flows) and melts the fissionable material, which may breach the containment vessel. The control rods at the Chernobyl reactor were accidentally and suddenly removed, which caused the runaway chain reaction that caused the reactor coolant to flash instantaneously to steam and blow the reactor vessel and its containment building apart. The operators disabled the control mechanisms to conduct an experiment.

---

23   Yes, reactors must become critical to work, unlike in bad sci-fi or submarine movies where a critical reactor is a scary thing.

Consider how reintroducing wolves into Yellowstone National Park brought the deer population under control, impacting the regrowth of forests (Smith *et al.*, 2016), stabilizing rivers and wetlands, and repopulating other species. Chaos occurs when a positive loop changes faster than the negative feedback loop can handle.

3.2.2.6 Leverage point 5: Information flows

The CPD Model embodies the flow of information, work, and innovation. Information flows become a leverage point when they change the behavior of a system. Consider using smart devices that monitor the user's physical condition and provide feedback on activities, calories burned, etc., and externally recorded body parameters such as weight, BMI, and other factors. This information might cause the user to change behavior before their clothes become ill-fitting.

One of the first bits of analysis focuses on how information flows within an organization (the complex system). Correcting the flow of information is often the fastest and cheapest way to change complex system behavior positively. Providing information that has not previously been available introduces a new feedback loop that helps other feedback loops to operate better within their desired tolerances. Communications 101 is about getting the correct information to the right place at the right time and frequency.

3.2.2.7 Leverage point 4: The rules of the system (incentive, punishments, constraints)

"The rules of the system define its scope, boundaries, degrees of freedom ... Rules change behavior. Power over rules is real power" (Smith *et al.*, 2016). You must determine how work flows, how communication flows, and how improvements (change) occur. The flows represent the behavior of a system: who sets the rules for behaviors, interprets them, and enforces them (are they enforced)?

Changing the rules that govern a system has a significant impact on the behavior within the system.

Consider the effect Sarbanes–Oxley (Wikipedia, 2022k) had on publicly traded companies in the US. The new rules established transparency and accountability, behaviors, and outcomes. Rules and rulemaking provide significant leverage points on a complex system.

3.2.2.8 Leverage point 3: The power of self-organization

Living systems change themselves: they create new structures and behaviors to evolve and adapt to their environment. Self-organization (Wikipedia, 2022l) can change any lower order of leverage points. As Meadows (1997) pointed out, "Self-organization is basically a matter of evolutionary raw material – a stock of information from which to select possible patterns – and a means for testing them."

Think of an organization with an existing set of systems that produces behaviors that enable it to function in its environment. That complex system came into being through self-organization, continual trial and error, and seeking a positive outcome that provides some advantage in its environment. If this sounds like a living organism, it mimics living systems. What is powerful about self-organization is that it can change all lower-order leverage points to optimize its existence in its environment. The power of self-organization lies in the organization of experiments, to try and fail and try again until it finds something that works. It makes things better for the organization. All too often, organizations stamp out experimentation while seeking control over conformity.

The gaps exposed via the overlay of the DVMS (Z-X Model capabilities) surface opportunities to improve performance, which provides new information that the organization can use to change the behavior of its systems to maintain or improve its ability to create, protect, and deliver digital business value for its stakeholders.

3.2.2.9 Leverage point 2: The goals of the system

Changing the organizational goals to create, protect, and deliver digital value is more effective than any combination of attempting to defend against a bad actor or protecting every digital asset. When the organization changes its goal to create and protect, it supports creating an adaptive system capable of responding to the evolving threat landscape with built-in resilience. It's somewhat akin to mimicking a living organism's immune system. Developing and standing firm for new systems goals is a high leverage point.

3.2.2.10 Leverage point 1: The mindset or paradigm out of which the system arises

A paradigm represents a shared mindset pattern. System purpose, feedback, stocks, and flows stem from paradigms. From James Burke's perspective, the paradigm becomes the universe. Meadows (1997) said, "Systems folks would say one way to change a paradigm is to model a system, which takes you outside the system and forces you to see it whole. We say that because our paradigms have been changed that way."

Paradigms change – that's part of the problem. The shared mindset inherent in a paradigm provides a mental model for the way things are – colored by our perceptions and perspective. If you've heard this phrase, you're already familiar with part of the concept: "That's not how we do things here." The essence of "how we do things" represents a paradigm.

The difficulty in changing the paradigm is that it forces you outside of your universe (what you know and embrace as reality) to look back at it and see it as a whole. Like the trite cliché, "think outside the box," thinking outside your current universe is difficult; sometimes, it's required. Recall that the threat actors continually try new things. We discussed the MITRE ATT&CK database in Chapter 2. This database contains only information about known vulnerabilities, a subset of the vulnerability universe. Also, don't forget ransomware, a "trick" that's been around for a while. All it takes is one person to fall for a phishing attack. [24]

Now, put this into the perspective of your organization and think about how to step outside the box. This creative leverage point has the most profound impact on complex systems.

The organization hits a pivotal event (or set of circumstances) that forces an adaptive or disruptive change. For example, discovering a critical vulnerability as part of a "be the menace" exercise, or a critical breach being reported in the organizational supply chain. The chosen response could be to "patch it and forget it," or to be more proactive and look to improve the protections for all related digital assets. Typically, the events that cause the pivot are less obvious or immediate. However, they involve a similar realization: there is a "survival" reason to stay ahead or play catch-up.

The world changes outside of our control, leading to a reminder about getting stuck in our thinking. Consider George Box's comment about models to ensure no one thinks these leverage points are sufficient or correct (in an "absolute" sense): "All models are wrong, but some are useful." (Wikipedia, 2022a). Paradigms change over time.

---

24   On the dark side, what if this individual was a plant or a mole, embedded to ensure the attack succeeded?

3.2.3   Adaptive cyber resilience

How does an organization become an adaptive cyber-resilient organization? To answer that, we need to explore the concepts of adaptation and resilience.

Adaptive is the adjective form of *adapt*, which means to adjust to new conditions. The adaptive organization can adjust its behavior to respond to environmental changes. Resilience is "the ability to recover from or adjust to change" (Merriam-Webster, n.d.-e). When we consider these two words within a cybersecurity context, the adaptive cyber-resilient organization must do both: recover from and adjust to new conditions.

The concepts associated with cyber resilience provided the basis for our thinking that led to the development of the CPD Model (see Figure 3.5), which represents a complex system and enables the creation, protection, and delivery of digital business value. The minimum viable set of capabilities that the Z-X Model represents provides the means to operationalize the CPD Model.

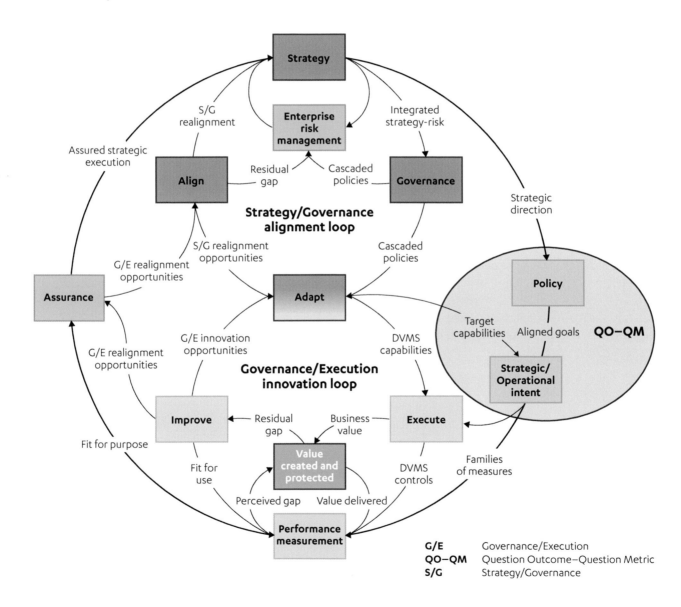

Figure 3.5 The CPD Model

The Governance/Assurance loop is the outer CPD Model loop (starting at strategy, through QO–QM, performance measurement, assurance and back to strategy). The governance side turns organizational strategy into policies executed to create, protect, and deliver digital business value for stakeholders. The assurance side examines the performance of the organizational capabilities that execute the strategic policies to ensure those capabilities are fit for use and purpose. The assurance side also assesses whether the value created is appropriately protected to meet stakeholder expectations.

The Strategy/Governance loop (top inner loop) turns strategy into policies adapted and executed via organizational capabilities, actions, and feedback that may cause a realignment of policy or strategy.

The Governance/Execution loop (bottom inner loop) turns policies into organizational capabilities that create, protect, and deliver digital business value. It measures organizational capability to execute its strategic and operational intent to produce value for its stakeholders. It produces feedback from innovation opportunities actioned in either the Governance/Execution or the Strategy/Governance loop.

The CPD Model subsumes the concept of innovation. Our model of innovation has four aspects:

- **Incremental** Incremental innovation applies when the organization takes continual improvement steps. Each step builds on the progress of the previous steps. This approach is the most common aspect of innovation that applies to incremental improvements of business and technical processes or capabilities. Improving an existing feature in a software product in a series of successive sprints is one example of incremental innovation. The NIST-CSF seven-step model (NIST, 2018) is representative of this approach.

- **Sustaining** Sustaining innovation addresses more significant steps that an organization takes to improve capabilities. The seven-step model also characterizes this approach to implementing new functionality, for example, adding two-factor authentication.

- **Adaptive** Adaptive innovation occurs when the organization changes policy to achieve a new organizational capability that opens new opportunities. The policy change typically results in a corresponding change in practice or technology. An example of this innovation occurred when Amazon developed the logistic capacity to shift its small package deliveries to its fleet.

- **Disruptive** Disruptive innovation occurs when the organization changes strategy, resulting in a breakthrough shift that directly or indirectly disrupts the organizational context and all who share its environment. One of the most disruptive examples occurred when Apple introduced the iTunes music store with per-song purchases as an alternative to buying a whole album or CD. That was an extinction event for many industries, including record stores.[25]

The CPD Model uses the four aspects of innovation to provide objective feedback for the organization to make informed decisions; it establishes the extent of innovation in the complex system. Think back to two discussions: the leverage points within a system and the scope of the four aspects of innovation. Once you have connected these two dots, what comes into focus is a way for an organization to adapt its complex system to its environment based on actionable objective performance measures.

Figure 3.6 illustrates how the CPD Model continually adapts to changes in the environment with appropriately scoped innovation levels. The red ellipses in the figure indicate points to apply leverage to the system. The organizational strategy establishes the "what and why" it wants to perform in its environment. Innovations at this level require the identification of a higher-order leverage point. At this level, you can potentially change the system paradigm, the rules or the rule makers, its goals, or its ability to self-organize. The CPD Model treats this as a realignment of policies or strategies via adaptive or disruptive innovation.

---

25   While record stores still exist, the number and associated business value are significantly lower today. When Netflix shifted to a streaming model instead of DVD-by-mail rental, that was a similarly disruptive event for the bricks-and-mortar video rental business.

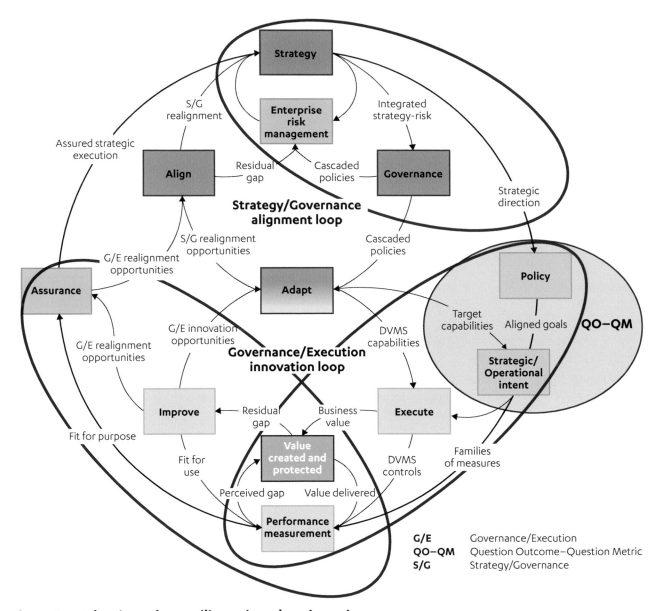

Figure 3.6 Adaptive cyber resilience in a chaotic environment

The Governance/Execution loop limits the extent of innovation to incremental or sustaining improvements. Effectively the organization is tweaking its existing capabilities within the tolerances established for the system. The extent of innovation focuses on the lower-order leverage points. The organization must thoroughly understand the scope of any innovation within the context of using each leverage point to effect desired outcomes of a complex system.

3.3   Knowledge management and systems

Have you heard the phrase "Knowledge is power?" While it sounds good, it misses the mark. Merely "knowing" (or having the knowledge) does not confer power or competitive advantage. The efficient and effective *use* of knowledge provides a potential competitive advantage. We define knowledge management in this context. However, effectively and efficiently using knowledge requires that knowledge be gathered, stored, appropriately managed, and shared. Knowledge management, therefore, is the art and science of three Rs: getting the right information to the right people at the right time to make informed decisions.

Knowledge management is an essential "flow" in systems thinking. Figure 3.2 shows one aspect of this idea of "flow." In this case, it's a perception flow of behavior and communication. This type of flow model of knowledge management suggests that knowledge management participates in creating an organizational culture. Effective knowledge management contributes to a positive culture that supports staff retention and a faster response to the inevitable cybersecurity incident. The ineffective application of knowledge management leads to a bureaucratic or toxic culture that negatively impacts staff retention and the bottom line.

3.3.1   Knowledge management versus repositories

While tools support knowledge management, getting knowledge into a repository is not the goal. The typical perspective holds that there is a stock[26] (or store, or repository) of knowledge; this is insufficient. Recall that we suggested that systems thinking considers multiple perspectives. Knowledge exists in numerous places, not just in some tool (or repository); it exists throughout the organization, including people's heads.

We've already discussed the idea of examining system behavior over time. We can ask how the system changed or evolved throughout the examination period. Studying behaviors over time helps us glimpse the underlying system structure. We can determine trends over time, and potentially why something occurred. In many cases, this allows us to piece together how the system participants used knowledge management to craft the decisions that led to the exhibited behaviors.

In this broader system context, collective organizational wisdom is a different way to think about knowledge management. Some of the knowledge resides in physical repositories, whether digital or analog. Some of the knowledge exists in "this is the way we do things here"; other aspects of knowledge reside in the individuals, past and current, who act within the system.

The key takeaway about knowledge management is the requirement to shift thinking about it as a store of knowledge; instead, think of it as supporting an adaptive organization that can make decisions quickly, effectively, and efficiently.

Knowledge management and history

In the late 1990s, one of the authors was asked to help a client company streamline the ordering process from Europe. Orders from the US took anywhere from an hour to a day to process; orders from Europe could take nearly a week. The company internationalized its website to present information in the local language. Pricing, specifications, special conditions, and more appeared in the native language, yet orders could take a week to process. Behind the scenes, the European customers never saw that the website translated everything into English.

It took more than a month to track down the source of the problem – eventually finding a retired employee who knew the history. In the 1950s, the company received its first international order from France. At that time, only one person, Mary, spoke French. She translated the order specifications from French to English. Over time, the one-person translator became an entire international department headed by Mary. As time passed, every international order passed through this group. At the time of this author's engagement, all international orders still passed through this group.

There was a simple solution: change the process to allow these orders to be handled exactly like the US orders, and figure out what to do with the people in "Mary's department." The solution would've been obvious had any of this history been preserved. There was a gut feeling that eliminating Mary's group was the right thing to do, but people at the organization were reluctant to act without knowing the history.

---

26   Systems thinking, stocks, and flows – there's more information in Aronson and Angelakis (n.d.) and at Wikipedia (2022m). The former provides a mini-quiz to help you distinguish between the two.

3.3.1.1 Knowledge management, mentorship, and complexity

There are aspects of organizational knowledge that should or must be stored in one or more repositories, such as:

● Project lessons learned
● Risk and improvement registers
● Specifications, requirements, and design documents
● The questions and answers suggested in Chapter 2
● Documentation to meet regulatory and compliance requirements.

The preceding list is just a sample; it's up to the organization to define and enforce the requirements for the physical storage of organizational knowledge. What about the information stored in people's heads? How do you share the knowledge that supports the organizational need, regardless of staff turnover?

One way to address this is to make mentorship a part of organizational policy. We're not referring to skills training – we're talking about the background required to make decisions as part of applying those skills. What does the new person (new hire or transfer) need to know to make appropriate and correct decisions that support the group, team, department, or organizational direction? The 3D Knowledge Model™ provides a guide to handling knowledge management mentorship (see Figure 3.7).

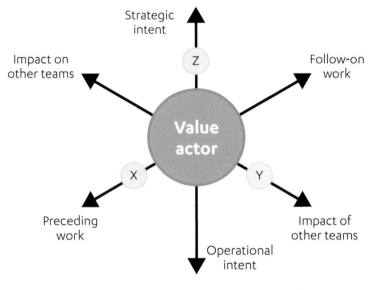

Z forms strategic intent
Z+X and Z+Y form operational intent
Z+X forms value intent

Figure 3.7 The 3D Knowledge Model

In this case, the X-axis represents what somebody needs to know about a given team's past and future work. The Y-axis represents what the individual needs to learn working collaboratively with other teams. The Z-axis represents what the individual or team needs to know regarding how their efforts contribute to strategic and operational intent.

The DVMS FastTrack approach (covered in Chapter 5) originates from lessons from work in agile environments. It assumes the application of the 3D Knowledge Model to manage complexity. Two rules support this contention:

● Provide appropriate autonomy to foster cooperation and collaboration
● Ensure the application of this autonomy is effective in service of the overall mission and vision.

These rules, encapsulated in the 3D Knowledge Model, are critical to ensuring efforts don't go off the rails. The model has wide-ranging applicability, including an approach to managing complexity, which starts with the understanding that everyone needs to know what people are doing and why. The model also surfaces the need for people to understand the consequences of their actions.

3.3.1.2   Organizing for knowledge management

There isn't an ideal or specific org-chart structure to support knowledge management. A better way to organize knowledge management is to base the organization on a flow model inherent in the 3D Knowledge Model. Ensure appropriate mentorship and easy, frictionless communication within a team (essential for a distributed workforce, including homeworkers) and between teams.

3.3.2   The flows

Once you understand that a system is not the sum of its parts but the product of the interactions between them, it's easier to conceptualize a diagram or model as representative of flows within the system. The structure of a system influences the behaviors within it (see the beer game, described in section 3.1.2). If you map the behaviors, that will give you insight into the system structure. Behaviors/actions/flows produce results that shape future actions. For this mental model, we consider three flows: the flow of communication, work, and innovation.

- **Communication** How do teams receive and generate communication, intra-team and inter-team?
- **Work** How does work flow? How is it apportioned within a team and between teams? How is it distributed, and aggregated to form a whole?
- **Innovation** How are opportunities to innovate (including incremental or sustaining innovation) identified, recorded, and actioned?

An additional question occurs when you combine the flows: how does the combination create or contribute to a flow of value for stakeholders?

Note: It is essential to map the flows based on reality, not how people say or think the flows occur. In many organizations, the mapping will differ significantly from the org chart. Understanding flows within the organization is essential without relying on static charts of movement.

3.3.3   Knowledge management, system structure, and system behavior

Discussions of knowledge management typically focus on the technical aspects of the capability. The word "capability" is deliberately used; when you view knowledge management as discussed in this chapter, it's difficult, if not impossible, to treat it as the province of technology. Technology enables and supports knowledge management as a capability; it isn't the endpoint.

Managing and using knowledge effectively is a critical aspect of an adaptive way of working (covered in detail in Chapter 5) and is essential for rapid response to a cybersecurity incident.

3.3.3.1 Knowledge management and culture

Robert Westrum (2004) defined a three cultures model, which determined how culture contributed to how organizations process information:[27]

- **Pathological cultures** are power-oriented, demonstrating low cooperation, with responsibilities shirked or scapegoated and with messengers punished. This type of culture typically views information as a personal resource to be used as necessary to exercise power
- **Bureaucratic cultures** are rule-oriented, exhibit modest cooperation with narrow responsibilities, and ignore messengers. This culture type typically uses standard channels or procedures, which may be insufficient when a rapid response is required, for example, to respond to a cyber breach
- **Generative cultures** are performance-oriented with high cooperation, shared risk, and messengers trained. This culture is typically proactive about getting the correct information to the right people quickly and by any means necessary to support efficient and effective decision-making.

Think about Westrum's culture model in the context of the 3D Knowledge Model. The mentorship program recommended in section 3.3.1.1 is consistent with a generative culture. It supports deliberate and policy-driven efforts to keep team members informed and stocked with the appropriate knowledge to do their jobs effectively and efficiently, providing a proactive approach to knowledge management.

3.4 Working at the edge of chaos

Let's start with an understanding of chaos. The Merriam-Webster definition of "chaos" is "The inherent unpredictability in the behavior of a complex natural system" (Merriam-Webster, n.d.-b). This is a good start to our discussion because we've already covered complexity in section 3.2.1. Two parts of the definition are essential to understanding the concepts we'll explore in this section: "inherent unpredictability" and "behavior of a complex natural system."

Working at the edge of chaos differs from living at the edge of chaos. The idea is similar to what we described when discussing the difference between working *in* and working *on* a system. Working *in* a system is what you experience within constraints imposed by the system structure and "normal" system behaviors. Working *on* a system is when you seek to change its structure and related behavior.

All organizations live on the edge of chaos because that is the nature of their environment. They seek to understand and seek order in their environment and formulate strategies based on the best-guess understanding of how their future environment works, combined with expectations for behaviors and outcomes.

The organization seeks to optimize its performance within that environment. Impactful things totally out of control happen, such as natural disasters, strategic material shortages, currency manipulation, and rogue nations developing nuclear weapons. It seeks to understand and mitigate its risk as best it can in an unpredictable world.

Every organization has evolved to optimize its performance within its environment. It's one thing to let chaos happen to you; it's another for the organization to create chaos or seek to be impactful in its environment. This section explores how organizations can work within a system on the edge of chaos.

---

27 There are ways to map and improve organizational culture that are beyond the scope of this book to cover. You can find one such reference at the Harvard Business Review site (Groysberg *et al.*, 2018; subscription required).

3.4.1   Understanding chaos

> *"(A) seemingly chaotic situation that results in desirable outcomes can be said to contain order despite producing unexpected outcomes bringing to the fore the term, organized chaos. This theory is anchored on the premise that there lies a natural order by which all organisms are governed, and it is this that governs situations, which might seem disorganized."*
> Peter Elijah Lungu (2014)

We start with the CPD Model to understand organizational environmental touchpoints.

The organizational strategy represents complex adaptations (behaviors) that serve an essential function in achieving evolutionary success. The CPD Model integrates strategy with its understanding of enterprise risk to form a risk-informed strategy (strategy-risk). This strategy-risk represents what the organization "thinks" describes the best adaptations of its behavior in its environment to optimize its ability to survive and thrive (succeed). Think back to our discussion in section 3.2 (Leverage, change, and adaptive resilience), where we discussed the difference between complicated and complex and then discussed the application of leverage to change system behavior. Add to that consideration of the current situation the organization faces. The organization seeks to change the behavior of its complex system in the context of its environment, which is another complex system. What can possibly go wrong?

The organization must use high-order leverage points to impact its paradigm, set the rules by which it operates, and changes its goals or the way it self-organizes. The results are new or updated strategy-risk policies, which result in new/additional management policies that create or improve organizational capabilities and performance by creating more favorable circumstances to achieve the desired outcomes. This idea is part of an ongoing set of activities to learn, adapt, make changes, and evaluate how those changes impact system outcomes.

The CPD Model Governance/Assurance loop (the outer loop in Figure 3.5), in conjunction with the Strategy/Governance loop (Figure 3.8), is used to effect change based on feedback from its environment and input of its performance in its environment and the performance of its capabilities.

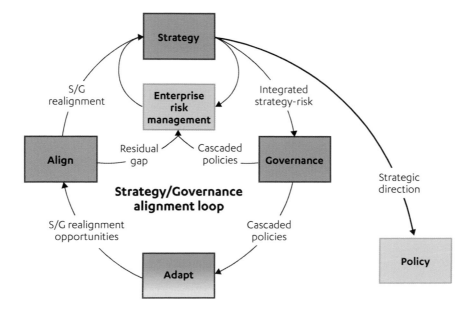

Figure 3.8 Strategy/Governance loop: Strategy and a chaotic environment

Policies provide the guidance that management uses to create or improve organizational capabilities to achieve the desired outcomes that change the system behavior and structure. The CPD Model policy takes two different and essential paths:

- In the first path, management adapts policies to create or improve existing organizational capabilities
- The second path expresses the strategic and operational intent, establishing organizational measures and metrics to instrument[28] capabilities and ensuring that it appropriately creates, protects, and delivers digital business value.

The Governance/Execution loop (Figure 3.9) uses the lower-order leverage points. The activities in this loop operate within engineered tolerances established by higher-order leverage points. In all practicality, the Governance/Execution loop works more like a complicated system than a complex one.

The Governance/Execution loop manifests the strategic and operational intent to create, protect, and deliver digital business value, measured against stakeholders' expectations, in the context of its chaotic environment.

The QO–QM loop shown in Figure 3.9 provides the basis to align Governance/Execution loop tolerances with the strategic and operational intent in the Strategy/Governance loop (Figure 3.8).

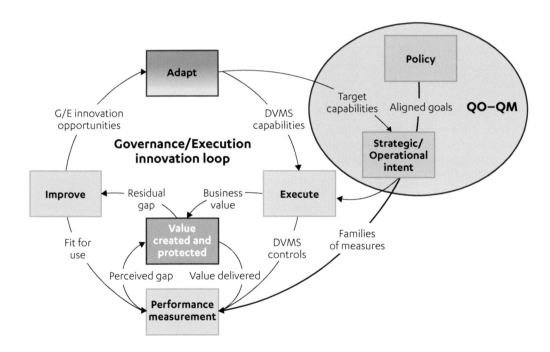

Figure 3.9 Governance/Execution loop: Capability performance in a chaotic environment

---

28   We use the term "instrument" to mean the subject of the instrumentation provides both formal and appropriate means to use measurement to determine whether the resulting behaviors or actions meet defined expectations.

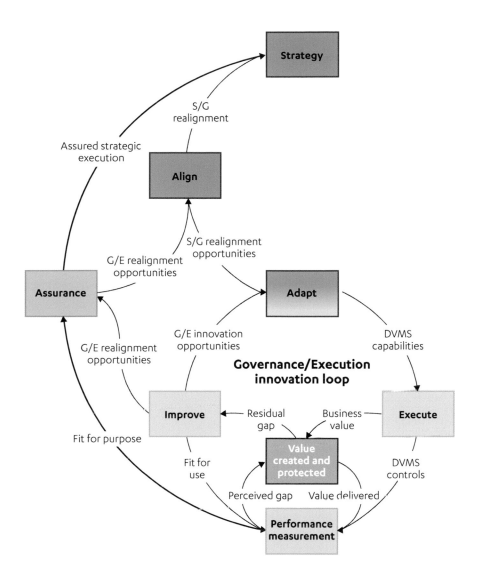

Figure 3.10 Governance/Execution loop: Utilizing Innovation in the context of chaos

The Governance/Execution loop (Figure 3.10) applies the organizational capabilities to create, protect, and deliver digital business value within the tolerances set out by strategic policies.

Measures and metrics derived from the strategic and operational intent provide the basis to evaluate performance. The object is to consider the "what" and "how" in the context of verifiable proof.

- What are we going to do?
- How will we do it?
- How will we prove we've done it?

A capability is fit for *use* when it operates as designed; it is fit for *purpose* when it effectively and efficiently achieves the desired objectives. Performance gaps (i.e., out-of-tolerance performance) are closed in the Governance/Execution loop. Similarly, this loop addresses value gaps that result from capability gaps. The Strategy/Governance loop addresses results from misaligned policy or strategy, which result in the realignment of policies, necessitating a change in policy or a realignment of strategy. Use both high- and low-order leverage points in section 3.2 to adjust organizational complex system behavior (and potentially structure) that creates, protects, and delivers digital business value.

3.4.2 Applying leverage

Once you understand how the organization receives feedback from its environment, the next step is to examine how it applies the leverage points to change behaviors.

Section 3.2.3 examined how innovation contributes to the organization becoming adaptive and cyber-resilient. Here we address each aspect of innovation related to applying leverage within a system.

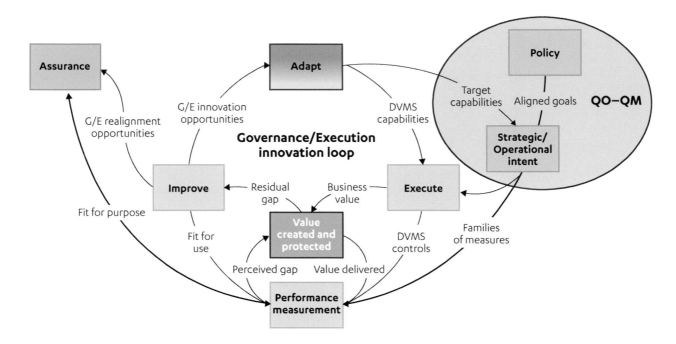

Figure 3.11 Governance/Execution loop: Applying low-order leverage

In the CPD Model, the Governance/Execution loop (Figure 3.11) does the heavy lifting. This loop is where stakeholders' experience and the capabilities to create, protect, and deliver digital business value come together. It is also the place where low-order leverage is applied.

The QO–QM loop (covered in detail in Chapter 7) provides the basics to establish performance measures. This loop is where strategic policies are expressed as aligned goals and then decomposed using the GQM methodology to develop a set of measures and metrics to monitor performance within strategic policy tolerances. These are the same policies that management adapts to create or improve the organizational capabilities to create, protect, and deliver digital business value. Later in this book, we'll cover how the implementors and auditors of the organizational capabilities work collaboratively to ensure the proper instrumentation of capabilities to produce the measures and metrics that assure system performance.

The CPD Model performance measurement measures the actual capability performance and value delivery. Each gap represents an innovation opportunity, evaluated by the responsible approval authority within a clearly defined extent. The term *extent* refers to the leverage points to best impact system behavior within a determined and agreed scope. The innovation model gaps provide the context for evaluating organizational capabilities.

Incremental and sustaining innovations improve or implement organizational capabilities using low-order leverage points. These innovations occur within the Governance/Execution loop and tweak system performance within established tolerances. These are not innovations triggered by realignment of policy or strategy. Incremental changes make minor adjustments to system performance. Sustaining changes typically result in new or improved performance, but not new capabilities.

Gaps in delivered value may represent a residual gap in part of a system that provides value to stakeholders. Residual gaps typically result from a phased delivery approach. The gap represents the remainder value delivered with subsequent improvement iterations. However, consider what happens when the value gap results from an unanticipated change in the business environment. While the organizational capabilities provide value within tolerances, the value delivered may no longer meet stakeholder expectations. This value gap requires a realignment of the policies governing organizational capabilities or strategy (i.e., an adaptive or disruptive innovation).

When an organization faces either an adaptive or a disruptive change, it must look at the possibility of realigning its policy or strategy to adapt the organizational capabilities relative to a change in the environment. An adaptive change looks at the policies derived from strategy, and may realign those policies relative to the response to an environmental change. Realignment of policies occurs within the scope of the existing strategy.

Consider a pizza delivery driver stuck in traffic. Company policy requires the customer to receive hot pizza within 10 minutes from when it leaves the store, using the optimized route chosen by the store-provided GPS. The delivery person is on the route selected by the GPS. In this scenario, the customer will likely receive a cold pizza. What if the store policy allowed the driver to reroute given unanticipated traffic delays, or upgrade the GPS to use real-time traffic data to provide automatic rerouting? Changes in policy deal with both solutions.

What if the store used automated drones to deliver pizza within five minutes of leaving the store, eliminating traffic delays and the added customer expense of tipping the driver? That is a change in strategy. That new delivery strategy would require updated policies to improve or develop new delivery capabilities actioned in the Governance/Execution loop. This approach is an example of high-order leverage points impacting system behavior.

3.4.3   It's about time

Section 3.2 discussed what makes complex systems complex. It is essential to understand the interrelationships among the components of the system. One of the most critical aspects of these interrelationships is *latency* – the time between an event and when its impact is felt or observed. Latency exists in all systems. It is a vital aspect of thinking in systems to understand the role latency plays in system performance (see the discussion in section 3.1.2.3 about behavior-over-time graphs).

Think about piloting a Jet Ski. It has a very high power-to-weight ratio and can turn in a circle within its length. Now think of piloting a super container ship. It's very long and heavy and has a low power-to-weight ratio; if you want to turn, it will take many times the ship's length, and many minutes, to make that turn. Both vessels represent a complicated water transportation system; both take directional input from their pilot. Yet the same input results in much different behavior of the system. The primary difference is the delay between steering input and the rate of change in the vessel's direction of travel.

Consider your organizational recruitment and talent development system (human resources or HR). With the approval of an opening for a senior accountant, how long does it take to fill the position? Where are the built-in delays? When can the hiring manager expect to have a new hire start?

Here's an interesting exercise: Examine your organizational systems to identify latency. How many ways can you think of to address latency?

Examples of delays include communication and information flows, the time it takes to do something, or how long it takes to improve existing processes or activities. What are the intermediate steps? Does every step contribute to value? If not, why is it necessary? Consider creating behavior-over-time graphs to make latency visible.

In systems thinking, any observer of system performance must identify and understand how much time separates an event from its impact on the system. Think back to the beer game. Failure to understand delays in a system will often result in overcorrecting input to speed up or slow down the result, causing the system to go into oscillation.

An example is a highly successful marketing campaign that drives a sharp spike in demand. The organization responds by adding a second shift to produce more to meet the demand. Before the additional product is available for sale, there is a sharp reduction in demand – due to the delay in delivering the product. The result is excess product sitting in a warehouse. How many ways can you think of to address this scenario?

Fundamental to understanding any system is to understand built-in latency. Only then can you confidently seek to change the system's behavior without sending it into oscillations or chaos.

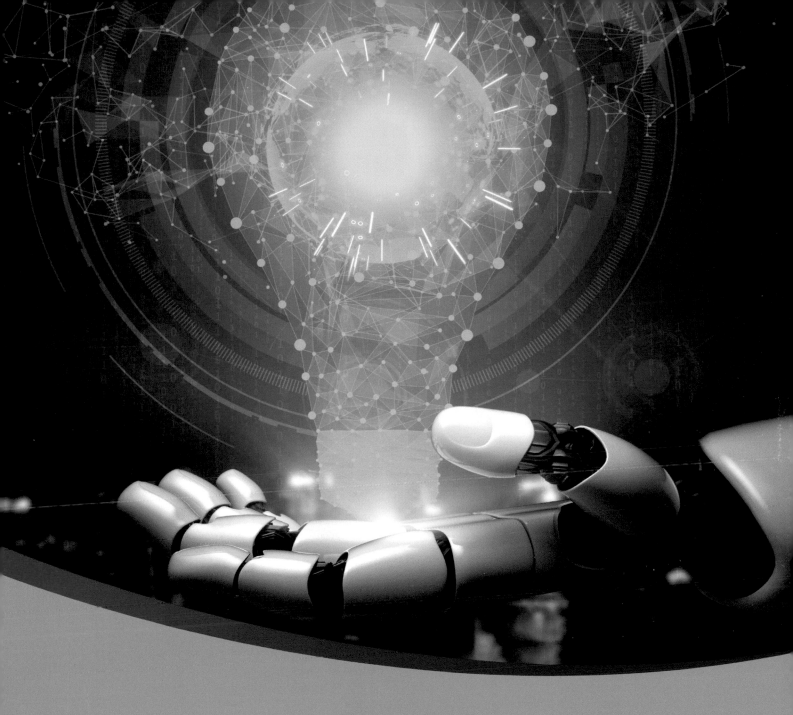

CHAPTER 4
Cybersecurity and the Digital Value Management System™

4 Cybersecurity and the Digital Value Management System™

Up to this point, we've discussed high-level concepts that help us think about cybersecurity differently. The most important concept we've discussed is a change in approach that focuses on value creation and protection being inseparable – different sides of the same coin. Once an organization has made that paradigm shift, the rules and goals of the complex systems it uses to create value must change to align resources to include value protection with value creation, enabling the delivery of appropriately protected value to stakeholders.

4.1 Exploring the DVMS

This section explores how an organization operationalizes the governance and assurance required by a complex system to execute its strategic policies, and to assure that these policies create and deliver protected digital business value for stakeholders.

We'll discuss how an organization becomes adaptive and cyber-resilient in the context of the concepts in Chapter 3.

This section establishes the context for the Z-X Model; section 7.2 details the model's capabilities.

4.1.1 The DVMS and the Z-X Model core capabilities

The DVMS represents our model of the minimum viable capabilities (MVCs) necessary to create, protect, and deliver digital business value. The model represents a three-layered system to be used by organizations as an overlay to their existing capabilities. Gaps between the current organizational capabilities and the DVMS overlay of Z-X Model capabilities provide an improvement roadmap to deliver adequately created and protected digital value.

The idea of an overlay is essential: the DVMS is not one-size-fits-all, but a systems model applicable to all, regardless of size. Conceptually, the existing organizational capabilities are a black box. The DVMS acts as a white box that, when overlaid, exposes performance gaps. The Z-X Model describes the MVCs, not processes or activities, expressed as practice outcomes. The "how" associated with the adaptation to produce the required outcomes is unique to the organization. The DVMS Model is agnostic concerning the underlying service management system, not a replacement for it.

The following sections describe each of the DVMS core capabilities and associated practice areas. The DVMS does not cover the implementation and execution of the activities required to achieve the expected outcome; the typical way to address these activities is via one or more processes. This approach is deliberate and results from the DVMS's overlay nature. The organization must define the necessary activities, procedures, and processes[29] based on resources, need, etc.[30]

Five core organizational capabilities comprise the DVMS, as shown in Figure 4.1.

---

29   The DVMS does not address processes which are an organizational responsibility to define and use. A process implements or executes one or more practices, grouped by the practice areas covered in section 4.1.1.1. Our use of the term "process" refers to the set of activities, tasks, procedures, etc., that provide the basis to manifest the outcomes expressed for a practice. The level of process implementation rigor is left to the organization. There is more detail about the practices in Chapter 7.

30   The nature of internal DVMS relationships, a maturity capability model, and demonstrable artifacts for each outcome at each capability level are explained in section 7.2.

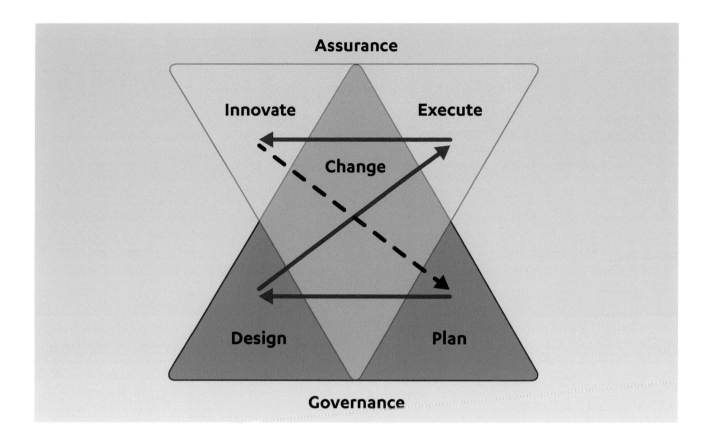

Figure 4.1 The Z-X Model of DVMS capabilities

4.1.1.1 Z-X Model capabilities

Plan

This capability enables the organization to plan for operationalizing the governance and assurance of the Z-X Model core capabilities. It develops the plans for organizational performance necessary to create and execute a risk-informed business strategy, manage its portfolio of programs, risks, and projects, and manage organizational knowledge. The practice areas of the Plan capability subsequently enable the organization to create, protect, and deliver digital business value.

The purpose of the Plan capability subsumes two goals: creating and delivering digital business value, and appropriately protecting the value.

Five practice areas comprise the Plan capability:

- Governance (planning)
- Assurance (planning)
- Strategy-risk management
- Portfolio, program, and project management
- Knowledge management.

Design

The Design capability enables the organization to create a straightforward, cohesive approach to creating, protecting, and delivering digital business value. It seeks to develop designs through the system architecture and configuration management practice areas that enable the organization to deliver protected digital business value.

Practice areas:

- System architecture
- Configuration management.

Change

The Change capability is a fundamental organizational capability that enables the organization to adapt to its environment. Internal needs, external requirements, and a dynamic threat environment drive the Change capability. It affects digital solutions that meet the design requirements necessary to create, protect, and deliver digital business value. It establishes the governance structure required to coordinate solutions that affect digital business value.

Practice areas:

- Change coordination
- Solution adaptation
- Release management
- Deployment management.

Execute

The Execute capability represents the practice areas that create, protect, and deliver digital business value. These practice areas encompass providing access to digital products, services, and systems to authorized users; mitigating disruptions in the delivery of digital business value; identifying and resolving systemic interruption or degradation of digital business value; and the overarching management of the infrastructure platforms.

Practice areas:

- Provisioning
- Incident management
- Problem management
- Infrastructure/platform management.

Innovate

The Innovate capability seeks opportunities for improving the creation, protection, and delivery of digital business value. The organizational context drives achieving its expressed strategic and operational intent. It measures the overall performance of the components and systems that create, protect, and deliver digital business value, analyzes performance gaps, and catalogs innovation opportunities. The Z-X Model capabilities enable the organization to adapt to its dynamic environmental context.

Practice areas:

- Continual innovation
- Performance measurement
- Gap analysis.

4.1.1.2   Integrating cybersecurity controls with Z-X Model capabilities

When an organization adopts the NIST Cybersecurity Framework, it's making the strategic decision to take a structured, risk-based approach to cybersecurity. Typically, the adopting organization already has some cybersecurity capabilities. Using the DVMS as an overlay exposes gaps in the current cybersecurity posture. The adopting organization must adapt control requirements to meet its internal needs, external conditions, and threat landscape. The gaps determine whether it must improve existing capabilities or create new ones.

The adopting organization must establish the baseline, the critical first step, to meet its cybersecurity needs – understanding that this baseline continually evolves. The organization must clearly understand its own internal needs based on its perception of its performance in its environment relative to the value it produces for its stakeholders. External considerations – legislative, regulatory, statutory, etc. – represent fixed external requirements placed on the organization that it must accommodate as part of its performance within its environment. The competitive landscape (applicable to commercial, military, or governmental organizations) potentially imposes another class of external requirements. Lastly, setting the bar for cybersecurity is also informed by the organizational threat surface (review Chapter 2) and the highly dynamic threat landscape.

Once this baseline has been established, the adopting organization seeks an optimal approach to identify, prioritize, and integrate the selected cybersecurity informative references with its existing Z-X Model capabilities. Some organizations might need to create or improve their DVMS capabilities to integrate cybersecurity control requirements. Chapter 5 introduces the DVMS FastTrack model, which enables an organization to rapidly establish a cybersecurity beachhead and expand its defensible cybersecurity perimeter with additional cybersecurity control requirements.

Integrating cybersecurity controls with the organizational DVMS capabilities ensures that it achieves the minimal organizational capability to create, protect, and deliver digital business value.

4.1.1.3   The 3D Knowledge Model and the flow of communication, work, and innovation

The 3D Knowledge Model (Figure 3.7) is essential to understanding how communication, work, and innovation happen in a complex system.

Put yourself in the middle of the model. You are a software developer on a team creating a mobile application that enables a sales engineer to capture the specifications for a custom power supply for a new product for a customer. What does the 3D Knowledge Model mean to you in this context, specifically the flow of communication, work, and innovation?

Communication

Communication flows through all three axes of the 3D Knowledge Model.

The Z-axis (strategic and operational intent) provides the capability basis for you (the value actor) to capture the customer's onsite technical specifications. It allows you to provide the customer with design, unit pricing, and lead time to shipping. This approach drastically shortens the sales cycle and improves your organizational manufacturing and procurement capabilities.

Now put yourself in the position of the programmer who writes the code to reformat the sales engineer's specifications as input to the legacy design configurator. You create this software (the "what") and know its value for the overall product development cycle (the "why").

In addition, you know what the next value actor will do with your code. Their job is to integrate your work into the larger application; part of your job is to ensure this occurs smoothly and seamlessly. You provide the appropriate documentation for your code to facilitate their efforts – you've tested it in a mock live environment and documented the discovered issues so that the handoff to the next steps proceeds cleanly. You don't work in isolation; communication flows to and from other teams. Other teams may inform you of some critical aspect of their work that impacts what you are doing.

Similarly, your work may impact how others complete their job. Applying this model, you know the "what" and "why" of your job, what preceded your efforts, and what follows. Other teams have kept you informed about their work, and you have, in turn, kept other teams informed of yours.

Work

Work flows through the value stream as individual value actors perform some action that adds to the overall value of the work – in our example, writing software code that reformats input data to be used by an existing legacy system. Value actors developed the software architecture; others did the system and subsystems design, developed the detailed specifications for the software modules, and coded them. Someone will test and integrate it into the subsystem, etc. Everyone added some value in the form of work as your contribution flowed through to completion. Your team may integrate another team's work into your work product. Similarly, something your team did might be repurposed or reused by another team.

The critical thing to note here is the cooperation and collaboration required to make this happen. The 3D Knowledge Model represents the antithesis of silos. Each team uses aspects of the 3D Knowledge Model to ensure the scope of its work meets the strategic and operational intent. Each group becomes aware of its work efforts and understands the impact on the actions of others.

Innovation

Innovation flows within each axis of the 3D Knowledge Model. Incremental change (slight improvement) might be the province of a single team (Z-axis) or multiple teams (Z- and Y-axes). In our sample case, a front-end software module exists to communicate with the legacy system. Your job is to improve it slightly to accept additional or different data from a new source. The effort requires other teams to either contribute to the development of the improvement, test it, release it to a new environment, or deploy it (i.e., make it operational) in a new environment. In this case, the application of the Z-axis is likely to be implicit.

Active engagement across the Z-axis occurs when the project represents a sustaining, adaptive, or disruptive innovation. Examples of these three types of innovation:

- The **sustaining** innovation development of a standard capability that allows the company to keep up with the competition
- The **adaptive** innovation that changes policies to enable the development of support tools to reduce the design, acquisition, and cycle time drastically to deliver better value for customers faster, producing a corresponding competitive advantage
- The **disruptive** innovation that crafts a replacement for the legacy system to allow the company to enter new markets, and also frees resources assigned to maintain the front-end modules.

Think about the advantages of working in an environment where you know what you are doing and why it is essential to the organization. You clearly understand the work you do and the value your efforts add. Additionally, you know what other teams expect: those working on the same aspect of the project, and the next group picking up the effort. Everyone involved continually keeps everyone apprised of their work – in a productive way.

The 3D Knowledge Model is not limited to internal use. Arrange contracts so that partners and suppliers participate in the model; imagine the transparency. Applying the model to internal and external use, would your job be less stressful and more rewarding if you worked in this environment?

4.1.2   The Digital Value Capability Maturity Model

A capability maturity model provides a basis for an organization to gauge various organizational capabilities and the maturity of management or the level of rigor the organization applies toward achieving and maintaining those capabilities.

We've adapted the US Department of Energy's Cybersecurity Capability Maturity Model (C2M2) (US Department of Energy, 2022) for use with the DVMS and the Z-X Model capabilities to create the Digital Value Capability Maturity Model (DVCMM).

An organization adopting the NIST Cybersecurity Framework takes a risk-based approach to cybersecurity. It sets its bar for cybersecurity based on its internal needs, its external requirements, and the threat landscape. The DVMS represents the minimum viable capability the organization must demonstrate to create, protect, and deliver digital business value; the DVCMM has four levels (numbered 0 to 3). To meet those minimum capabilities, an adopting organization must achieve level 3 (the fourth level) to ensure the value created is appropriately protected.

The DVCMM (Table 4.1) is an uncomplicated approach for determining the organizational capability to create, protect, and deliver digital business value. It's a binary evaluation: the organization either does something or doesn't; the outcomes and associated process maturity must be measurable (documented and auditable).

Existing organizational policies establish the basis for execution. The organization measures process[31] performance to ensure that the Z-X Model capabilities fit its intended purpose and deliver digital business value that meets expectations.

4.1.2.1   DVCMM capabilities, characteristics, and management

The Z-X Model overlays existing capabilities and practices (grouped into the practice areas identified in section 4.1.1.1). Consequently, the characteristics of the model are intentionally broad; they represent the organizational capabilities necessary to achieve a given maturity level. The term "management" connotes the organizational level of rigor applied to the Z-X Model's practice-area-related processes.

Level 0

- **Capability** The organization has no awareness or structure that can create, protect, and deliver digital business value with any reliable level of repeatability. It has no measures or metrics to provide a basis for the assurance of policy execution, fitness for use, or fitness for purpose
- **Characteristics** There are no discernible Z-X Model capabilities. This characteristic is typical of an organization that does not know or understand how to use the Z-X Model as an overlay to improve performance
- **Management** The organization does not know or understand the capabilities necessary to create, protect, and deliver digital business value, or to exhibit discernible or objectively measurable action.

---

31   The Z-X Model capabilities do not extend to process; the model covers practice areas and practices that form the basis for areas of improvement. Processes execute the activities associated with one or more practices.

Table 4.1 The DVCMM

Level	Characteristics	Management	Artifacts
Level 0	There are no processes to perform the capability-related practice areas	None	None
Level 1	Processes to perform the capability-related practice areas are unplanned and informal	Ad hoc	Some processes are repeatable There is documentation for some processes There are measures and metrics for some processes There are policies that provide some (potentially incomplete) guidance governing establishing measures and metrics Existing measures and metrics provide the basis for action
Level 2	There is documentation for the processes that execute the capability-related practice areas Stakeholders are identified and involved There are adequate resources to support the process Uses standards or guidelines to support the implementation of processes related to capabilities and practice areas	Structured	The organization adopts a structured approach to creating, protecting, and delivering digital business value The organization uses risk-based policies to create measures and metrics that express the organizational strategic and operational intent There is a traceable link between business value and resource allocation to create, protect, and deliver The organization implements relevant processes to support the Z-X Model practice areas There is process documentation There are measures and metrics to determine that the processes are fit for use Auditable documentation shows stakeholder identification and their respective involvement with the appropriate processes Evidence shows the adopted standards have supporting adaptation documentation with the appropriate fit-for-use measures and metrics There are staff awareness and training plans to enable skilled and knowledgeable staff to support the Z-X Model practice areas and associated processes

Level	Characteristics	Management	Artifacts
Level 3	Governance and policies guide activities Policies include compliance requirements for specified standards or guidelines Activities are periodically reviewed for conformance to policy Responsibility and authority for each process are assigned Personnel performing the processes related to capabilities, and processes related to capabilities and practices, processes have adequate skills and knowledge	Controlled	Measures and metrics are used to determine that the processes: • Are fit for purpose • Comply with relevant internal and external requirements • Assure strategic policy execution There is proof that stakeholders are identified, accountability is established, and responsibilities are detailed All Z-X Model-associated practice areas and the resulting processes are adequately staffed at the level required to create, protect, and deliver digital business value Policies and procedures are applied to periodically assess personal skills and knowledge, to ensure staff have and use the required skills and knowledge to create, protect, and deliver digital business value

Level 1

- **Capability** The organization performs processes that create, protect, and deliver digital business value at an ad-hoc level. Performance assessment might involve some measures and metrics. However, these measures and metrics don't provide meaningful or actionable information without overarching policies to establish performance goals
- **Characteristics** The organization performs an initial set of associated Z-X Model practice-related processes that are unplanned or informal. There is little or no documentation used in the performance of these processes, and no assurance of repeatability
- **Management** The organization may perform some activities associated with Z-X Model practice areas, but only on an ad-hoc basis. There is no assurance of reliable or repeatable outcomes.

Level 2

- **Capability** The organization adopts a structured approach to creating, protecting, and delivering digital business value. It establishes risk-informed policies that drive strategies to develop measures and metrics that express the organizational strategic and operational intent. Resource allocation is value-based. The organization has adopted and adapted the relevant Z-X Model practice areas to close identified performance gaps. The processes associated with each practice area support appropriate measurements and metrics to ensure they are fit for use
- **Characteristics** The organization documents associated Z-X Model practice-area-related processes based on established strategy-risk-informed policies and governance. It identifies and assigns accountable and responsible stakeholders for process performance, metrics, and outcomes. The organization provides adequate resources to implement Z-X Model practice-area-related processes

- **Management** The organization establishes a structured approach to creating, protecting, and delivering digital business value. Z-X Model practice-area-related process activities conform to process documentation. The stakeholders in the outcomes of these processes play an active role in those processes. The organization provides the necessary funding and resources to create, protect, and deliver digital business value consistent with the organizational strategic and operational intent. The organization follows established standards, frameworks, and methods.

Level 3

- **Capability** The organization is "under control." Governance and strategy-risk-informed policies guide all activities. Z-X Model capabilities, internal needs, external requirements, and the dynamic threat landscape are part of the ongoing assessment, balanced against the organizational strategic and operational intent. The organization identifies and assigns stakeholder accountability and responsibility. Part of accountability and responsibility includes finding and closing gaps in Z-X Model capabilities, personnel skills, and value performance

- **Characteristics** All organizational DVMS-related activities are guided by policy and subject to oversight. The policies address internal needs and external requirements to establish a basis to respond to the dynamic threat landscape. The organization periodically reviews DVMS-related activities to ensure policy compliance. Personnel has assigned responsibility and authority for practices and conformance to policy

- **Management** The organization ensures the execution of strategic policies consistent with its strategic and operational intent. It establishes a reporting schema that identifies gaps in performance and ensures that Z-X Model practice-area-related processes are fit for use, are fit for purpose, and deliver the desired digital business value.

4.1.2.2 DVCMM quality is (almost) free

Unprotected value contributes to higher costs. By separating the inseparable, creating value without appropriate protections, the organization elects to pay a higher rate to respond to a cybersecurity breach and recover from the damages it causes.[32] Why? How is this possible?

Consider the following analogy. You should take your car to your auto mechanic to perform the recommended preventative maintenance. For example, suppose you ignore changing the oil. You're likely to experience complete engine failure and a voided warranty, and incur an expense that could be at least 10% of the car purchase price – to say nothing about aggravation, lost productivity, cost of a rental car, and more. The decision to ignore recommended maintenance puts you in a self-insuring position against engine failure. Take the small incremental steps to "appropriately protect" the car's value, and you avoid the unnecessary expense of engine replacement.

With the incremental cost of performing regular oil changes for your car, even if you keep the car for ten years and change the oil and oil filter every quarter, the total cost for the oil changes will likely be less than 25% of the cost of replacing the engine.

The same is true for digital value. There is a relatively small incremental cost to combine value creation with value protection. The perspectives of both implementor and auditor must be represented on the solution development team. Ideally, fill the roles with different people. In a small organization with insufficient resources, one person must provide the two perspectives.

The DVCMM provides a roadmap supporting incremental improvements to create and protect digital business value for stakeholders.

---

32   It is also likely that it will pay higher premiums on cybersecurity insurance.

4.2   A systems view of the CPD Model

Our view of systems thinking is an approach that integrates the belief that the components of a system, when separated from the whole system, will behave differently. So, in complex systems, isolating parts of the system to "fix" how the system behaves often results in unexpected system behavior.

---

*"Systems thinking in practice encourages us to explore **inter-relationships** (context and connections), **perspectives** (each actor has their own unique perception of the situation) and **boundaries** (agreeing on scope, scale and what might constitute an improvement)"*
Learning for Sustainability (n.d.)

This section introduces some basic systems archetypes that provide a context for an in-depth examination of the CPD Model's interrelationships and perspectives, and an understanding of boundaries when making innovative changes to the system's behavior.

4.2.1   Because stuff happens

The human brain has evolved to recognize patterns of behavior. These create what we call expertise in our subconscious mind, which enables a fast response to similar situations. It's an evolutionary survival capability. Human organizations mimic natural behavior patterns, and can be identified or modeled with various tools and techniques. We can use these multiple tools to ask and answer, "Why?" Each question and answer build our understanding of behavior patterns and a deeper understanding of how things work. Our leverage discussion (section 3.2) explained that an entire spectrum of leverage points in a complex system affects system behavior.

But before we do a deep dive into the CPD Model, let's look at some of the basic building blocks of a system by examining a causal loop.

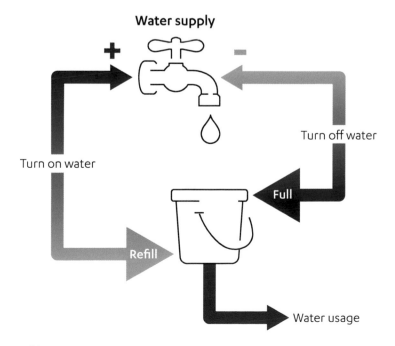

Figure 4.2 Simple causal loop

In Figure 4.2, we have a simple causal loop. This loop causes the bucket to maintain a water level between the refill and full levels. The water level reaching either "refill" or "full" causes the faucet to turn on or off. This diagram represents an example of a reinforcing and balancing loop. When the water level falls to the "refill" level, the water is turned on (reinforcing). When it reaches the "full" level, the water is turned off (balance).

Thinking in (and working on) systems requires a basic understanding of how to talk about complex systems, much like diagramming a sentence: there are nouns, verbs, and modifiers.

> *"A causal loop diagram consists of four basic elements: the **variables**, the **links** between them, the **signs on the links** (which show how the variables are interconnected), and the **sign of the loop** (which shows what type of behavior the system will produce). By representing a problem or issue from a causal perspective, you can become more aware of the structural forces that produce puzzling behavior."*
> Colleen Lannon (2018)

As simple as this diagram is, it is fundamental to understanding the patterns and behaviors of the complex systems you work in and on.

Daniel H. Kim's booklet *Systems Archetypes I: Diagnosing Systemic Issues and Designing High-Leverage Interventions* (Kim, 1992) is an excellent reference to learn more about systems thinking and different archetypes.

4.2.2 Working *on* or *in* a system

Frameworks describe what an adopting organization should think about and why it's essential. A framework is descriptive because it leaves the "what to do" and "how to do it" to the adopting organization. We've discussed how the CPD Model describes a complex system that enables an organization to achieve and maintain cyber resilience.

The CPD Model represents an organizational adaptation of the guidance in the NIST Cybersecurity Framework, realized in two parts. The first part is implementing or improving the current organizational cybersecurity capabilities to achieve the desired cybersecurity posture. The second is executing and improving the "new normal" or updated state of cybersecurity capabilities. [33]

When an organization adopts the NIST-CSF and uses the CPD Model to guide its adaptation, it must clearly understand the differences between working *on* and working *in* the system.

Working *on* the system is what an adapting organization does to create or improve its cybersecurity capabilities, including people, practice, and technology. It includes the points of view of the implementor and auditor. This dual viewpoint is a critical aspect of the CPD Model because both perspectives are necessary for the capabilities to plan, design, change, execute, and innovate to create, protect, and deliver digital business value. The combined perspectives enable the adapting organization to instrument its systems so that both the implementor and auditor can determine whether the new or changed systems deliver the expected business value, meaning the changes are fit for purpose and fit for use.

Working *in* the system is what the people in the adapting organization do within the system that realizes the desired organizational cybersecurity capabilities. It also explains how the organization utilizes the data collected from the system to make informed decisions about the system's ongoing fitness for purpose and to identify potential innovation opportunities.

---

33   This is described in section 5.4.

4.2.3   Understanding the flows within the CPD Model

This section decomposes the CPD Model (Figure 3.5) to demonstrate how communication, work, and innovation flow within each loop.

There are five loops of the CPD Model that we'll examine in detail:

- Governance/Assurance
- Strategy-risk
- Strategy/Governance
- Governance/Execution
- Value delivered.

4.2.3.1   Governance/Assurance

A fundamental aspect of the CPD Model is that it provides the system abstraction used by the Z-X Model to operationalize an organizational capability for governance and assurance. Governance provides the overall guidance used by the management team to execute its strategic policies. Those policies shape how management creates and executes organizational business objectives.

Assurance examines organizational performance and assures the execution of strategic policies. The easiest way to think about this is that governance is what we're going to do, and assurance proves that it has been done.

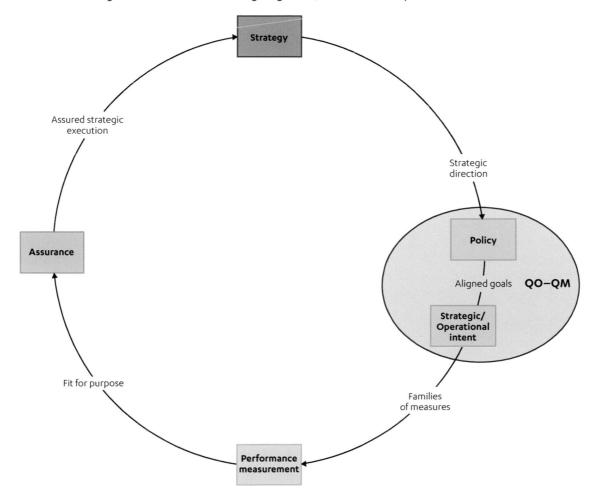

Figure 4.3 Governance/Assurance loop

Let's examine the Governance/Assurance loop (Figure 4.3).

- **Strategy** Strategy represents the best estimation of how the organization needs to perform within its environment. The policies developed as part of strategy represent its strategic direction. Strategy development considers internal and external organizational needs (e.g., legal, regulatory, and compliance). It also assesses the organizational presence in its environment and evaluates what it needs to adapt, survive, and thrive. The flow of communication is critical because changes to the strategic direction represent a high-order leverage point for how the entire system behaves. Strategy makes or changes the governing organizational rules and goals; it shifts the paradigm to value creation and protection to enable the organization to become adaptive and cyber-resilient. All communication, work, and innovation flow from strategy.

- **Policy** Policy turns strategic direction into a cascading set of policies[34] that provide the guidance management uses to create or improve the organizational capability necessary to execute and achieve the strategic direction and business objectives. Policies consider the need to work *on* the system to develop or enhance the required capabilities to achieve the business objectives. The achievement of the business objectives results from working *in* the system. This distinction is important because policy also ensures aligned strategic goals across the organization. QO–QM (discussed in detail in Chapter 7) decomposes those goals to identify the measures and metrics used to assure the organizational capabilities to execute the strategic policies. Communication flows in the form of cascading policies that provide management guidelines. Work to create policies, and the subsequent expression of the strategic and operational intent in the form of measures and metrics, provide the basis for performance measurement.

- **Performance measurement** Performance measurement collects the information that serves as the basis for the organization to evaluate its overall performance in its environment and its internal capabilities to execute its strategic policies. This information is covered in more detail in section 4.2.3.4. This area of the CPD Model measures stakeholders' delivered value against their expectations. It is a measure of the delivery of value from the system. It also provides an external view of the organizational performance within its environment, as a combination of value delivered and assurance of executing strategic policies. Think of it as, "Did we deliver the value we needed and perform as expected in our environment?" We also measure the organizational capabilities in two ways:

  - Did we perform as designed?
  - Did our capabilities achieve their purpose?

  These ideas help determine whether performance is fit for use and purpose (also covered in detail in section 4.2.3.4).

- **Assurance** Assurance assesses organizational performance against its strategic policies. In other words, did we do what we said we were going to do? Did we achieve our objectives? The assurance of the execution of strategic policies measures the capability to perform satisfactorily in its environment. It signals any gaps in organizational performance that might cause a change or realignment of policies or strategy (innovation). This information completes the Governance/Assurance loop. Notice that everything in this loop involves high-order leverage points (Figure 4.4) that impact how the system behaves.

The Governance/Assurance loop provides the organizational touchpoints to its environment and feedback on its performance. This loop causes the organization to innovate and adapt internally and externally. Becoming an adaptive cyber-resilient organization requires senior management to accept the responsibility to define the rules that establish the paradigm to create, protect, and deliver digital business value for its stakeholders.

---

34   This set of cascading policies forms the basis for organizational governance.

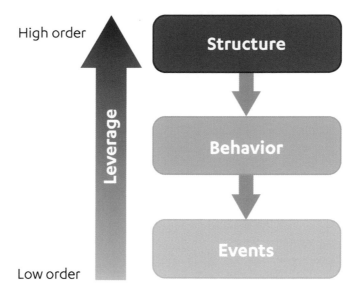

Figure 4.4 System structure and leverage

4.2.3.2 Strategy-risk

Strategy-risk is a sub-loop of the Strategy/Governance loop (Figure 4.5). A critical aspect of the CPD Model is that enterprise risk management (ERM) plays an integral role in forming organizational strategic direction. In the CPD Model, we've created a construct called "strategy-risk," which connotes that strategy and risk management are inseparable, similar to the idea of space-time. Strategy-risk becomes fundamental to the CPD Model representation of an adaptive cyber-resilient organization.

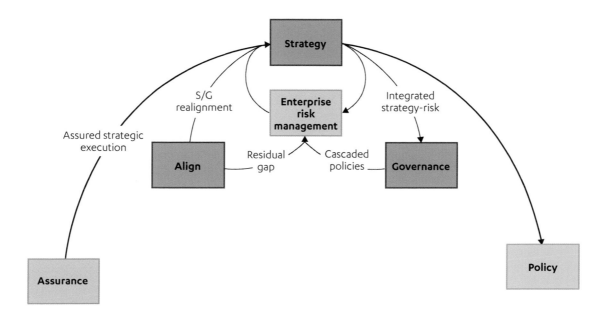

Figure 4.5 Strategy-risk loop

ERM requires the organization to look at how it deals with risk. We've adopted the principled approach to ERM expressed in the COSO framework. While it represents a superset of our cybersecurity focus, it's still an integral part of the organizational ERM efforts due to the pervasive use of digital technology to achieve business objectives.

The COSO framework uses five major components or areas: [35]

- **Governance and culture** The framework posits that the combination of governance and culture forms the basis for all other components of ERM. Governance establishes the tone for reinforcing the importance of cyber vigilance and establishing oversight responsibilities

- **Strategy and objective-setting** Integrating cyber risk management into the strategic plan requires establishing business objectives that include the requirement to create and protect digital business value. With an understanding of the business context, the organization can gain insight into internal and external factors and the corresponding effect on risk. An organization sets its cyber risk appetite in conjunction with strategy. The business objectives allow strategy-risk to be put into practice and shape the capabilities to become an adaptive cyber-resilient organization

- **Performance** An organization identifies and assesses risks, including cyber risks, that may affect its ability to achieve its strategy and business objectives. Prioritize risks according to their severity, with consideration for the organizational cyber risk appetite. Then the organization selects risk responses and monitors performance for change via the Governance/Assurance loop. This approach also provides the organization with a portfolio view of the amount of risk it assumes pursuing its strategy and organization-level business objectives (expressed in the CPD Model as *strategic and operational intent*)

- **Review and revision** Reviewing strategy-risk capabilities, practices, and organizational performance relative to established targets enables the organization to determine how well the cyber risk management capabilities and practices have increased value over time and will continue to drive value in light of substantial changes. Performance measurement is part of the Governance/Assurance loop and is adjusted based on the assurance feedback to strategy

- **Information, communication, and reporting** Communication is the continual flow and sharing of information. Management uses relevant information from internal and external sources to support cyber risk management, addressed in the Governance/Assurance, Strategy/Governance, and Governance/Execution loops. The organization leverages information from the performance measurement in the Governance/ Assurance loop, appropriately shared across the entire organization.

The strategy-risk loop of the CPD Model is critical to establishing the rules and goals of the system that create, protect, and deliver digital business value for its stakeholders in an adaptive cyber-resilient organization. The organizational capabilities of the Z-X Model subsume the organizational ERM capabilities into developing strategy-risk.

---

35   The source for the COSO principles is the COSO Internal Control – Integrated Framework (2013), which is used with permission of AICPA. On the COSO website, you can find the executive summary (COSO, 2017) and a summary of the COSO principles and approach (COSO, 2019).

4.2.3.3 Strategy/Governance

The Strategy/Governance loop (Figure 4.6) turns strategy-risk into cascading policies that develop or improve organizational capabilities to create, protect, and deliver digital business value for its stakeholders.

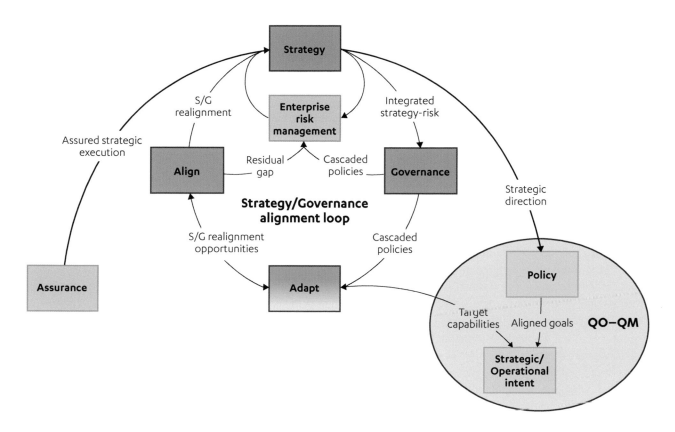

Figure 4.6 Strategy/Governance loop

- **Strategy** As discussed in section 4.2.3.1, the system rules and goals enable the organization to adapt, survive, and thrive. The output from strategy includes an integrated risk-informed strategy that we call strategy-risk. Assurance of the execution of strategic policies is one feedback input from that Governance/Assurance loop. It represents feedback on strategy performance and the capabilities to execute the strategy. All communication, work, and innovation flow from strategy-risk.

- **Governance** Governance parses strategy-risk system rules and goals into a cascading set of policies used to adapt the organizational capabilities to create, protect, and deliver digital business value. Policies are also fed back to ERM for use within the ERM framework.

- **Adapt** This aspect of the model enables management to apply policy guidance to create or improve organizational capabilities. Management guides the activities that create or improve capabilities, and establishes the operational intent by expressing its target capabilities (see section 4.2.3.4). This is used later in combination with the strategic intent to form strategic/operational intent, which plays a role in performance measurement within the Governance/Assurance and Governance/Execution loops. This feedback serves as input to possible policy realignment opportunities.

- **Align** The align aspect turns policy alignment opportunities into actionable activities via strategy. These policy innovations are still high-order leverage points that significantly impact system behavior.

This is an excellent time to cover *delay* (or *latency*) and its role in complex system behavior. The Governance/ Assurance, Strategy-risk, and Strategy/Governance loops all operate over timescales that, depending on factors such as the organizational size, levels of management, and geography, may span anything from days to years. It's critical to understand that an effect of a change to system behavior or structure may be separated in time (sometimes a significant amount of time) from the application of leverage discussed in section 3.2. (Large complex systems don't change their behavior on a dime. Everyone must understand system latency and its potential impact on changes to strategy-risk. Review section 3.1.2.3.)

4.2.3.4 Governance/Execution

The Governance/Execution loop (Figure 3.11) is where "the action" happens. This loop represents how organizations try to impact system behaviors. And yet, this loop is primarily suitable only for low-order leverage points. In the Governance/Execution loop, capabilities serve to create or improve the achievement of the desired behaviors expressed in strategic/operational intent. In essence, this loop engineers the capabilities to behave within the tolerances established by the Strategy/Governance loop. Think about designing a complicated system to operate within its design envelope.

- **Adapt** As described in section 4.2.3.3, Adapt turns policy into guidance used to create or improve the organizational capabilities to create, protect, and deliver digital business value. Essentially it provides the specifications for the organizational capabilities, which extends to the people, practice, and technology necessary to achieve the desired system behaviors. If you think this seems more like a complicated system rather than a complex system, you probably could make a good case. However, this becomes more of a matter of scope than anything else. For this book, we treat it as a complicated system within a complex system. Business objectives embed the requirements for new or improved capabilities. The essence of the CPD Model paradigm is simple: value created must be protected. Any recognized gap in the underlying organizational capabilities is closed, in whole or in part, as part of the innovation necessary to achieve the desired organizational capability. The adapt aspect also provides the desired target capabilities to the QO–QM (discussed later in this section) to express operational intent, and provides input to performance measurement. Adapt receives feedback from the improve aspect, which may result in a need to change the behavior of organizational capabilities or perhaps offer the opportunity to realign policies. Information in the form of policy flows through adapt; work involves designing and planning new or improved capabilities. The Governance/ Execution loop handles the incremental or sustaining aspects of the Innovate capability.

- **Execute** This is where the "rubber meets the road," so to speak. Execute is what the organization does to work both *on* and *in* the system. Work *on* the system by creating or improving existing capabilities; work *in* the system by executing the organizational capabilities to create, protect, and deliver digital business value. Execute represents the face of the organization to its stakeholders. It is one of the points where the organization interfaces directly with its environment. Adapt creates the specification to create or improve capabilities; it also provides target capabilities to QO–QM (discussed below). This is an essential aspect of the CPD Model, because the implementors and the auditors work together to identify the measures and metrics used to assure performance, each providing a different point of view. Implementors want to know whether what they built is operating as designed; auditors want to know whether the capabilities achieve their purpose efficiently and effectively while delivering the expected value to stakeholders. The implementor and auditor work together to "instrument" the organizational capabilities to produce the measures and metrics used by performance measurement to determine whether the capabilities are fit for use and purpose while meeting expected stakeholder value. Execute outputs the value combination of created and protected, and metrics that describe the performance of its capabilities.

- **Question Outcome–Question Metric** QO–QM is our modification of the GQM⁺Strategies® (Basili *et al.*, 2014). GQM is a method that asks questions about an expressed goal to identify the measures and metrics that accurately reflect achieving that goal. It's used in QO–QM to accomplish the same end, but it starts by asking questions to align organizational goals before drilling down into identifying capability measures and metrics.

This approach is not an egghead exercise,[36] but a very effective way of ensuring that the organization creates the right metric relative to achieving a goal. It is a critical aspect of the CPD Model because the organization identifies how it will measure itself, which makes it an Apollo 13 "failure is not an option" moment. Failure to accurately identify the suitable measures and metrics negatively impacts on how the system adapts to its environment. Failure here has a widespread impact on high- and low-order leverage points, and can cause the system to become chaotic or oscillate in behavior. QO–QM requires engagement and participation by the entire program team; it is not a "tick box" item. The resultant measures and metrics provide the basic information used by performance measurement.

- **Performance measurement** This aspect participates in every CPD loop. It is the nexus point to measure organizational capabilities, and value created and protected, against stakeholder expectations. It uses the measures and metrics supplied by QO–QM to express strategic/operational intent. From this, it assesses value and capability performance. Its outputs represent gaps in performance for subsequent evaluation as innovation opportunities. The outputs include value gap, fitness for use, and fitness for purpose.

- **Improve** Improve assesses innovation opportunities based on value gaps and the fitness of organizational capabilities. It doesn't close the gaps: it identifies the scope of the innovation and passes it along to the appropriate innovation authority (the individual or entity that decides whether the innovation opportunity should be pursued). It determines the type of innovation, with incremental or sustaining innovation handled in the Governance/Execution loop and adaptive or disruptive innovation handled in the Strategy/Governance loop. Performance measurement also assures the metrics used to assess that the execution of the organizational capabilities aligns with the strategic policies.

The Governance/Execution loop can change only three things: people, practice, and enabling technology. The organizational capabilities are engineered and operate within the tolerances established by the rules and goals of the system, determined by strategy-risk. The only thing you can do in the Governance/Execution loop is change behavior within design tolerances. If the innovation exceeds tweaking the system within tolerance, it becomes an adaptive or disruptive innovation that exerts change using high-order leverage points.

4.2.3.5 Value delivered

Value created and protected (Figure 3.11) enables stakeholders to realize the digital business value. While value is subjective, the CPD Model uses QO–QM and the subsequent strategic/operational intent expression to quantify objective and subjective or perception values. Assessment of value is *not* an exact science: experience and common sense come into play. The delivery of value is the direct organizational interface with its environment. Feedback about value is critical because it drives innovation opportunities across the spectrum.

A perceived value gap has many causes. It is also essential to consider the impact latency has on the performance of a system (see sections 3.1.2.3 and 4.2.3.3). We use the term *perceived* to describe gaps in value because value is subjective. The organization must apply appropriate measures and metrics as it filters value feedback. When filtering feedback, it's essential to consider the environment, organizational drivers, and expected performance. This is probably the "squishiest" part of the CPD Model. That is why it's essential to filter value feedback through objective measures of capability performance. Any subjective gap not reflected in objective measures requires extra scrutiny.

---

36   For a reminder of the importance of questions, review section 2.1.1.

4.2.3.6   The CPD Model and the DVCMM

The CPD Model focuses on organizational capabilities and their associated practice areas (see section 4.1.1.1); the DVCMM focuses on practice areas (aggregating one or more practices) and processes, which implement and execute the necessary activities to produce specific outcomes. We cover this in more detail in Chapter 5. For now, consider how the Plan capability covers these practice areas:

- Governance:
  - Creating organizational structures
  - Sustaining organizational structures

- Assurance:
  - Performance
  - Review and revision
  - Information sharing and reporting

- Strategy-risk management:
  - Policy integration
  - Identify improvement opportunities
  - Digital business continuity management
  - Supply chain risk management

- Portfolio, program, and project management:
  - Establish a digital business value portfolio
  - Program/project management

- Knowledge management:
  - Manage the flow of information
  - Audit and manage the information lifecycle
  - Manage stakeholder information flow.

It is up to the organization to define and document appropriate processes for each practice. This step is a requirement of the DVCMM, which assumes processes exist except at level 0. These practice areas are not siloed; we'll explore their relationships in Chapter 5.

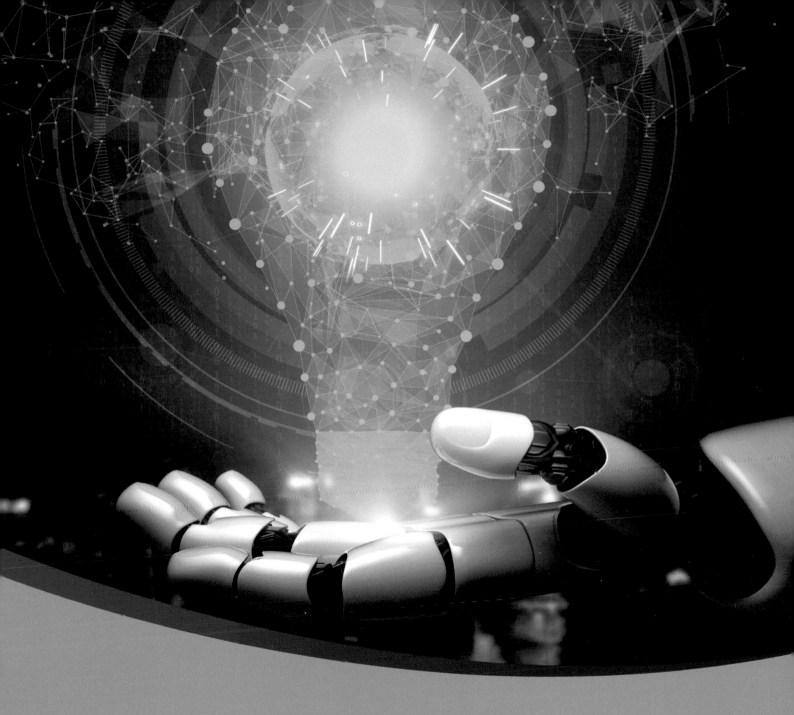

CHAPTER 5
Adapting the way we work

5 Adapting the way we work

---

*"Managers are not confronted with problems that are independent of each other;
but with dynamic situations that consist of complex systems of changing problems that
interact with each other. I call such situations messes ... Managers do not solve
problems, they manage messes."*
Russell Ackoff (1979)

Why did we include a chapter on an adaptive way of working? Cyber resilience requires the organization to cycle through the NIST Cybersecurity Framework's core functions (Identify, Protect, Detect, Respond, and Recover) quickly and efficiently. Besides having the requisite cybersecurity controls in place, the organization requires a degree of agility to adapt to the rapidly changing threat landscape. Agile approaches aren't just for software development – they apply to the entire organization; in that context, we call this *organizational agility*. We are not discussing a particular agile method or approach: we're talking about a generic approach to agile.

If an organization is to follow an adaptive way of working when taking a strategy-risk-informed approach to cybersecurity as an aspect of creating and protecting digital business value, this requires a principle-based approach to enterprise risk management. There are two perspectives to consider regarding this principle-based approach to an adaptive way of working. The implementor perspective addresses doing the right thing by delivering strategy-risk-informed expected outcomes. The auditor perspective addresses the assurance that the value delivered has appropriate strategy-risk-informed protections.

5.1   An adaptive way of working

---

*"The flattening of the world has happened faster and changed rules, roles,
and relationships more quickly than we could have imagined."*
Thomas Friedman (2005)

The Friedman quote that begins this section raises a few questions:

- How do we respond?
- How do we adapt?
- How do we remain competitive in a flat world?

These questions address our ability to respond to rapid changes regarding customer expectations, marketplace conditions, and the ever-changing cybersecurity threat landscape.

You may notice a similarity to generic agile – this is intentional. We do not advocate for or against a particular agile approach or methodology. As noted above, the context is the speed with which an organization can adapt and respond to conditions.

In section 3.3.3.1, we discussed Robert Westrum's taxonomy of cultures. We suggested a link between organizational structure, behavior, and culture – including the need to train and encourage messengers.

For an organization to have the capability to respond rapidly to cybersecurity incidents and changes to the threat landscape demands a mission focus requiring that messengers are trained and, most importantly, encouraged and empowered. The organization cannot keep pace unless it "knows" what is happening – it's the role of the empowered messengers to supply this information.

5.1.1 Adaptive working explained

Let's start with, "Why an adaptive way of working?" The answer to this question rests partly with the quotation from Dr. Russell Ackoff that began this chapter. Managers don't solve problems – they manage messes. Telling and all too true. Typical management is reactive to a situation without considering the larger and more complex business system. Not only is a systems view about the overall business activities usually lacking, but so is a view that includes how the business interacts within the larger environment – how the organization provides digital business value. What is the best way to get out of managing messes and the likelihood of being highly reactive? Before answering the question, we need a bit more context.

Today we do business in a hyper-connected world. Getting out of the rut associated with "managing messes" requires a different way of thinking: thinking in the context of a system. It also requires us to recognize that solutions may not be obvious. Combining these ideas leads to our conceptualization of an adaptive way to work: adaptive work is a way to lead and manage change in a situation where both the problem and the solution are unclear, and all the participants (may) require new learning.

Notice that the context includes leadership and two related ideas about "managing," how individuals handle change, and the management practices that facilitate the necessary organizational adaptation. If we aggregate both individual and management perspectives, we establish a different context – cognizant of both points of view and the typical change cycle.

An adaptive way of working is a generic approach to agile.[37] The goal is to incrementally deliver expected outcomes (product, service, value) [38] in short work intervals while reducing or eliminating waste. Figure 5.1 expresses this idea.

Short, rapidly incremental improvements support faster learning, less wasteful failures, faster customer response, and quicker adaptation to changing conditions, which accelerates innovation and decreases response time – essential to deal with the rapidly evolving threat landscape. Notice that each broken-line slope becomes steeper with successive attention to little gaps, with more value delivered sooner as the iterative cycles approach the desired state.

When the focus is on the big gap, there is a higher probability of increased waste along the way and missed expectations at the time of delivery. A big-gap focus requires more time and effort to estimate the required effort because the delivery event horizon is typically far in the future. It also makes it harder for the development teams to rapidly formulate responsive and midcourse corrections without a potential negative impact on cost and schedule.

---

37 It's beyond the scope of this book to get into a detailed treatise on agile approaches and methodologies. If your organization is not applying an agile approach, there are several to choose from, such as Scrum Kanban, lean, DSDM/AgilePM, SAFe, Crystal, and RAD. Even DevOps, done correctly, represents a form of agile (though not usually at the enterprise level). You can find more about the benefits of an agile approach in an article by Forbes Technology Council (2016). While the article refers to Scrum, the benefits are not limited to that framework.

38 Two terms in agile may be confusing to some people: "increment" refers to an aspect of functionality; "iteration" refers to time (e.g., sprint or timebox).

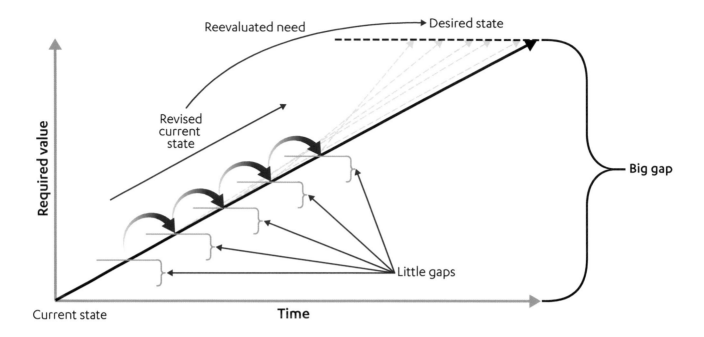

Figure 5.1 Little gaps versus big gap

Focusing on little gaps, combined with incremental delivery and stakeholder feedback, facilitates and potentially encourages minor midcourse corrections. The little-gap delivery horizon is typically one to four weeks, making it easier to estimate and plan.

The focus on little gaps still requires an appreciation of the whole, so everybody understands what they're doing, how it impacts others, and where it fits into vision and strategy – the 3D Knowledge Model restated.

5.1.2 Adaptive working as generic agile

Part of the goal of an agile approach is to find a better way to deliver value, leading to questions about what generates or contributes to value in the mind of customers and/or stakeholders. The same questions also help identify things that contribute to waste, such as partial work, rework, wasted motion (e.g., paper shuffling), communications latency, and implementing out-of-date requirements.

Each agile iteration seeks to deliver a minimum viable capability (MVC) or minimum viable product (MVP). This concept of *minimum viable* is critical to understand. The goal isn't to deliver everything, but to deliver a minimum viable subset that allows stakeholders to interact and provide immediate feedback to enable the developers to stay on track. The object is to deliver the needed solution that meets the need at the end of the development process, as opposed to the requested solution designed at the beginning. This approach requires a different way of thinking about prioritization from simply assigning high or low priority. We recommend the *MoSCoW* method (or MoSCoW prioritization; Wikipedia, 2022i). The vowels are just there to make a word; the key is in the capital letters: M, S, C, and W:

- The M stands for *must*. It is something that must be in the deliverables for "this" iteration, otherwise the product or service will not meet the bare minimum requirements for acceptability
- The S stands for *should*. It is something the product or service should have if the developers can fit it into the allotted time (sprint or timebox)

- The C stands for *could*. It is something the product or service could have to improve user experience or satisfaction. These items become part of the deliverables only if time and resources permit after delivery of the *musts* and *shoulds*

- The W stands for *won't*, meaning the product or service won't have it in this version, iteration, or increment.

A *should, could*, or *won't* could get a nonlinear promotion at any time. For example, something labeled as a *won't* could become a *must* to meet changed regulatory or compliance requirements.

Everything cannot be a *must*. The application of MoSCoW rules requires the capability to ask different questions. When there is an insistence that "too many" things are *musts*, apply a consistent theme in this book series – ask (potentially) different questions such as:

- Why is "x" a must (rather than a should or could)?
- What is the value to appropriate stakeholders of "x" versus the value of "y"?
- What is the risk of deferring "x" into the next iteration (or increment)?

Once the team has selected the tasks for an iteration, it is responsible for determining how the work will proceed. Teams should have cross-domain knowledge to ensure the application of a broader or systems perspective to the effort. Teams should be small, with no more than seven to nine members.

5.2 A principled approach to creating, protecting, and delivering digital business value

We use the term "principled" in the context of an expression of fundamental truth or theory, an idea that forms the basis of something. This book uses principles as building blocks of ideas that form the foundation of the DVMS, its underlying capabilities, and how they operationalize the CPD Model. This section discusses how we used our "first principles" to express the concept of creating and protecting digital business value. We used the COSO principles to ERM within the organizational strategy to develop the idea of "strategy-risk" and describe how it fits into the CPD Model in this chapter. These building blocks helped us understand how a systems approach enables organizations to become adaptive and cyber-resilient.

5.2.1 The first principles

We identified a set of four principles that express the fundamental truths organizations must understand if they are to become adaptive and cyber-resilient. We introduced these principles in *Fundamentals of Adopting the NIST Cybersecurity Framework* (Moskowitz and Nichols, 2022).

The first principles are:

- Customers drive value
- Change is a constant
- Adopt and apply systems thinking
- Risk is an intrinsic aspect of strategy.

This section reviews and discusses each of these first principles.

5.2.1.1   Customers drive value

There are three aspects of value:

- **Perception** A customer point of view is required to determine the value
- **Protection** Efforts to secure value must be proportionate to the customer's and the organizational perceived value
- **Maintainability** Value to the customer must be maintained in a dynamic and rapidly changing environment.

Value comes with multiple points of view. The same thing may have value to different stakeholders for different reasons. Value is also subjective, as discussed in section 4.2.3.5. It is essential to filter subjective viewpoints to understand objective performance. The CPD Model subsumes stakeholders and their points of view to develop strategic and operational intent. We covered this idea as part of the discussion of the Question Outcome–Question Metric approach (QO–QM) in section 4.2.3.4.

Providing appropriate value protection based on organizational needs and/or requirements is essential. Think about this for a moment. Have you ever heard someone say that cybersecurity prevented them from achieving their objectives, or made it more difficult to do so? Part of the reason may be related to Dr. Ackoff's quotation at the beginning of this chapter: "Managers do not solve problems, they manage messes." Part of the "mess" occurs when value protection is not an aspect of value creation, creating the need for rework, often under pressure.

The software development community learned long ago that bugs or defects caught early in the software development cycle cost less to fix than those caught later. Further, the required resources to "work the fix" aren't available for innovative projects, which forces managers to manage a mess. Why? Because value protection occurs later in the lifecycle.

W. Edwards Deming (1982), Philip B. Crosby (1979), and others discuss the escalating costs of low quality (fixing after the fact) versus designing and building quality at each product or service lifecycle stage. Why is this discussion about quality relevant here?

The *Fundamentals* book included the following in Chapter 3:

"Building on the idea of a relationship between quality and value, we suggest a relationship between quality and cybersecurity. Low quality, or lack of attention to cybersecurity at the board of directors level, increases costs … If it makes it easier to think differently about cybersecurity as an organizational responsibility rather than a technical one, then think of cybersecurity initiatives as a property of what the organization does to achieve a desired level of quality."

In the context established in the *Fundamentals* book, it makes sense to think of the terms *quality* and *value* as almost interchangeable synonyms. Once you have made that link, Crosby's statement in *Quality Is Free* takes on a different meaning for cybersecurity to create and protect digital business value:

"Quality is an achievable, measurable, profitable entity that can be installed once you have commitment and understanding, and are prepared for hard work."
Philip B. Crosby (1979)

Part of the "hard work" Crosby references relates to organizational culture. Both Deming and Crosby agree quality is the responsibility of everyone in the organization, not a single person (such as the quality manager or chief information security officer (CISO)). In the same way that the responsibility starts at the top, so does the responsibility for culture. In his book *Hit Refresh*, Satya Nadella, CEO of Microsoft, writes (emphasis ours):

---

*"No one leader, no one group, and no one CEO would be the hero of Microsoft's renewal. If there was to be a renewal, it would take all of us and all parts of each of us. **Cultural transformation would be slow and trying before it would be rewarding** ... When Microsoft's board of directors announced that I would become the next CEO, I put the company's culture at the top of our agenda. I said we needed to rediscover the soul of Microsoft, our reason for being. **I have come to understand that my primary job is to curate our culture** so that one hundred thousand inspired minds – Microsoft employees – can better shape our future."*
Satya Nadella (2017)

In Chapter 3, we said this:

"Tension metrics create inherent competition or conflict – good, fast, or cheap: pick two. The challenge is that by picking two of the three, we elevate the two selected to be more important than the one. Tension metrics seek to find the appropriate balance – in this case, good, fast, and cheap – while maintaining the relative importance of all three."

The organizational challenge is to find the proper balance.

Customers drive value; they expect (and sometimes demand) a level of quality. Value or quality exists in a dynamic environment and is subject to changes to internal needs, external requirements, and a dynamic threat landscape. The value of digital assets changes over time, which requires a continual evaluation of asset value and the appropriate level of protection. The CPD Model provides clarity and focuses on what matters to create, protect, and deliver digital business value. It enables the organization to adapt to those needs and close performance gaps, applying the first principle: *customers drive value*.

5.2.1.2   Change is a constant

The organization exists in a dynamic environment and must adapt its performance as an adaptive cyber-resilient organization, potentially changing *everything* (people, practice, and technology).

The CPD Model represents a dynamic system that accommodates change in organizational needs, requirements, and the threat landscape. It enables an organization to adapt by identifying gaps caused by continual change. Fundamentally, the organization approaches everything as an opportunity to innovate. No matter what, the current state represents the starting point to pursue continual innovation to close gaps between the current and desired states.

5.2.1.3   Adopt and apply systems thinking

"What is a system?" We introduced the idea of systems thinking in section 5.1.3 of the *Fundamentals* book and it is covered in more depth in Chapter 3 of this publication. A system is a group of interrelated and interacting parts organized to accomplish a purpose. In simple terms, a system is a "whole" that consists of parts with the following characteristics:

● Each part affects the behavior or properties of the whole
● Each part of the system, when it acts within or impacts the system, is dependent on the effect of some other part
● No part of a system (or collection of parts) has an independent effect.

A system is *not the sum of its parts* – it is the *product of interactions* between them.

We treat the interactions within a system as behaviors. These behaviors within a system create signals (messages) to other parts of the system or other systems (including external systems). These behaviors occur within a structure: the structure of the system. The idea of behaviors within a structure links these two concepts such that you cannot change one without impacting the other. System behavior and system structure are different sides of the same coin. Once we understand the idea of a system, we can address systems thinking – which requires developing a different perspective, a different approach to problem-solving, and applying the high- and low-order leverage points discussed in section 3.2.

5.2.1.4   Risk is an intrinsic aspect of strategy

You've probably heard the axiom about cyberattacks: "It's not a matter of if, but when." Another maxim also applies: "Failure to plan is planning to fail." Failure to plan for a cyberattack leaves the organization vulnerable.

Once they have accepted these ideas, it is essential that all organizations, regardless of size, adopt and adapt an ERM framework to ensure their business strategy is fully risk-informed. As we discussed in section 4.2.3.2, the CPD Model posits that business strategy includes understanding the elements of risk inherent in any strategy. The model presents this concept as *strategy-risk*. As with "space-time," the two parts of strategy-risk exist together: one cannot exist separately from the other.

In the same way that no plan is perfect, no strategy is, either: every strategy includes uncertainty and some risk aspect. The CPD Model incorporates the risk-informed strategy (strategy-risk) to create a set of cascading strategic policies that seek to mitigate cyber risk through guidance that creates business value and proportionally protects it.

In practical terms, the business objectives result in strategic and management policies that cause considerations for value protection from the beginning, instead of figuring out how to bolt it on after the fact, applying the high- and low-order leverage points discussed in section 3.2. This approach integrates strategy and ERM to change the dynamics associated with cybersecurity. The CPD Model combines value creation and protection into a single requirement to deliver the expected value for stakeholders. The model eliminates the idea that cybersecurity is a cost center or something to add (bolt on) later in the development cycle. Strategy-risk represents a high-order leverage point, with new rules and goals for the system.

The ideas in the previous two sentences bear repeating:

- Cybersecurity is not a cost center
- Strategy-risk provides a high-order leverage point for the system.

The best way to ensure that cybersecurity becomes an aspect of value creation and protection is to view the organization from the holistic perspective of a system. Previously we've linked the idea of value and quality. Value and quality are organizational responsibilities. In the context of creating and protecting value, this requires adopting, learning, and applying systems thinking.

5.2.2 The CPD Model and the first principles

The first principles provide the fundamental building blocks that underpin the CPD Model. The following discussion examines each first principle, focusing on operationalizing them.

5.2.2.1 Customers drive value

Let's start with the idea of "value." Value is often subjective, with potentially multiple stakeholder constituencies having different views of a specific digital asset. The organization must "rationalize" value in expressing its strategic intent, thereby defining how the organization seeks to survive and thrive in its competitive environment.

The CPD Model represents a scalable approach for the organizational requirement to protect the delivery of digital business value proportional to its value for stakeholders (Figure 5.2). The strategic policies define the requirement that appropriate value protection be a concurrent aspect of value creation. The organization adapts its policies to create or improve its capabilities relative to achieving its strategic goals. These capabilities allow the efficient and effective implementation of the policies to deliver protected digital value to the stakeholders.

We've already discussed the change in value that occurs in a dynamic environment. The CPD Model includes the necessary gap analysis in the Strategy/Governance and Governance/Execution loops that continually enables the organization to innovate and maintain value creation and protection within defined tolerances. These innovations will likely be predominately incremental or sustaining innovations within the Governance/Execution loop. As required, higher leverage points involving the Strategy/Governance loop provide changes to policy (adaptive innovation) or strategy (disruptive innovation).

We started with value, and we'll end with value. Digital business value represents an outcome. The CPD Model deals with the behaviors that produce outcomes. While value represents the subjective viewpoint of one or more stakeholders, there must be an objective measure of the capabilities that deliver appropriately protected value. This requires evaluating these capabilities against the strategic and operational intent combined with a balance of efficiency and effectiveness.

The principle that customers drive value provides the basis for creating, protecting, and delivering digital business value while continually adapting organizational capabilities within the dynamic environment.

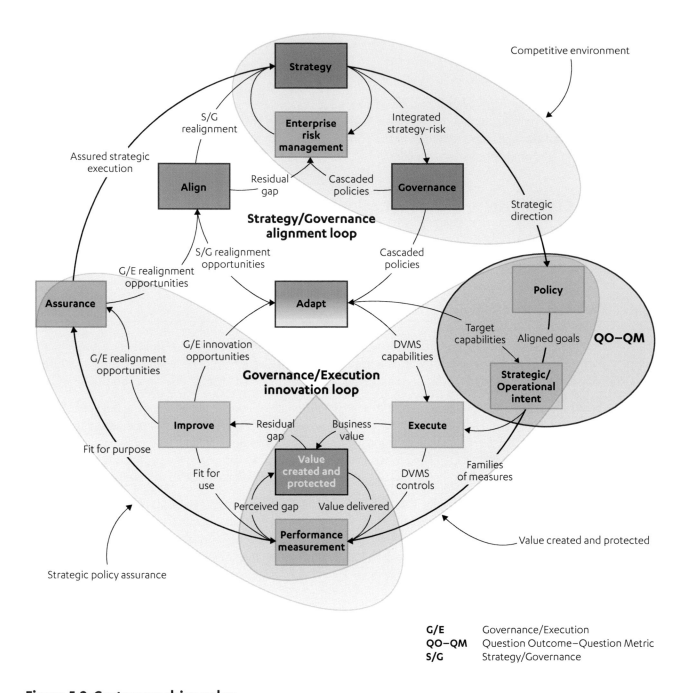

Figure 5.2 Customers drive value

G/E	Governance/Execution
QO–QM	Question Outcome–Question Metric
S/G	Strategy/Governance

5.2.2.2 Change is a constant

The model deals with change through its approach to innovation, as represented by the combination of the Strategy/Governance loop and the Governance/Execution loop shown in Figure 5.3, starting with the model's use of high-order leverage points.

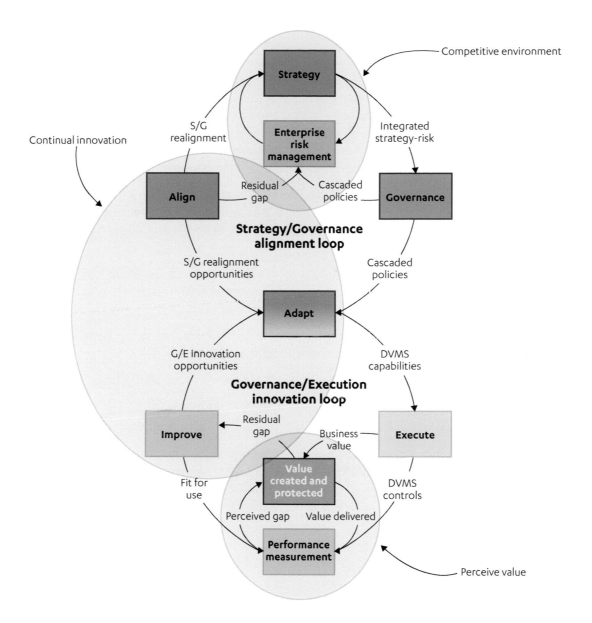

Figure 5.3 Leverage in the Strategy/Governance and Governance/Execution loops

The model accommodates changes in its competitive environment, including internal needs relative to external requirements and the threat landscape. The organization responds to its environment (business, military, or political) by changing the rules and goals to achieve an optimized posture. The resulting changes to strategy and policies change the behavior of the complex organizational systems. Of course, strategic or policy changes do not occur overnight, nor are their effects felt immediately. The organization expects that its strategy and policy changes will improve its capabilities to produce the desired changes to its behaviors, thus creating (or continuing) the expected value for its stakeholders.

What happens downstream from strategy and policy changes? As we said above, they don't happen overnight. There is latency inherent in the system. We're attempting to change a complicated system at the delivery end, so this is more of an engineering problem. Strategy and policy changes change the rules and goals. The organization seeks to transform its capabilities to operate within different tolerances. In other words, it's changed its operating envelope, representing how complex systems self-organize around these new rules and goals. Working in the modified system may reveal performance gaps, requiring additional system adjustments in the form of incremental or sustaining innovation. These changes occur within the Governance/Execution loop and impact system behaviors within tolerances (within the organizational operating envelope).

However, if gaps require a change outside the operating envelope, appropriate corrective actions should occur within the Governance/Execution loop. These actions arise due to a potential adaptive change to policy or a disruptive shift in strategy. In either case, there is a delay (latency) between the event (the change) and the effect of the change.

With this in mind, it becomes apparent that changing complex or complicated systems can have far-reaching and unexpected impacts on system behaviors. Experience is what you get when the results are unpredictable. Expect to gain some experience.

Think about this in the context of the fast-paced digital business environment. For an organization to survive, let alone thrive, in such a supercharged chaotic environment, it must actively seek to become an adaptive cyber-resilient organization.

5.2.2.3 Adopt and apply systems thinking

The CPD Model is a high-level abstraction of a complex organizational system to create, protect, and deliver digital business value (Figure 5.4). Each organization differs in the detail level of its adaptation based on its rules and goals. At a macro level, though, all organizations exhibit some form of this behavior. An organization seeking to become adaptive and cyber-resilient will adopt and apply a systems thinking approach to understand how to shape its system behaviors and outcomes.

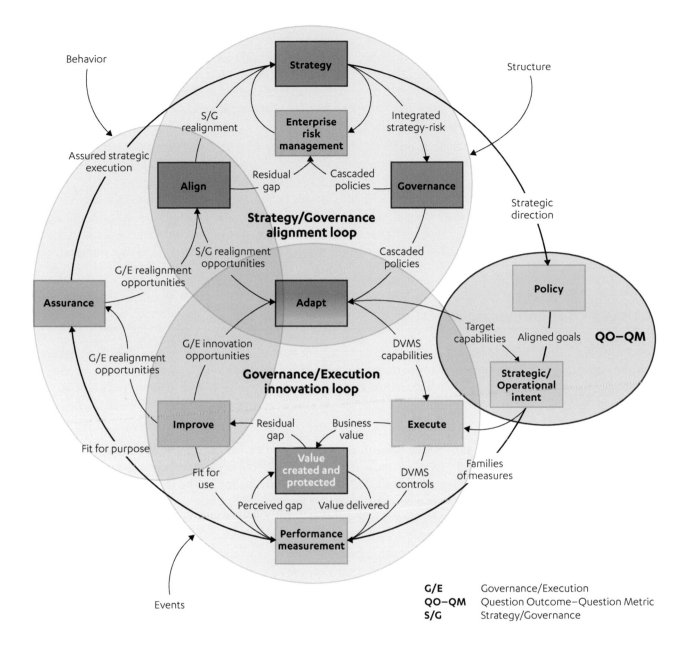

Figure 5.4 Adopt and apply systems thinking

Details on the three aspects (behavior, structure, and events) shown in Figure 5.4 are as follows:

● **Behavior** Based on the align aspect, system behavior is shaped within the Governance/Assurance loop. Performance measurement identifies performance gaps. The gaps are assessed and forwarded to the entity responsible for innovation. The resulting innovation is implemented in either the Governance/Execution or Strategy/Governance loop. The behavior of this complex system is best understood based on the following flow. The strategy establishes the system rules and goals; the remainder of the system self-organizes to function within the tolerances. Policies establish the tolerances for organizational capabilities that the adapt aspect creates or improves. Regular and ongoing assessment of the entire system (including components, interactions, and behaviors) occurs against established criteria. We'll explore these ideas in more detail in Chapter 6.

- **Structure** The whole model represents a system that includes complicated and complex system structures. The Strategy/Governance loop creates the risk-based strategies that provide the basis for developing the policy cascade that subsequently guides management to create or improve organizational capabilities. High-order leverage points, applied in the Strategy/Governance loop, set the system rules and establish the goals the system seeks. Adaptive innovation (based on feedback) causes the realignment of policies within current tolerances. Disruptive innovation (also based on feedback) impacts the strategy and causes a strategic realignment to adapt system performance to the environment.

- **Events** The Governance/Execution loop engineers the organizational capabilities guided by strategic policies. This loop works on the system by creating or improving organizational capabilities. It works in the system by executing its capabilities to produce outcomes that create, protect, and deliver digital business value. Strategic policies establish the basis for organizational capability tolerances; instrumentation produces the measures and metrics that help identify performance gaps. When performance gaps require changes in existing capabilities to maintain optimal performance, these changes are incremental or sustaining within the system tolerances. Performance gaps outside tolerance levels require the Strategy/Governance loop to tackle policy or strategy realignment.

5.2.2.4 Risk is an intrinsic aspect of strategy

The CPD Model reflects how an organization adapts to its environment. Like a living organism, the organization evolves by adapting to environmental changes that represent a threat to its survival or perhaps an opportunity it can exploit. Like in the living world, some organisms are more successful in adapting to positive and negative risks than others. Risk plays a critical role in the survival of an organism and an organization; survival depends on how they perceive and deal with risks.

In the CPD Model, ERM provides the organization with the mechanism that seeks to understand and mitigate the risk the organization faces (Figure 5.5). Through understanding the risks, the organization can formulate risk-informed strategies to mitigate the risks it needs to, and exploit the ones it should. The resultant risk-informed strategy, which we call *strategy-risk*, organizes organizational resources to bring about changes in its capabilities to capitalize on or avoid risks. If the strategy-risk is successful, the organization will realize the desired outcomes of its business objects. However, it may fall short in some instances, requiring some tweaks to strategy-risk. The CPD Model provides the necessary feedback loops so that strategy and ERM can adjust to its performance in the real world and seek to identify changes to better adapt to its environment.

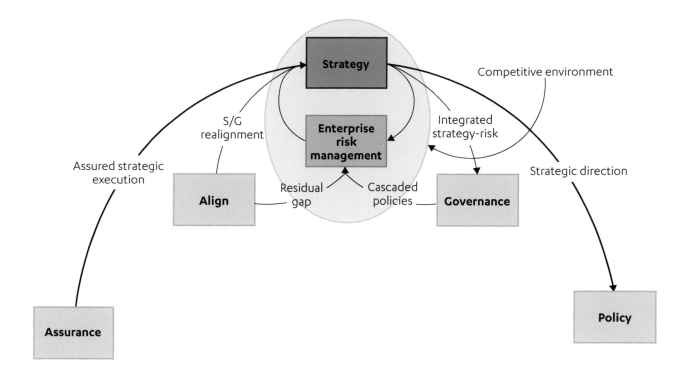

Figure 5.5 Risk is an intrinsic aspect of strategy

5.2.3   Operationalizing COSO principles in the CPD Model

We introduced the COSO principles in the *Fundamentals* book as an ERM framework, and have discussed them in this book as building blocks used in developing the CPD Model.

"Each enterprise risk management component includes principles that apply to creating, preserving, and realizing value in an organization regardless of size, type, or location. The principles and their components do not represent isolated, stand-alone concepts. Each highlights the importance of integrating enterprise risk management and the role of decision-making. The Framework outlines considerations to integrate culture, practices, and capabilities into each principle [and] into the entity. These considerations are not exhaustive, but they do demonstrate the range of inputs into decision-making and the exercise of judgment by personnel, management, and the board."
COSO (2013)

The emphasis of the first sentence in the above quote is ours: it demonstrates how these principles are universal and applicable across *all* organizations, irrespective of size, type, or location.

The COSO principles apply to the entire organization in a broader context than cybersecurity. However, digital business has become "the business." As you read the following material about these principles in the narrow context of cybersecurity, think about the other aspects of the principles related to the complex systems used to create, protect, and deliver digital business value.

5.2.3.1 COSO principles 1–5: Governance and culture

The COSO principles in this group are foundational to every aspect of ERM. Governance, informed by strategy-risk, establishes the tone, the approach, the expectations, and the basis for enforcement and underpins the attention and broad responsibility for cybersecurity. Each of the five principles establishes the rules and goals of the complex system essential for the organization to create, protect, and deliver digital business value.

1. **Establish board risk oversight** This principle defines the group with primary responsibility for risk management. The board of directors is responsible for the oversight and governance that supports management's ability to deliver the strategic intent. In general terms, the board oversees the Governance/Assurance loop. In specific terms, the Strategy/Governance loop creates the underlying support mechanism that enables board oversight. Since it's a loop, we can start anywhere; we begin with strategy for this discussion. The CPD Model strategy integrates with ERM to create strategy-risk. The 20 principles of COSO represent an ERM framework that we reference as our preferred ERM. In Figure 5.6, all of the first five COSO principles are operationalized in the Strategy/Governance loop. In the CPD Model, strategy-risk establishes the rules and defines the system goals. The assurance aspect provides everything the board needs to ensure adequate oversight of the operationalization of the COSO principles and the execution of its strategic policies.

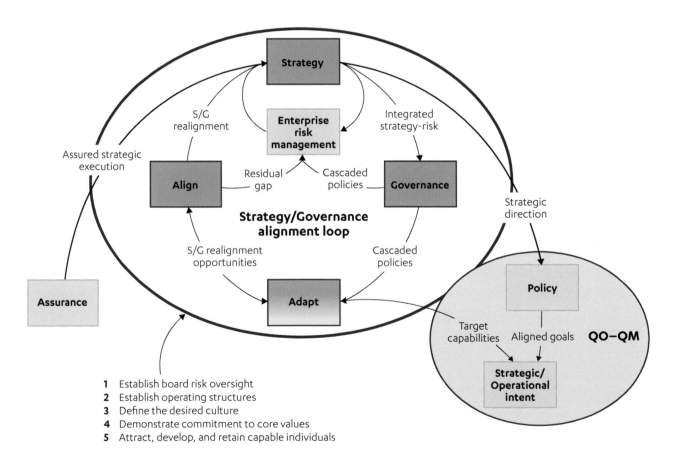

1   Establish board risk oversight
2   Establish operating structures
3   Define the desired culture
4   Demonstrate commitment to core values
5   Attract, develop, and retain capable individuals

Figure 5.6 COSO principles 1–5 and the CPD Model

2. **Establish operating structures** The integration of risk management with strategy forms strategy-risk, which establishes the rules and goals of the system. The system self-organizes to form the structures and behaviors necessary to create or improve the organizational capabilities to create, protect, and deliver digital business value. This includes the structures essential to assure the board of the execution of its strategic policies.

3. **Define the desired culture** Section 5.2.1.1 included a quotation from Satya Nadella, CEO of Microsoft, which included the following: "I have come to understand that my primary job is to curate our culture ..." Culture starts at the top, reinforced through leadership action. Culture defines the norms for expected and discouraged behaviors; it expresses the organizational beliefs, attitudes, values, and practices. Culture is not static: the organization can define a new culture and work to achieve it (Groysberg *et al.*, 2018). This concept is the essence of Nadella's statement. Discussing culture in the context of cybersecurity might seem a bit "warm and fuzzy," but organizational culture directly impacts organizational performance. To become an adaptive, cyber-resilient organization requires more than hardware and software. It requires leadership that "walks the talk."

4. **Demonstrate commitment to core values** Like the need to define the desired culture, the leadership must articulate and demonstrate an organizational commitment to the core values. Again, this may seem "warm and fuzzy" when we're discussing cybersecurity, but it's not. The basis for the CPD Model is to enable creating, protecting, and delivering value for stakeholders. Value delivered to stakeholders depends on the core organizational values expressed as mission, vision, and principles. Applying this COSO principle demonstrates organizational culture in action and has its genesis in strategy-risk.

5. **Attract, develop, and retain capable individuals** This principle highlights the critical need to consider the human resources that are essential to achieving business objectives. It requires optimizing people, practice, and technology to become an adaptive, cyber-resilient organization. People operationalize the culture. High-performance teams attract and retain the best people because they operate as a meritocracy. When organizations say what they do, do what they say, and reward performance, they adapt and operate as a high-performance team.

The first five principles of the COSO ERM framework support the creation of the human structures and patterns of behavior that live and breathe its core value, which, in the CPD Model, is the creation, protection, and delivery of digital business value.

5.2.3.2 COSO principles 6–9: Strategy and objective-setting

Strategy-risk is a fundamental construct of the CPD Model (Figure 5.7). The essence of strategy-risk requires the integration of cyber risk into developing plans that express the strategic intent within the context of consistent organizational objectives. To do this effectively requires the consideration of internal and external risk factors. The principles in this group look at the organizational environment (where it lives), what and how much risk the organization can take (its risk appetite), weigh the alternative strategies to adapt to its environment, and formulate its business objectives.

10. **Identify risk** Identified risks impacting performance behaviors that affect the delivery of the strategic intent and related business objectives provide the basis for strategy-risk. In other words, here are the things we've determined that might impact our ability to achieve our objectives. Strategy-risk considers internal needs, external requirements, and the threat landscape. It represents the optimal strategic alternative to attain the organization's objectives. It also presents the business objectives (new rules) and the subsequent development of cascading strategic, managerial, and operational policies for governance.

11. **Assess the severity of risk** Following risk identification, someone must assess the risk and determine the severity of its impact. The object of assessment is to determine "how bad, bad is" in the context of the risk associated with the digital asset. The assessment results determine the prioritization assigned to protect the asset. It's important to note here that the business-system level approaches this at the appropriate level of granularity. Digital assets aggregate into the business systems they enable. Many discrete digital assets may participate in delivering one or more business systems, potentially revealing that many essential business systems share a single digital asset representing a single point of failure. This realization presents a challenge in a large-scale heterogeneous system. The James Webb Space Telescope launched with 344 known single points of failure, with 80% coming into play after launch (EarthSky, 2022). An organization makes informed decisions about known risks, even in a complex system. This idea is vital to get right so that the organization can move forward, prioritizing risk.

12. **Prioritize risk** The root word for *prioritize* is *priority*: ranking, establishing order or precedence. In ERM, the organization looks at its assets, its risks, and the severity of the impact of those risks to make decisions. What come first are the business systems that provide the most value; the risks, vulnerabilities, probabilities, etc.; and the impact on the organization if that value is compromised or denied. The organization must prioritize its risks so that business objectives and strategy-risk produce policies that support creation and protection of value at an appropriate level.

13. **Implement risk response** The CPD Model implements the organizational risk response in the Governance/Execution loop, directed by policies developed in the Strategy/Governance loop and managed through adapt.

14. **Develop a portfolio view** A holistic view of risk enables the organization to view its assumed risk by aggregating its business systems and associated risk profiles. This view gives the organization a realistic view of its strategic assets and risk, enabling it to adjust its risk profile as necessary. A portfolio view of risk allows the organization to maintain a baseline of the organizational risk profile. This view is more than an executive dashboard: it provides a balancing feedback loop for strategy. How much is too much? What are our leverage points? What do we have to do to balance our risk profile across business systems? All good questions; the answers require a holistic view of risk relative to value.

5.2.3.4   COSO principles 15–17: Review and revision

The CPD Model's Governance/Assurance loop (Figure 5.9) expresses what the organization will do to adapt its performance to its environment. The Governance/Execution loop assures the execution of strategic policies so that the value delivered meets stakeholder expectations. It also ensures that the capabilities that created, protected, and delivered that value did so effectively and efficiently. The review and revision principles span assessing change, assessing its potential impact on risk and performance, and continually innovating organizational capability to manage enterprise risk.

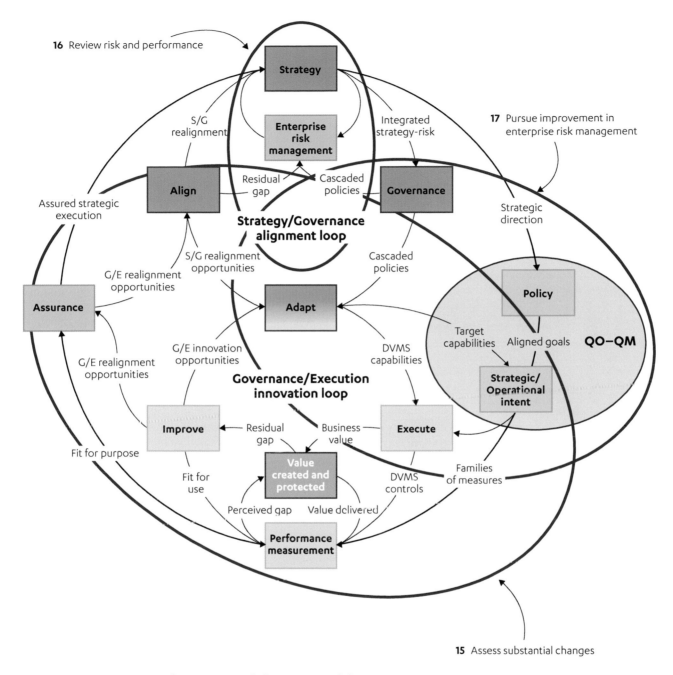

Figure 5.9 COSO principles 15–17 and the CPD Model

15. **Assess substantial changes** The CPD Model is an abstraction of a complex system enabling the organization to be adaptive and cyber-resilient. The assurance and align aspects determine whether an innovation opportunity represents a substantial change that warrants policy (adaptive) realignment or strategy-risk (disruptive) realignment. The idea of "substantial" is congruent with the requirement to apply high-order leverage points to change system behavior. For example, suppose the innovation opportunity requires strategic or managerial policy realignment. In that case, the scope is limited to realigning the policies (a tool to implement objectives) within the tolerances of strategy-risk. Rules and goals may change, but only so far as strategic direction will tolerate. If the innovation opportunity involves strategy, system rules and goals will change, necessitating the system to self-organize to accommodate these changes. "Substantial changes" don't often occur; when they do, they require serious due diligence by the board, executive, and managerial ranks.

16. **Review risk and performance** It is essential to provide ongoing risk-based organizational performance reviews. In other words, did we do what we said we'd do, and how well did we do it? Perform these reviews within the context of the Strategy/Governance loop with input in the form of innovation opportunities from the assurance and align aspects. This approach surfaces and assesses performance gaps that may require the realignment of policies and strategy. The organization exercises appropriate due diligence to determine the impact on the overall risk profile, and the nature and scope of the necessary leverage points to change system behaviors. None of this happens overnight. At the strategy and policies level, even a highly agile organization needs to understand the event and its impact on behavior, including latency.

17. **Pursue improvement in enterprise risk management** Strategy-risk makes the rules and sets the system goals that create, protect, and deliver digital business value. Any innovation that causes a realignment of strategy or policies is implemented through the adapt aspect in the Governance/Execution loop, resulting in changes to strategic and operational intent. New or improved capabilities are built, deployed, and operated to create, protect, and deliver digital business value. Performance measurement applies the schema produced by QO–QM (see Chapter 7) from strategic and operational intent to measure the performance of organizational capability and assure execution of strategic policies. Performance gaps that impact the Governance/Execution loop represent incremental or sustaining innovations. Gaps impacting policy or strategy are implemented in the Governance/Assurance or Strategy/Governance loops. The CPD Model enables the organization to identify performance gaps and appropriately respond to them, with a complete understanding of the application of leverage to achieve the desired system behaviors.

5.2.3.5 COSO principles 18–20: Information, communication, and reporting

Communication occurs when there is an exchange of information or news combined with comprehension. The ability to change, revise, and improve depends on continual communication. The practical application of pervasive (i.e., organization-wide) communication facilitates the organizational capability to respond to cyber risks. It is essential to use internal and external sources of information to support this endeavor. Leverage technology to capture, process, manage, and support communication throughout the organization. Communication focuses on all aspects of an organization, including culture, performance, and risk. The communication to support this effort depends heavily on knowledge management, both repository-based and personal experience-based (the latter is often referred to as *institutional knowledge*). See Figure 5.10 to understand where these principles fit into the CPD Model.

18. **Leverage information and technology** The CPD Model creates or improves organizational capabilities by adapting people, practice, and technology to create, protect, and deliver digital business value. It adapts the use of technology where appropriate. Technology represents a low-order leverage point within the system and can only impact behavior within the tolerances established by policies. However, technology enables organizations to scale. The idea of scalability is essential for complex systems that support vast amounts of information and communications flow between system components (including people), reducing the time needed to identify digital assets. Once identified, this approach enables appropriate technical protections, detection, and response to cybersecurity events and supports speedy recovery. The organization must understand that technology is only a means to the end.

19. **Communicate risk information** The CPD Model operationalizes the organizational flow of communication, work, and innovation. Any organization needs to understand how it communicates internally and externally. How the organization communicates risk is critical to creating, protecting, and delivering digital business value. Risk is communicated in three ways:

● As strategic integration of business strategy and ERM (strategy-risk)
● Through business objectives and resultant policies that create or improve organizational capabilities to create value and protect it at an appropriate level

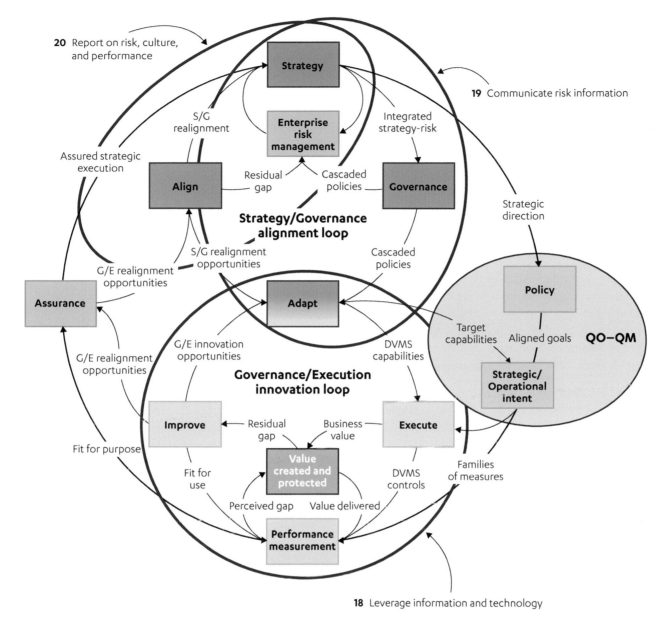

Figure 5.10 COSO principles 18–20 and the CPD Model

- In the operational delivery of digital business value. Each level of communication carries information relative to that level to appropriately address risk. Strategic and operational intent identify measures and metrics that the performance measurement aspect uses to identify performance gaps. This represents a reinforcing and balancing loop that seeks to optimize the value created and protected.

20. **Report on risk, culture, and performance** The Governance/Assurance loop uses the input from performance measurement to identify the organizational capability to create, protect, detect, and deliver digital business value as an adaptive, cyber-resilient organization – fundamental for the organization to adapt to its environment successfully. We've discussed risk and performance in other parts of this section, so let's focus on culture. Culture is the reflection of who and what you are as an organization. It is the most powerful leverage point an organization has to become adaptive and cyber-resilient. Organizational leadership is responsible for its culture, because it establishes the norms regarding how and why people behave. The difficulty is: how do you measure it? How do you examine the organization across the globe? An organization that treats its cyberculture as an unknown will fail as a cyber-resilient organization.

5.3 Organizing to create, protect, and deliver (CPD) digital business value

Organizing for CPD is not about organization (org) charts – it's about leadership that creates and communicates the vision and mission for CPD and then seeks to get organizational buy-in. This approach is consistent with applying the DVMS as an overlay rather than a framework or method. We'll cover this in more detail in Chapter 8.

Organizing for CPD requires the application of the 3D Knowledge Model. Part of "organizing for CPD" requires preserving institutional knowledge to avoid the situation discussed in the "Knowledge management and history" commentary in section 3.3.1.

5.3.1 Getting ready to organize for CPD

Before attempting to organize to create, protect, and deliver digital business value, it may be necessary for the organization to address the cultural issues raised previously. In their book *ABC of ICT: An Introduction to the Attitude, Behavior, and Culture of ICT* (Wilkinson and Schilt, 2008), Paul Wilkinson and Jan Schilt discussed the link between attitude, the resulting behaviors, and culture. While attending a conference, one of the authors talked with Paul about the precursor to attitudes, specifically belief. It's impossible to change attitudes if you can't change the underlying belief system that serves as their basis.

Robert Westrum's paper on the taxonomy of cultures (Westrum, 2004) indirectly reflects the idea of belief systems. The organization can't work to provide a generative culture without first addressing the underlying beliefs of the people operating in either a pathological or a bureaucratic culture. Stephen M. R. Covey's book *The Speed of Trust: The One Thing that Changes Everything* (Covey, 2008) addresses why this is true. If there isn't sufficient transparency, consistency, and integrity between what management says and the observed behaviors, trust is likely to be low.

With this in mind, the concept changes from "ABC of ICT" to "BABC of the organization": belief, attitudes, behavior, and culture.[39] There are ways to address this in the *Harvard Business Review* (HBR) article by Groysberg *et al.* (2018), Covey's book on trust (Covey, 2008), and John P. Kotter's *HBR* article "Leading change: Why transformation efforts fail" (Kotter, 1995). Specifically, while all eight reasons in Kotter's article are relevant, check error #8: "Not anchoring changes in the corporation's culture."

---

39   During the conversation we mentioned, Paul agreed with this author that at an organizational level, BABC was critical.

5.3.2   What does organizing for CPD mean?

As we noted at the beginning of this section, organizing for CPD does not mean creating or redoing org charts. Organizing for CPD requires that the appropriate organizational stakeholders understand their role and responsibilities to contribute to the ongoing effort to create, protect, and deliver digital business value. This idea is consistent with W. Edwards Deming's view that "Quality is everyone's responsibility."

Another aspect of organizing to create, protect, and deliver digital business value is that it may require a change in beliefs from treating cybersecurity as a cost center to treating it as a contributor to the bottom line. Consider the following extract from an *MIT Technology Review* article:

"Companies have not figured out how cybersecurity makes them money, [Michael] Daniel says. The market fails at measuring cybersecurity and, more importantly, often cannot connect it to a company's bottom line – so they often can't justify spending the necessary money."
Patrick Howell O'Neill (2022)

Chapter 3 of the *Fundamentals* book included the following quotation from the Executive Summary of the NIST-CSF:

"Similar to financial and reputational risks, cybersecurity risk affects a company's bottom line. It can drive up costs and affect revenue."
(NIST, 2018)

One way to look at the CPD Model is to understand that it addresses quality and cybersecurity. Value not appropriately protected has little to no value to the intended stakeholders who link value and quality; if the quality doesn't meet expectations, the perception of value diminishes. *Unprotected value is an aspect of low quality.*

5.3.2.1   Not about the org chart

The typical org chart addresses management command-and-control. Organizing to create, protect, and deliver digital business value requires managing the flows – specifically the flows of work, communication, and innovation. The trick is to do it in the proper context: in this case, cybersecurity. We need to start with the program structure to understand how to build the cybersecurity program team.

Figure 5.11 illustrates how the resources in the program team collaborate. The board or executive-level equivalent charters the cybersecurity program and ensures the appointment of an executive sponsor who is accountable to the board for program performance. The strategy-risk manager acts as an advisor. Depending on the size and complexity of the organization, it may have an entire executive-level risk team that supports the executive sponsor and program manager. The head auditor of the organization acts as an advisor to the program manager. The organization may also seek external support in the form of a program consultant and program trainers.

Figure 5.11 represents groups or departments for large organizations. For small organizations, it represents roles, not positions – yes, although it may be challenging, one person may fill multiple roles.

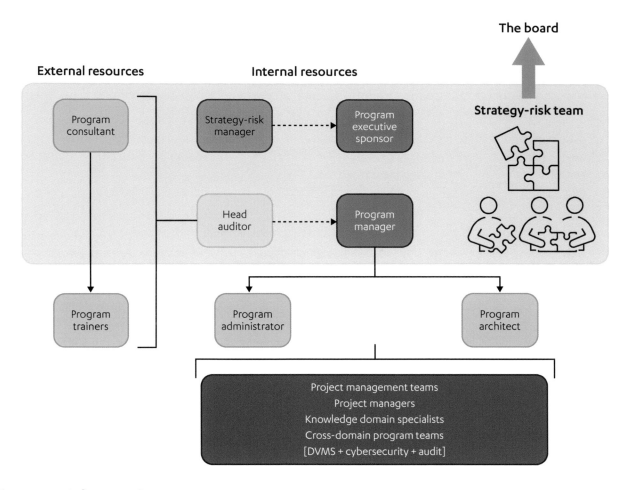

Figure 5.11 Cybersecurity program team resources

5.3.2.2   The DVMS and the Z-X Model

There are seven generic capabilities that most organizations should have in place in one form or another, including the capabilities to plan, design, change, execute, and innovate. While every organization somehow also addresses governance and assurance, larger organizations will do so formally. If you've read our *Fundamentals* book, these seven capabilities should be familiar as part of the Z-X Model part of the DVMS [40] (see Figure 4.1 in this book).

5.3.2.3   The generic capabilities and practice areas

These seven generic capabilities[41] aggregate *practice areas* that may be more familiar to readers. The Z-X Model represents the nonlinear flows within an organization. In addition, they broadly apply to the entire organization. While some of the labels given to the practice areas may be reminiscent of other frameworks, our use here is broader. For example, the Governance capability includes practice areas to create and sustain organizational structures. When applied to an organization, the practices and processes associated with human resources fall into

---

40   The DVMS represents an overlay of the minimum viable capability set to create, protect, and deliver digital business value, which is applicable to any organization regardless of size or geography. It provides a basis to assess the current organizational state. As a scalable system, the DVMS supports the necessary adaptation of the organization to achieve the desired cybersecurity capabilities.

41   The seven generic capabilities are: Governance, Assurance, Plan, Design, Change, Execute, and Innovate. This section focuses on the five core capabilities: Plan, Design, Change, Execute, and Innovate.

this capability. Similarly, a record of the knowledge and skills of the people who work in the organization becomes part of configuration management,[42] which is part of the Design capability.

Neither ownership nor individual accountability is associated with these seven capabilities and the corresponding practice areas and practices. The resulting processes created by the organization have associated accountability and ownership consistent with a RACI model.[43]

Plan

The Plan capability enables the organization to govern; assure performance; create and execute a risk-informed business strategy; manage its portfolio of programs, risks, and projects; and manage the organizational knowledge. The practice areas of the Plan capability subsequently enable the organization to create, protect, and deliver digital business value. The Plan capability aims to create and deliver digital business value with a level of protection proportional to its value to the business. The Plan practice areas (Figure 5.12) are:

- Governance
- Assurance
- Strategy-risk management
- Portfolio, program, and project management
- Knowledge management.

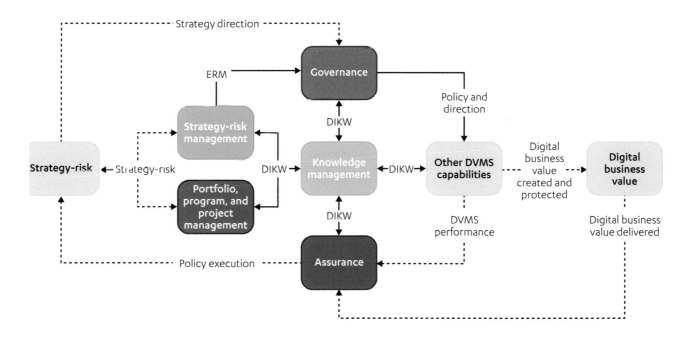

DIKW Data, information, knowledge, wisdom

Figure 5.12 Plan practice area relationships

---

42   The names of some practice areas may seem familiar because of their similarities to those used in service management frameworks and standards. If it aids understanding, mentally change the wording to "the practice area associated with (incident management, for example)" or "the practice of managing incidents."

43   RACI stands for "responsible, accountable, consulted, and informed." You can find more information on Wikipedia (2022j).

Design

The Design capability enables the organization to create a straightforward, cohesive approach to creating and appropriately protecting and delivering digital business value. It seeks to develop designs through the system architecture and configuration management practice areas that enable the organization to deliver digital business value and protect it. Large organizations will need to focus on enterprise and system architecture; small ones might need to focus on system architecture only. The Design practice areas (Figure 5.13[44]) are:

- System architecture
- Configuration management.

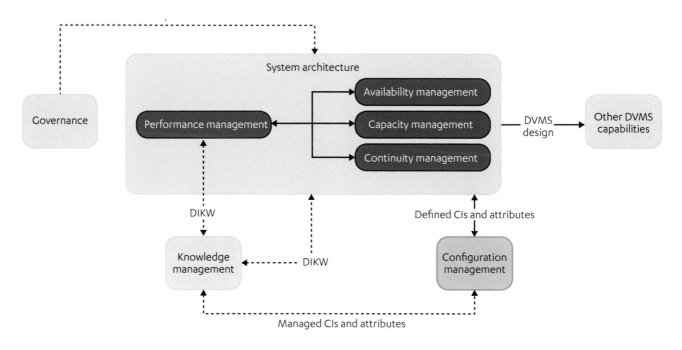

CIs	Configuration items
DIKW	Data, information, knowledge, wisdom

Figure 5.13 Design practice area relationships

Change

Change[45] is a fundamental organizational capability that enables the organization to adapt to its environment. Three distinct areas drive the Change capability: internal needs, external requirements, and a dynamic threat environment. It influences digital solutions that meet the design requirements necessary to create, protect, and deliver digital business value. It establishes the governance structure required to coordinate solutions that impact digital business value. The Change practice areas (Figure 5.14) are:

- Change coordination
- Solution adaptation
- Release management
- Deployment management.

---

44 DIKW in the figure is discussed in detail in section 7.2.4.5.
45 In their Harvard Business Review article "How good is your company at change?," David Michels and Kevin Murphy propose a new system for measuring and improving an organizational ability to adapt. It is recommended reading (Michels and Murphy, 2021); subscription required, reprints available).

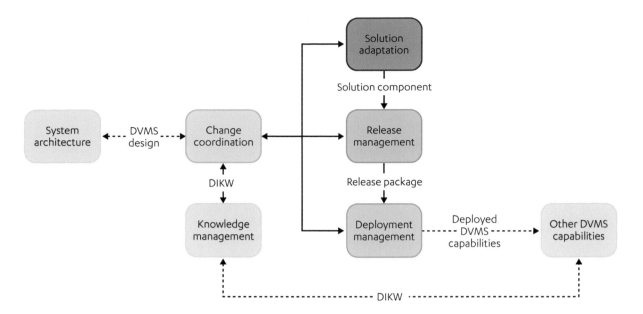

Figure 5.14 Change practice area relationships

Execute

The Execute capability represents the practice areas that create, protect, and deliver digital business value. They encompass providing access to digital products, services, or systems to authorized users; mitigating disruptions in the delivery of digital business value; identifying and resolving systemic interruption or degradation of digital business value; and the overarching management of the infrastructure and platforms. The Execute practice areas (Figure 5.15) are:

- Provisioning
- Incident management
- Problem management
- Infrastructure/platform management.

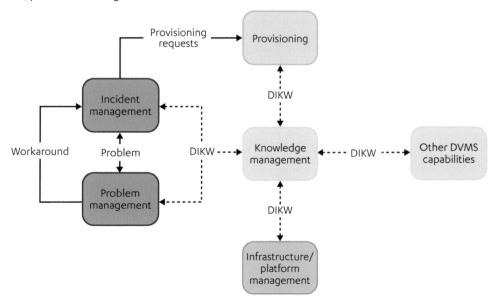

Figure 5.15 Execute practice area relationships

Innovate

The Innovate capability seeks opportunities for improving, creating, protecting, and delivering digital business value. The communicated strategic and operational intent drives incremental, sustaining, adapting, or disruptive innovation. Innovation measures the overall performance of the components and systems that create, protect, and deliver digital business value, analyzes any performance gaps, and catalogs opportunities to innovate. The Innovate practice areas (Figure 5.16) are:

- Continual innovation
- Performance measurement
- Gap analysis.

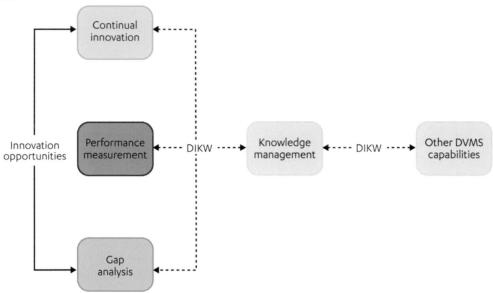

Figure 5.16 Innovate practice area relationships

5.3.2.4   The practices

Each practice area aggregates related practices;[46] the actual execution of each practice occurs in one or more defined organizational processes. While some of the names of the practices might suggest technical information technology exclusively, that is not the case. The capabilities, practice areas, and practices apply to the entire organization (i.e., throughout the system).

Plan (associated practices by practice area)

- **Governance:**
  - Create organizational structures
  - Sustain organizational structures
- **Assurance:**
  - Performance assurance
  - Review and revision
  - Information sharing and reporting

---

46   There's more detail on this in section 7.2. In addition, read this section with an understanding of the COSO principles discussion in section 5.2.3.

- **Strategy-risk management:**

  - Policy integration
  - Identify improvement opportunities
  - Digital business continuity management
  - Supply chain risk management

- **Portfolio, program, and project management:**

  - Establish digital business value portfolio
  - Program/project management

- **Knowledge management:**

  - Manage the flow of information (to/from repositories and between people; see section 3.3.1.1)
  - Audit and manage the information lifecycle
  - Manage stakeholder information flow.

Someone reading the list might ask: "You said this applies to the entire organization; where, for example, is HR?" The answer is that it's part of governance: creating and sustaining organizational structures. HR is also part of assurance; portfolio, program, and project management; knowledge management; and other practices associated with the Z-X Model. Every organizational function maps to one or more practice areas.

Design (associated practices by practice area)

- **System architecture:**

  - Performance management
  - Availability management
  - Capacity management
  - Demand management
  - Continuity management

- **Configuration management:**[47]

  - Configuration item management
  - Configuration administration.

Change (associated practices by practice area)

- **Change coordination:**

  - Change orchestration
  - Change performance assessment

- **Solution adaptation:**

  - Commercial solution acquisition
  - Digital hardware solution
  - Software solution
  - XaaS (something as a service)

---

47 Configuration management applies to more than just inanimate objects. It applies to people and their skills, resources, and responsibilities; training requirements; establishing baselines; configuration policies (including naming conventions); and more. See Wikipedia (2022f) for more information.

- **Release management:**

  - Release planning
  - Monitor component build and test
  - Release testing

- **Deployment management:**

  - Manage release transition
  - Validate release transition.

Execute (associated practices by practice area)

- **Provisioning:**

  - Access management
  - Request management

- **Incident management:**

  - Manage incident models
  - Execute incident model

- **Problem management:**

  - Manage problem models
  - Execute problem model

- **Infrastructure/platform management:**

  - Event monitoring
  - Event management.

Innovate (associated practices by practice area)

- **Continual innovation:**

  - Innovation management
  - Model innovation types
  - Use innovation models

- **Performance measurement:**

  - Instrument practice outcomes
  - DVMS reporting

- **Gap analysis:**

  - Determine the gap
  - Model and assess the gap.

Remember to consider these practice areas and practices in the context of each associated capability. It is essential to understand that the actual execution of the activities related to each practice occurs in organizationally defined processes. Practice areas (and the associated practices) describe what an organization does; processes define the "how." Each organization must create and adapt appropriate processes to accomplish its objectives, preferably in the context of the DVCMM (Digital Value Capability Maturity Model) presented in section 4.1.2.

5.3.2.5 How strategy-risk fits

Some background about the idea of *strategy-risk* might be helpful. The ideas behind this idea grew out of ongoing discussions we (the authors) had about an underlying concept or central theme to which to apply the concepts required for successful cybersecurity efforts. Everything else flowed from that idea once we had settled on strategy-risk as a single entity. With the internalization of single-entity strategy-risk, we couldn't separate the notion of value creation from its protection.

Strategy-risk is an aspect of a reimagined holistic or systems view of an organization. Combining strategy and risk into strategy-risk becomes an enabler, not an inhibitor. Typically, a strategy focuses on creating value; strategy-risk focuses on creating *and* protecting value.

Consider Mintzberg's five "P"s of a strategy: plan, ploy, pattern, position, and perspective (Wikipedia, 2022n). For strategy-risk, expand each "P" to consider what it takes to create and deliver value and ensure it is appropriately protected. While it might be argued that this is little more than the role of managing strategy, many articles in the field focus on creating value and associated risk; what is typically not included is the aspect of protecting value as a part of its creation.

Strategy-risk is a deliberate attempt to get people within organizations to think differently and organize differently to ensure that the value created is appropriately protected. Businesses must be more nimble to respond to changes in the threat landscape, perceived quality or value, marketplace, and trends. The required agility necessitates thinking differently, which leads to organizing around strategy-risk.

Something to think about

The nimble eat the cautious. There are several historical examples of nimble organizations disrupting or killing overly cautious organizations. For example, streaming services disrupted the brick-and-mortar video rental business, which started when Netflix transitioned from a DVD rental/mail service to a streaming service. Another example, viewed from a different perspective, is Kodak. The company was responsible for the invention of the digital camera. However, because its strategic business pattern was as a coating and film company, it wasn't nimble and agile enough to change to become an imaging company.

Organizing to create and protect digital business value is, at its core, a cultural issue, not an org chart (or reporting or chain-of-command) issue.

5.3.2.6 Consulting experience to adopt agile applied to cybersecurity

Over years of working with organizations to adopt and adapt to an agile approach, applying this to cybersecurity suggests there are five components to success.[48]

The first is senior management ownership and accountability for the leadership team's behavior. A disciplined approach to collaboration is required to support the development of a team mindset that integrates strategy-risk so that it becomes pervasive throughout the organization. This approach ensures that value creation and protection become part of the organizational DNA. It is also essential to create a sense of urgency that becomes organization-wide. Remember, bad actors continually adapt, and the organization must learn to do the same.

The second component requires the senior management teams – what Kotter calls a "guiding coalition" – to focus on driving the acceptance of strategy-risk, making every department and individual aware of the requirement to combine value creation and protection. This is not something accomplishable by fiat: it takes time, effort, and

---

48 Although this is derived from personal experience, many readers will recognize its relationship to John P. Kotter's 8-step process for leading change (Kotter, 1995) and his book Leading Change (Kotter, 2012).

consistency, combined with the potential need to change the organizational culture. In other words, there isn't a magic bullet or path to overnight success.

The third component provides small quick wins by assembling teams of the right people (i.e., people with the right mindset), working in small increments and at short intervals. These teams must have cross-domain knowledge, with the appropriate diversity and talent to think differently, making creating and protecting digital business value a mantra within the organization.

The fourth component may require the development of new roles and responsibilities to meet the demands of making cybersecurity enterprise-wide. For example, if the organization has two roles, one responsible for strategy and the other for risk, consider having just one role responsible for strategy-risk.

The fifth component is to expect bumps in the road and be ready to deal with them. As mentioned above, we suggest small increments and short intervals, treating each of these as an experiment. If it works, document what you learned and move on. If it doesn't work, treat the effort as an experiment, record what you learned, and move on to the next experiment.

5.3.2.7 Rules of engagement

There are a few simple ideas that are nonetheless essential considerations. While they might not be part of "organizing" for anything, they depend on knowledge management and the 3D Knowledge Model covered in section 3.3:

- Know and understand what people do and how they perform – not what they say, but what they do
- Empower and encourage self-organization that supports collaborations within teams and cooperation between teams. This idea also distributes decision-making to the lowest and most appropriate level – something essential for a rapid reaction to a cybersecurity event
- Make the Z-axis of the 3D Knowledge Model an essential aspect of team behaviors. It conveys the future strategic and operational intent
- Provide appropriate rewards for people who actively seek to work within the model. Applying this idea requires the transparency and approach to innovation we've discussed before. It also must include the aspiration of people to become the best they can be (i.e., the personal mastery that contributes to team mastery – concepts we've discussed originate in Peter Senge's *The Fifth Discipline* [Senge, 1990]).

5.4   The DVMS FastTrack approach

A critical aspect of adopting and adapting a structured approach to cybersecurity (e.g., the NIST Cybersecurity Framework) is the capability of the organization to internalize cybersecurity as a core, mission-critical capability, along with the ability to innovate the required cybersecurity controls. In other words, cybersecurity becomes a defining characteristic of the organization, not just something it does.

The DVMS FastTrack approach is based on the Z-X Model for the rapid adoption, adaptation, and continual innovation of cybersecurity controls necessary to protect the value created. It originates from agile experience; to make any genuine improvement to the current state, an organization must achieve stability (i.e., things reliably perform the same way every time). Once the environment is stable, the organization can optimize its existing capabilities (make existing things as good as they can be). Then, the work shifts to innovation opportunities to create, protect, and deliver digital business value. FastTrack provides a structured approach to enable an organization to do that quickly.

The last aspect of the DVMS FastTrack approach is embedding an organizational capability to adapt quickly and efficiently to threats, and internal and external changes, that might impact the desired cybersecurity posture.

While continual innovation isn't exclusive to cybersecurity, it's a must for any organization that aims to become adaptive and cyber-resilient.

5.4.1 Understand and apply the DVMS FastTrack approach

A well-known quality expert, Philip Crosby, noted author of *Quality Is Free* (Crosby, 1979), said, "Quality has to be caused, not controlled." Think about that for a second as applied to the discussion of leverage points and complex systems (section 3.2). Everything we've discussed up to this point has been about using leverage at the appropriate points and levels to cause the system behaviors to change. Crosby's point about built-in quality is one of the reasons we suggested treating cybersecurity as an aspect of quality – built-in – that creates and protects digital business value, not a bolt-on.

Think about that in the context of cybersecurity. We'll paraphrase something Crosby said about an organization that "needs" to implement a quality program: "It's like building a raft from the debris of your business, as it floats down the rapids." That's what it feels like to "need" a cybersecurity program. The idea of a cybersecurity program raises questions such as the following:

- Who do we need to do this? Who is going to do it?
- What do we do first? Where do we start?
- When and how will we know we're done?
- Why are we doing this?

Before we talk about DVMS FastTrack, let's establish some context.

5.4.1.1 Stabilize, optimize, and innovate

In any chaotic, out-of-control environment, the first order of business is to control the things you can and mitigate those you can't. In the raft analogy, you try to swim and not drown until you clear the rapids, and gather as much floating debris as possible. Now, cobble together a raft (this is an analogy, not an engineering exercise). You've stabilized the situation; you are alive and have a raft.

There will be more rapids, so it's time to make what you have as good as possible so you and your raft can survive the next set of rapids intact. While you haven't ensured survival, the raft is as good as possible. So what's next? Most likely, what's next are more rapids. Somewhere along the way, you find material suitable for a rudder and other debris suitable to build a shelter on the deck, oars, containers to store food, etc. You are innovating from a condition of stability.

Hopefully, your organizational "need" for cybersecurity doesn't originate from the aftermath of a significant breach, but more from the leadership awakening to the cybersecurity role in organizational value. What do you do next? Stabilize, of course, and then control what you can and mitigate the rest. Then you have a stable platform to optimize your capabilities before you innovate capabilities to create, protect, and deliver digital business value.

5.4.1.2 DVMS FastTrack approach

The DVMS FastTrack approach is not a framework nor a methodology. It is an approach based on the Z-X Model capabilities, enabling organizations to adopt the NIST-CSF rapidly. The approach adapts the cybersecurity control requirements from one or more informative references (IRs).[49] This adaptation of control requirements integrates them with the underlying capabilities to deliver digital business value. It represents a phased approach to stabilize,

---

49 We use the term "informative reference" in the context of cybersecurity. The following are examples of informative references: NIST Special Publication 800-53 (NIST, 2020) and ISO/IEC 27001 (ISO, 2013).

optimize, and innovate the capability to protect the created value. We present an overview of this integration in section 5.5.2.

FastTrack assumes that the organization has decided to adopt the NIST-CSF as its structured approach to cybersecurity. It also assumes that strategy-risk objectives embed creating, protecting, and delivering digital business value into existing practice areas (as enumerated in section 5.3.2.3 and discussed in section 5.5.2). The resultant policies provide management guidelines to create or improve organizational capabilities. That means that resources are available to create, protect, and deliver digital business within the tolerances established by strategic policy. Now, all that's left to do is to make it happen. Piece of cake, right?

The DVMS FastTrack approach (Figure 5.17) to the adaptation and implementation of IR guidance uses the capabilities of the underlying organizational DVMS. The initiation phase prepares the organization to adapt the NIST-CSF cybersecurity controls and establish a beachhead by ensuring basic cybersecurity hygiene controls. Once the beachhead is secure, the foundation phase expands the defensible perimeter. The last phase establishes the capability to innovate continually.

For each phase, we'll discuss an abstraction of cybersecurity control families derived from NIST Special Publication (SP) 800-53 (NIST, 2020). These control families are a suggested set and not intended to represent a prescriptive approach. Each organization must assess its needs, requirements, and threat landscape, in the context of its capabilities and digital assets. We selected NIST SP 800-53 because it contains a superset of control requirements expressed in other IRs – under the theory that it's easier to cut what you don't need than to figure out what's missing.

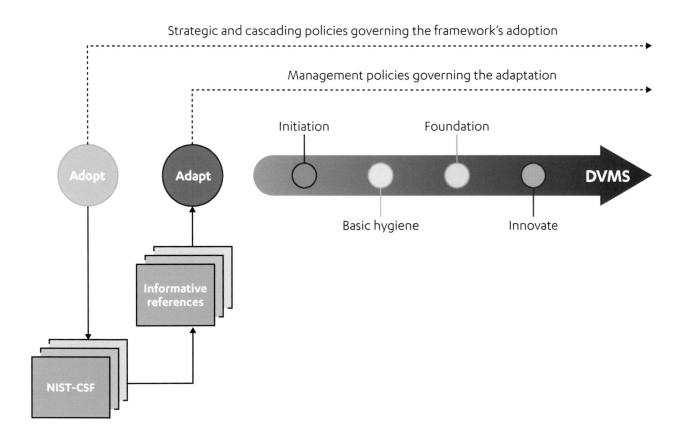

Figure 5.17 DVMS FastTrack approach

Phase 0: Initiate

We'll start the discussion of DVMS FastTrack with Phase 0, or "getting ready to get ready": it defines the baseline for subsequent phases. This phase lays the groundwork for the efforts in the subsequent three phases. Phase 0 enables the organization to stabilize its current capabilities.

- **Planning** The organization aligns its business objectives with its internal and external requirements and the dynamic threat landscape. This alignment involves objectives, policies, and the expression of strategic and operational intent. Policies are the tools used to execute strategic objectives, and to guide the creation of new organizational capabilities and the improvement of existing ones

- **Awareness and training** Cyberculture starts at the top and flows throughout. It is imperative to make the entire organization cyber-aware. This requires much more than a "Don't click on stuff" video course, followed by wrist-slapping of violators when they do. Cyber awareness involves everyone in the organization: it requires them to understand cyber business risk, and why it's essential to understand its context and role in keeping the organization cyber-secured. This is where the organization establishes the cybersecurity program team and executes a comprehensive role-based training plan for the core team and those that will integrate cybersecurity control requirements with the underlying organizational DVMS capabilities

- **Incident response** Developing or improving the capability to respond to a cyber incident is essential for this "getting ready" phase. In all likelihood, the organization can manage incidents impacting its digital assets. A cybersecurity incident is just a different incident category with a corresponding incident model (that, among other things, identifies the composition of the response team). As the organization moves through the FastTrack phases, it continues to innovate its cyber incident response capabilities, with subsequent integration of cybersecurity control requirements in later phases

- **Contingency planning** Similarly to incident response, the organization revisits its contingency planning in the context of a cybersecurity event. Again, similarly to incident management, expand existing contingency plans to include a response to a cybersecurity event

- **Program (and project) management** The issue is integrating cybersecurity control requirements, combined with the overarching goal to create and protect digital business value, into the planning and conduct of every program and project. This approach is not exclusively a Phase 0 "thing" – it is ongoing in every subsequent phase

- **Risk assessment** Like program (and project) management, risk assessment spans every phase. It is part of the essence and expression of strategy-risk. Consequently, we integrate supply chain risk management into this practice area.

Although this is about "getting ready to get ready," it is not a once-and-done phase. Progress achieved in subsequent phases, and other internal and external factors, will dictate revisiting each area as needed. Planning, cybersecurity awareness and training, risk assessment, and so on are ongoing activities with ongoing requirements to update and improve the initial baselines.

Phase 1: Basic hygiene

In Phase 1, the organization takes an 80/20 approach to establish its basic cybersecurity capabilities. It closes any performance gaps in a basic set of cybersecurity control requirements in the following control families. Think of the DVMS FastTrack approach as building a layer cake of cybersecurity control requirements. This layer cake idea leads to some control families appearing more than once in the list; subsequent phases add additional rigor and new requirements for cybersecurity controls. As part of the DVMS FastTrack phases, each adopting organization *must* adapt its chosen cybersecurity controls to suit specific organizational needs or regulatory requirements.

A quick note: starting Phase 1 does not signal the end of Phase 0. While program and project management and risk assessment (strategy-risk) are ongoing in every phase, appropriate innovations might still impact the other aspects of Phase 0 concurrently with work in different phases.

Phase 1 establishes the cybersecurity beachhead.[50]

- **Configuration management** The configuration management control family establishes baselines for hardware, software, and secure configuration. The organization must establish these three baselines to ensure complete and accurate knowledge of its digital assets. Implementing these control requirements depends on the organization's fundamental DVMS capability to manage its digital assets (configuration management, a practice area in the Design capability). If the organization does not have this Design practice area, it must establish the organizational practice before implementing the associated cybersecurity controls. The cybersecurity control requirements for configuration management depend on the Z-X Model practice area; the organization *must* integrate these three cybersecurity control requirements into its configuration management system. It must maintain the configuration management system so that every change to the baseline requires a supporting change to configuration data

- **Access control** Access control is essential to basic cybersecurity hygiene. The organization must know who or what accessed each protected asset; what was accessed; when it was accessed; how often; and, if relevant to the organization, why it was accessed, and the authorizing party. The organization must have complete knowledge of its digital assets before granting access with any assurance that the right individual has the correct access rights. In Phase 1, administrative rights are an essential first step. Subsequent phases add more fine-grained controls. As the organization integrates more cybersecurity controls and its maturity and capabilities expand, all aspects of the existing controls are examined and re-examined continually to innovate its cybersecurity capabilities

- **Assessment, authorization, and monitoring** In Phase 1, these controls are involved in vulnerability management to establish a cybersecurity beachhead. We haven't secured the beach yet. The organization establishes the capability to maintain its vigilance for existing or evolving vulnerabilities. It becomes proactive by continually examining its dynamic context for a performance gap that exposes an organizational vulnerability

- **Audit and accountability** In Phase 1, the organization audits its capabilities, practices, processes, activities, and events. This activity examines several factors: what happened, when it happened, the location, who or what was involved, and the identification of the accountable individual. This activity presents a high-level view. Chapter 6 reviews this in more detail. Audit and accountability enable the organization to track who does what in broad strokes

- **System and information integrity** This control family provides the controls necessary to maintain and audit the logs produced by the systems. What good does logging do if the resulting records are neither monitored nor maintained? These capabilities span both human and machine controls to monitor logging. This can combine automated event monitors and human scrutiny of flagged events. The integration of these controls and their dependencies within the DVMS is discussed in Chapter 7.

Progression through the DVMS FastTrack phases will not be linear. Each cybersecurity control integrates with or depends on an underlying DVMS capability. Innovation to improve DVMS capabilities might be a prerequisite to implementing cybersecurity controls. In addition, recall our discussion about unintended consequences in a complex system (Chapter 3): every control implementation might cause one or more teams to revisit "this" control as part of implementing new control requirements to reduce adverse side effects. Remember, the organization is changing a complex system, and must understand the selected leverage point(s) and the impact on other system components. Like the children's game of pick-up sticks, everything touches everything else.

---

50   Section 5.5.2 introduces the dependencies between cybersecurity controls and the underlying DVMS capabilities. Section 7.2 discusses these in more detail.

Phase 2: Expand

In Phase 2, the organization builds out the remainder of its cybersecurity foundation by expanding Phase 0 and 1 controls and integrating new control families. This is where the organization expands its defensible cybersecurity perimeter.

As the organization expands its capabilities, it must revisit its earlier integrations and improvements to ensure any new Phase 2 control capability impacts are understood and any residual performance gaps are identified and mitigated. Like in Phase 1, the organization must assess its current Phase 2 capabilities and close the gaps in the order and degree that meets its needs, requirements, and approach to the threat landscape.

- **Access control** With its expanding cybersecurity controls and maturity, Phase 2 addresses "need to know" or the principle of "least privilege." It tightens access controls to ensure that individuals and groups are granted only the minimum access necessary to complete their assigned work. This approach spans systems, services, hardware, software, network, storage, etc., and is implemented as a combination of technical and management controls integrated with the underlying DVMS capabilities
- **Audit and accountability** In Phase 2, the organization expands the scope of these controls by adding more control requirements and integrating them into the DVMS capabilities while also increasing the maturity level of those capabilities. In each iteration, incremental or sustaining innovation requires revisiting these controls and closing performance gaps
- **Assessment, authorization, and monitoring** As the cybersecurity capabilities and maturity improve, revisit this control family as necessary to mitigate performance gaps. This primarily involves expanding the controls within underlying DVMS capabilities and maturing the capabilities as discussed in the material about the DVCMM (see section 4.1.2)
- **Configuration management** Configuration management expands secure network configuration controls and adds network ports, protocols, and services. It also adds controls necessary to monitor and control accounts. It might not be evident now, but the organizational configuration management capability and associated change capability are essential to becoming an adaptive, cyber-resilient organization
- **Contingency planning** Contingency planning is revisited during each phase as it incorporates the necessary capabilities. Phase 2 results in a significant increase in organizational capabilities and the subsequent update to the organizational contingency planning – for business and IT continuity. Suppose the organization takes a system thinking approach to the DVMS FastTrack phases and integrates the cybersecurity control requirements. In that case, it's reasonable to assume that the organization must understand the scope of that change for each new or improved cybersecurity control. DVMS FastTrack acts as an approach for an organization to engineer the capabilities within the Governance/Execution loop of the CPD Model, typically confined to incremental or sustaining innovations. This also implies using low-order leverage points to change system behavior within the tolerances established by strategic policies. The phased approach of DVMS FastTrack addresses new or residual performance gaps to integrated cybersecurity controls as the organization expands its capabilities and maturity. It is also essential to be mindful that every innovation in organizational or cybersecurity capabilities considers the potential impact on other controls – in this case, contingency planning
- **Identification and authentication** Phase 2 matures the capabilities relative to the email and web browsers. It is dependent on access management and executes the organizational policies for appropriate usage. It establishes controls to ensure safe use within the tolerances established by management policies. This relates to Phase 0 cybersecurity awareness and training controls: these address the technical and human boundaries respectively. Cyberattacks exploit human factor weakness (the threat actor technique is social engineering). Good cybersecurity hygiene seeks to mitigate the human element with controls on policy, and hardware and software
- **Media and data protection** As organizational capabilities mature, it is essential to expand the appropriate cybersecurity control requirements related to handling digital media, including how it is stored, transported, backed up, and, if necessary, recovered. Expanding the defensible perimeter includes expanding the capability to protect digital media. Greater capabilities and maturity also require integrating controls that ensure

compartmentalization and isolation of digital assets

- **System and communication protection** Phase 2 controls provide separation of system and user functionality. User access is appropriately limited so that only those with an approved need to know can view the communication

- **System and information integrity** As the organization expands its defensible cybersecurity perimeter, it expands the scope of this control family to include malware, system boundaries (including system isolation), and wireless access. This extends beyond just the boundary and includes ensuring any malware can't move around within the infrastructure (i.e., network segmentation).

Phase 3: Innovate

Once an organization enters Phase 3, it has reached a stable and optimized state. It now expands its capabilities as needed to improve the depth and breadth of its cybersecurity capabilities. The organization continually examines performance to discover and mitigate gaps. Because the needs, external requirements, and dynamic threat landscape are in constant flux, it may have to revisit some of its control requirements and the underlying DVMS capabilities.

- **Access control** In Phase 3, continually innovate this control to provide appropriate incremental or sustaining changes within established tolerances. As the internal needs, external requirements, and threat landscape change, access control is revisited as needed

- **System and services acquisition** Thoroughly vet all new or changed services, irrespective of source, to ensure their impact on existing systems is well understood, and externally sourced software applications meet the organizational cybersecurity control requirements

- **Assessment, authorization, and monitoring** The organization adds controls to address inter-system connections at this level. Is the network traffic between systems monitored, authorized, and logged?

- **System and communication protection** The organization adds denial-of-service protections at this level

- **System and information integrity** Once the organization has established its defensible perimeter, it must proactively probe those defenses. Penetration is one technique used as part of robust cybersecurity control requirements. Thinking like a bad actor helps an organization design, build, and operate digital business systems. For more information, review Chapter 2

- **Contingency planning** By the time an organization reaches Phase 3, it has made continual incremental or sustaining changes to its contingency plans. There is no difference in Phase 3 other than expanding the cybersecurity controls to ensure data and business recovery within the information security aspects of the business continuity management plans.

Now what?

The organization has stabilized, optimized, and improved its cybersecurity capabilities through a phased approach to integrating the cybersecurity control requirements with the underlying DVMS capabilities. So, you are all done, right?

Nope: now that you have a "new normal" of adaptive cyber resilience, your organization must continually assess and innovate to close performance gaps in its DVMS capabilities, with integrated cybersecurity control requirements that create, protect, and deliver digital business value.

Following the phased approach that is DVMS FastTrack also supports progressing through the DVCMM (see Figure 5.18).

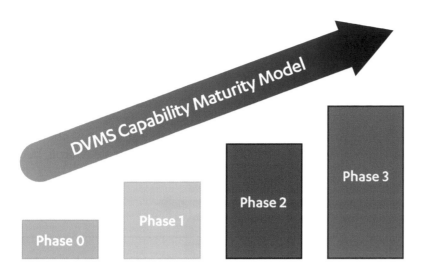

Figure 5.18 DVCMM and DVMS FastTrack phases

5.5 Agility and resilience (the CPD Model and cybersecurity)

What is the relationship between agility and resilience? The answer to this question starts with the definition of "cyber resilience" (or 'resiliency'):

"The ability to anticipate, withstand, recover from, and adapt to adverse conditions, stresses, attacks, or compromises on systems that use or are enabled by cyber resources. Cyber resiliency is intended to enable mission or business objectives that depend on cyber resources to be achieved in a contested cyber environment. Note: cyber resiliency can be a property of a system, network, service, system of systems, mission or business function, organization, critical infrastructure sector or subsector, region, or nation."
NIST (2021)

Within limits, external threat actors depend on a lack of cyber resilience to achieve their aims. The organizational goal should be cyber resilience,[51] not becoming bulletproof. Every organization must plan for the aftermath of an attack. Treat resilience as an architecture issue that starts with understanding risk and incorporating it as an essential aspect of organizational strategy (this is strategy-risk).

There is a special type of resilience to address the insider threat. An "Insider threat mitigation" guide published by the Cybersecurity and Infrastructure Security Agency (CISA) provides the following guideline:

"To combat the insider threat, organizations should consider a proactive and prevention-focused insider threat mitigation program."
CISA (2022)

---

51 The NIST-CSF includes resilience as a part of the Recover function.

5.5.2   Cyber resilience

An organization demonstrates cyber resilience when it continually delivers the intended outcomes regardless of cyber incidents, something that is nearly impossible when cybersecurity is a bolt-on. Part of cyber resilience requires preparation. It also requires not trying to reinvent the wheel by implementing cybersecurity controls as if they had no relationship to things the organization is already doing. We define a set of generic cybersecurity controls based on the control families specified in NIST SP 800-53 (NIST, 2020).[54] These control families are as follows:

● Access control
● Awareness and training
● Audit and accountability
● Assessment, authorization, and monitoring
● Configuration management
● Contingency planning
● Identification and authentication
● Incident response
● Maintenance
● Media and data protection
● Personally identifiable information processing
● Personnel security
● Physical and environmental protection
● Planning
● Program and project management
● Risk assessment (includes supply chain risk management and physical and environmental protection)
● System and communication protection
● System and information integrity.

As you look at this list, you might see elements of it that look familiar and are not exclusively the province of cybersecurity. For example, consider the following, which represent just under 50% of the list above.

● Awareness and training (for cybersecurity)
● Configuration management
● Contingency planning
● Incident response
● Maintenance
● Planning
● Program and project management
● Risk assessment.

The proper approach requires integrating cybersecurity into existing organizational practices rather than treating these controls as something extra to do. The same technique works for every cybersecurity control, regardless of the IR used by the organization.

---

54   If you want to use the control families in the NIST publication, feel free. To be consistent with our concept of strategy-risk, we combined the 800-53 supply chain risk management and system and service acquisition into risk assessment.

This idea suggests that improving the organizational cybersecurity posture does not start with trying to implement the selected cybersecurity IR. Instead, read the IRs to understand the impact of the cybersecurity control requirements on existing capabilities. For example, one of the things typically required for cybersecurity configuration management is a baseline of hardware and software – and in that order: hardware first, then software. If you already have an up-to-date baseline, you've met the first requirements to integrate cybersecurity configuration management.

This approach changes what might appear to be a huge task to implement the controls in a cybersecurity IR to one that integrates cybersecurity into the practices, processes, and activities that the organization is already performing.

Table 5.1 provides information regarding dependencies and integration points between the DVMS practice areas and the cybersecurity controls listed above. [55]

Table 5.1 The relationship between DVMS practice areas and cybersecurity controls

Cybersecurity control families mapped to practice areas of the DVMS/Z-X Model capabilities	Access control	Awareness and training	Audit and accountability	Assessment, authorization, and monitoring	Configuration management	Contingency planning	Identification and authentication	Incident response	Maintenance	Media and data protection	Personally identifiable information processing	Personnel security	Physical and environmental protection	Planning	Program and project management	Risk assessment	System and communication protection	System and information integrity
PL: Governance	D	D	D	D	D	D	D	D	D	D	D	D	D	D	D	D	D	D
PL: Assurance	D	D	D	D	D	D	D	D	D	D	D	D	D	D	D	D	D	D
PL: Strategy-risk management	D	D	D	D	D	D	D	D	D	D	D	D	D	D	D	D	D	D
PL: Portfolio, program, and project management	I	I	I	I	I	I	I	I	I	I	I	I	I	I	I	I	I	I
PL: Knowledge management	I	I	I	I	I	I	I	I	I	I	I	I	I	I	I	I	I	I
DE: System architecture	I	-	D	D	D	D	D	D	I	D	D	I	D	D	I	D	D	D
DE: Configuration management	I	-	D	D	D	D	D	D	D	D	I	D	D	I	D	D	D	D
CH: Change coordination	I	I	D	D	D	D	D	D	I	D	D	I	I	D	I	D	D	D
CH: Solution adaptation	I	-	D	D	D	D	I	I	I	I	I	I	I	I	I	D	I	D
CH: Release management	I	-	D	D	D	D	I	I	I	I	I	I	I	I	I	D	I	D
CH: Deployment management	I	-	D	D	D	D	I	I	I	I	I	I	I	I	I	D	I	D
EX: Provisioning	D	-	I	I	D	D	I	I	I	-	I	I	I	I	I	D	I	D
EX: Incident management	D	I	I	I	D	D	I	D	-	-	I	I	-	I	I	D	I	I
EX: Problem management	D	-	I	I	D	D	I	D	-	-	I	I	-	I	I	D	I	I
EX: Infrastructure/platform management	D	-	I	I	D	D	I	I	D	D	I	I	D	I	I	D	I	D
IN: Continual innovation	I	-	I	I	D	D	I	-	-	-	I	I	-	D	I	D	I	I
IN: Performance measurement	I	-	I	I	D	D	I	-	-	-	I	I	-	D	I	D	I	D
IN: Gap analysis	I	-	I	I	D	D	I	-	-	-	I	I	-	D	I	D	I	I

Key to practice areas

Plan capability   Design capability   Change capability   Execute capability   Innovate capability

---

55   In Table 5.1, the abbreviations PL, DE, CH, EX, and IN are the first two letters of the five core capabilities Plan, Design, Change, Execute, and Innovate.

The letter "D" in the table indicates that the cybersecurity control depends on the existence of the DVMS practice area covered in the discussion on configuration management (above). An "I" indicates that the control requirements are integrated into the practice area. We discussed this area as part of the incident response narrative in section 5.4.1.2. An aspect of every cybersecurity control is creating appropriate planning and policies for the control, which are reflected in the "D" for governance, assurance, and strategy-risk management. Similarly, appropriate integration with portfolio, program, project, and knowledge management is required.

This approach is consistent with several themes introduced in the *Fundamentals* book and this one. The idea is to think about systems: the whole, not a hole. This approach supports cybersecurity as an enterprise endeavor with primary responsibility resting with the board or the most senior management. You'll find a phased approach to this method in Chapter 6.

True cyber resilience requires the integration of cybersecurity into every part of the fabric of the organization, not treating it as a bolt-on.

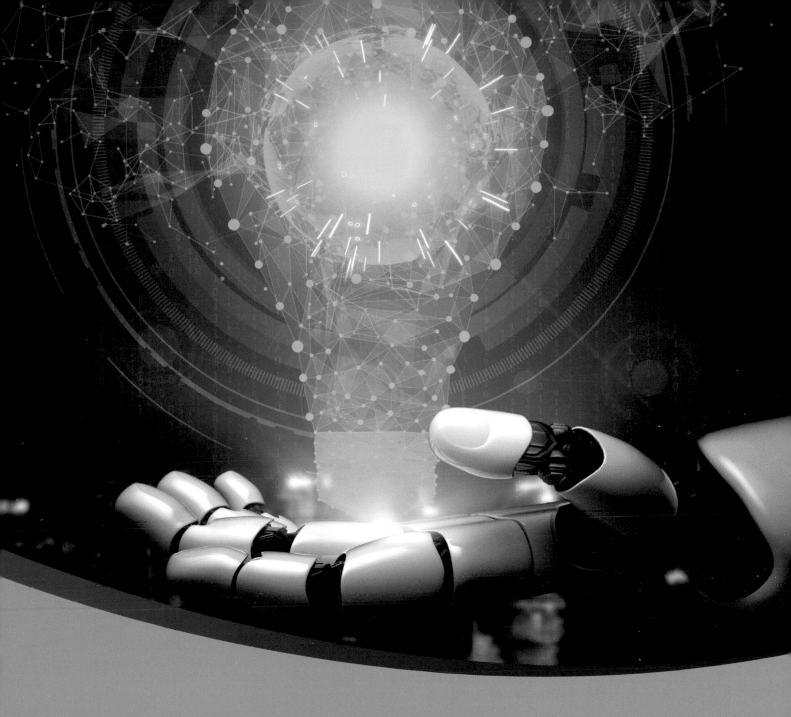

CHAPTER 6
Cybersecurity within a system

6 Cybersecurity within a system

We began section 3.1 with a question about why the typical treatment of cybersecurity is as a bolt-on, which relegates it to the technical departments. The answer we suggested was that C-level folks commissioned an assessment and tossed it over the wall to the IT folks to "fix" without also providing an appropriate budget for the effort.

This "throw-it-over-the-wall" approach demonstrates the idea that C-level believes cybersecurity "is not our problem," and the IT folks accept it as a technology issue. These perspectives represent two different sides of the same coin. Neither point of view is associated with long-term success.

We've also suggested a connection between cybersecurity and quality and the link between quality and value (section 4.1.2.2). Applying a bit of mathematical transitivity provides consistency with the central theme of linking cybersecurity to value. This approach is consistent with our first principles (sections 5.2.1 and 5.2.2). This chapter explores first principle number three (adopt and apply systems thinking) in more detail – how cybersecurity is a critical aspect of the system that creates and protects digital business value.

6.1   A systems approach to cybersecurity

Chapter 3 explored ideas that are essential to thinking in systems. This section explores cybersecurity and systems thinking – and why it's vital to "think this way." We've discussed the idea of "see the whole, not a hole" several times in this book and the *Fundamentals* book (Moskowitz and Nichols, 2022). In this case, the "whole" is critical to creating and protecting value. We justified this approach in section 3.1:

"The essence of creating, protecting, and delivering digital business value requires a holistic look at everything the enterprise does. Creating and protecting value are parallel efforts, not serial. This perspective is at the core of the CPD Model. Once this perspective is adopted, it's impossible to treat cybersecurity as a bolt-on."

Section 5.5.2 introduced a set of cybersecurity control families based on NIST Special Publication 800-53 (NIST, 2020). The section provided an introductory overview of integrating cybersecurity into existing organizational capabilities. Table 5.1 provides information regarding the dependencies that cybersecurity control families have on existing capabilities.

Each "D" in the table suggests a prerequisite dependency on the existence of the practice area in the left-most column with the corresponding control family in the top row. These capabilities must exist in the organization.

A letter "I" in the table suggests the requirements for the cybersecurity control family be integrated into existing practice areas, rather than creating a separate set of practices to support cybersecurity. What Table 5.1 does *not* reveal is the relationships between the practice areas.

Working through the DVMS FastTrack approach (section 5.4) and adding more rigor (i.e., tightening tolerances, etc.) to the practices associated with capabilities is a by-product of working with the approach combined with appropriate diligence (see Figure 5.18 and the discussion under "Now what?" in section 5.4.1.2).

This alignment of practice areas probably does not align with traditional thinking for someone familiar with other frameworks. This arrangement of practices represents an aspect of systems thinking, which requires us to think differently. Part of the thinking that leads to this approach appeared in section 5.3. The lead sentence in the section read:

"Organizing for CPD is not about organization (org) charts – it's about leadership that creates and communicates the vision and mission for CPD and then seeks to get organizational buy-in."

In the following sections, we start with the practice areas shown in Table 5.1 that have the prefix "PL" (for Plan), and continue through to "IN" (for Innovate). Consider why each of the cybersecurity control families has either a "D," "I," or "-" in the associated table cell.

6.1.1 Practice areas in Plan

6.1.1.1 Governance, assurance, and strategy-risk management

Table 5.1 suggests that every cybersecurity control requires the organization to establish capabilities to govern, assure, and manage strategy-risk. Why? First, it is critical to think of cybersecurity controls from any informative reference as a "statement of requirements," not as a "control" in the sense of a light switch. Second, examine NIST SP 800-53, starting with section 3.1, "Access control" (NIST, 2020). Every set of controls starts with the requirement to address policy and procedures. The first control requirement establishes a template for the information required, the assignment of an accountable individual for the controls in the family, and the need to review and audit the policies and procedures to ensure that they meet the organizational needs.

Without a system view of the organization that includes cybersecurity, the tendency might be to create separate policies and procedures just for cybersecurity. This point is essential and summarizes the entire approach. Taking a systems view changes this approach. The board of directors or a similar governing body is accountable for (i.e., owns) cybersecurity. Even in a small organization, someone at the top holds this responsibility.

6.1.1.2 Portfolio, program, and project management, and knowledge management

Moving down the list of practice areas in Table 5.1: portfolio, program, and project management, and knowledge management, show the letter "I" across all cybersecurity control families. In these cases, the formal practice areas might not exist, but the organization still demonstrates some aspects of them. For example, the organization must know the products and services provided to stakeholders and customers. It also must have a way to capture and record knowledge about what it is doing. Without either of these practice areas, the organization is unlikely to exist for much longer.

For these two practice areas, it is essential to integrate the requirements for the cybersecurity control families into whatever does exist to support the related activities. This approach is part of adopting and adapting. The "D" cells require expanding existing organizational capabilities to support the selected cybersecurity informative reference. If the "D" practice area does not exist, the organization should develop that capability – not just for cybersecurity but also to support the organizational objectives. This approach is an aspect of getting ready to address cybersecurity, recognizing the existing practice areas that enable the organization to create and protect digital business value – practice areas that must exist.

6.1.2 Practice areas in Design

6.1.2.1 System architecture and configuration management

The table cells with a "D" depend on system architecture and configuration management. For example, systems require an architecture that supports the ability to assess, audit, and monitor. Similarly, system maintenance depends on configuration management; it is essential to document things such as patch levels. On the other hand, while maintenance might be an architectural consideration, it is not dependent on the system architecture practice area.

6.1.3 Practice areas in Change

The practices in this section of Table 5.1 are all associated with the organizational capability to manage change. Notice there isn't a central change authority; we have change coordination as a practice area. Within any organization, there might be concurrent projects. Remember, projects are temporary units of an organization that introduce change (something new or a change to something already existing).

6.1.3.1 Change coordination

We talk about capabilities, practice areas, and practices directly related to coordinating one or more parallel change-related efforts, knowing there isn't a one-size-fits-all approach that will work to address the situation in every organization.

Notice that every cybersecurity control family has some relationship to change coordination. For example, access control is integrated into change coordination (shown by the letter "I" in the intersecting cell in Table 5.1). By contrast, the cybersecurity control family for configuration management (letter "D" in the intersecting cell) depends on change coordination. In other words, you cannot implement the controls in this family without the existence of at least a rudimentary level of the practice area.

This also suggests a bidirectional dependency[56] between the DVMS configuration management practice area that is part of the Design capability and the practices associated with the Change capability.

6.1.3.2 Solution adaptation, release management, and deployment management

Solution adaptation reflects the practices required to implement a change. Release management and deployment management represent traditional organizational behaviors. While there is a "-" for these three practice areas under awareness and training, some organizations might integrate the cybersecurity control family into these practice areas. The point is that this table is suggestive, not absolute.

6.1.4 Practice areas in Execute

While the previous three capabilities (Plan, Design, and Change) are associated directly or indirectly with the entirety of the CPD Model, the Execute capability is related to the Governance/Execution loop in the model.

---

56   Section 6.2 provides a table that covers these relationships.

6.1.4.1 Provisioning

Provisioning addresses the things the organization does to "provide for" something. That is why the "D"s and "I"s appear the way they do in the table.

6.1.4.2 Incident management and problem management

The relationship between incident management and problem management exists outside of a cybersecurity context. Incident management aims to maintain or restore an acceptable level of productivity; problem management seeks to fix (or develop workarounds) for causes of incidents.

We define an *incident* as something that does or could impact stakeholder productivity. The focus of incident management becomes identifying and restoring an acceptable level of productivity. *Problem* management addresses the underlying cause of an incident. This different approach leads to the slight difference in the table between these two practice areas. Specifically, it is more likely for an incident to lead to cybersecurity awareness and training changes, so the letter "I" appears at the intersection of this practice area and this cybersecurity control family.

6.1.4.3 Infrastructure/platform management

Infrastructure addresses every "thing" the organization has or uses, including physical or virtual stuff and cloud-based resources. The dependencies and integration points recorded in the table for the cybersecurity controls apply to all three of these areas (types of resources).

6.1.5 Practice areas in Innovate

We've devoted considerable space to continual innovation and performance measurement. Because of the rapidly changing threat landscape, we recommend organizations develop gap analysis as a separate practice area. There must be a way for the organization to efficiently and effectively identify gaps in organizational performance as close as possible in time to the emergence of the gap. If the gap is within organizational tolerances,[57] no immediate action is required. However, someone should monitor the gap to ensure it does not exceed tolerances. If the initial recognition of the gap exceeds organizational tolerances, the organization must take immediate corrective action.

---

57   The basis to establish tolerances is policies maintained by adaptive or disruptive innovation.

6.2 Overview of the practice relationships within the DVMS

As noted in section 6.1, there are relationships between the cybersecurity control families and the DVMS practice areas; there are also relationships between the DVMS practice areas, as shown in Table 6.1.

Table 6.1 Practice area relationships

DVMS practice areas	PL: Governance	PL: Assurance	PL: Strategy-risk management	PL: Portfolio, program, and project management	PL: Knowledge management	DE: System architecture	DE: Configuration management	CH: Change coordination	CH: Solution adaptation	CH: Release management	CH: Deployment management	EX: Provisioning	EX: Incident management	EX: Problem management	EX: Infrastructure/platform management	IN: Continual innovation	IN: Performance measurement	IN: Gap analysis
PL: Governance	-	B	B	B	B	B	-	B	-	-	-	-	-	-	-	B	B	B
PL: Assurance	B	-	B	B	B	B	-	T	-	-	-	-	-	-	-	B	T	B
PL: Strategy-risk management	B	B	-	B	B	B	B	T	T	T	T	-	-	-	-	B	T	B
PL: Portfolio, program, and project management	B	B	B	-	B	B	-	T	-	-	-	-	-	-	-	B	T	B
PL: Knowledge management	B	B	B	B	-	B	B	B	B	B	B	B	B	B	B	B	B	B
DE: System architecture	B	B	B	B	B	-	B	B	F	-	-	-	-	-	-	B	B	B
DE: Configuration management	-	-	B	-	B	B	-	T	B	T	T	-	T	T	T	B	B	B
CH: Change coordination	B	F	F	F	B	B	B	-	B	B	B	-	-	-	-	B	B	B
CH: Solution adaptation	-	-	F	-	B	-	B	B	-	F	F	-	-	-	-	B	B	B
CH: Release management	-	-	F	-	B	-	F	B	T	-	T	-	-	-	-	B	B	B
CH: Deployment management	-	-	F	-	B	-	F	B	T	F	-	-	-	-	-	B	B	B
EX: Provisioning	-	-	-	-	B	-	-	-	-	-	-	-	F	F	T	B	B	B
EX: Incident management	-	-	-	-	B	-	F	-	-	-	-	T	-	B	T	B	B	B
EX: Problem management	-	-	-	-	B	-	F	-	-	-	-	T	B	-	T	B	B	B
EX: Infrastructure/platform management	-	-	-	-	B	-	F	-	-	-	-	F	F	F	-	B	B	B
IN: Continual innovation	B	F	F	F	B	B	B	B	B	B	B	B	B	B	B	-	B	B
IN: Performance measurement	B	B	B	B	B	B	B	B	B	B	B	B	B	B	B	B	-	B
IN: Gap analysis	B	B	B	B	B	B	B	B	B	B	B	B	B	B	B	B	B	-

Key to practice areas

■ Plan capability ■ Design capability ■ Change capability ■ Execute capability ■ Innovate capability

A letter "B" in Table 6.1 indicates a bidirectional relationship. A "T" denotes a "to" relationship from the practice area in the row to the one in the column. For example, the "T" at the intersection of the "PL: Assurance" row and "CH: Coordination" column indicates the relationship to coordination from assurance. Similarly, the "F" at the intersection of the "CH: Coordination" row and "PL: Assurance" column indicates a relationship from assurance to coordination. In other words, the table is symmetrical.

The table shows the relationships between the DVMS practice areas. Practice areas aggregate practices. Adding more elements to the system increases complexity because it adds possibilities for interaction.

The following sections provide a brief overview of suggested practices in each area.[58] It is up to the organization to adopt and adapt appropriate practices and related processes that meet its needs.

Note: You may notice a similarity between the practices and the COSO principles covered in section 5.2.3. In addition, someone familiar with IT service management may recognize the reorganization of ideas typically associated with IT structures.

6.2.1   Suggested Plan practices

- Governance (both practices also create and/or maintain appropriate governance policies):

  - **Create organizational structures** For existing organizations, this practice comes into play typically due to adaptive or disruptive innovation
  - **Sustain organizational structures** This practice applies across existing structures, including human resources, financial, strategy-risk management, etc. Sustaining organizational structures also includes innovating or improving associated capabilities and considerations for strategy-risk

- Assurance:

  - **Performance assurance** Establishes the means to monitor and measure performance
  - **Review and revision** Addresses COSO principles 15 to 17 (section 5.2.3.4), establishing the relationship with the practice areas in Change (see Table 5.1)
  - **Information sharing and reporting** Embodies COSO principles 18 to 20 (section 5.2.3.5)

- Strategy-risk management:

  - **Policy integration** Ensure the efficient and effective integration of policies consistent with the organizational risk appetite and strategy-risk management
  - **Identify improvement opportunities** For strategy-risk management
  - **Digital business continuity management** Inclusive of business and IT
  - **Supply chain risk management** This should be part of strategy-risk, not other areas

- Portfolio, program and project management:

  - **Establish digital business value portfolio** Inclusive of digital services and systems (see section 2.1)
  - **Program management** Classic program management
  - **Project management** Classic project management

- Knowledge management:

  - **Manage the flow of information** Ensure the appropriate level of knowledge availability and transparency (includes the mentorship discussed in section 3.3.1.1)
  - **Audit and manage the information lifecycle** Ensure the flow of information and knowledge continues to meet organizational requirements
  - **Manage stakeholder information flow** Ensure stakeholders are appropriately informed (i.e., "kept in the loop").

---

58   It is beyond the scope of this book to delve into the practices. The DVMS book *Living on the Edge of Chaos* has more detail (to be published in 2023).

6.2.2 Suggested Design practices

- **System architecture** Rather than being standalone practices, these are an integral part of the architecture
  - Performance management
  - Availability management
  - Capacity management
  - Demand management
  - Continuity management
- **Configuration management** It is impossible to craft an architecture without some record or accounting of the available resources. Configuration management is an essential aspect of architecture and critical for Change and the other DVMS capabilities
  - Configuration item management
  - Configuration administration.

6.2.3 Suggested Change practices

- **Change coordination** Coordinating multiple changes requires orchestration (central control) and choreography (reactive, more trust transparency)
  - Change orchestration
  - Change performance assessment
- **Solution adaptation** Applies to developing a solution, whether developed in-house, purchased, or used as a service
  - Commercial solution acquisition
  - Digital hardware solution
  - Software solution
  - XaaS (something as a service)
  - Performance assessment (for solution adaptation)
- **Release management** Release management stages "packaged" releases into new environments (including withdrawal from service)
  - Release planning
  - Monitor component build and testing
  - Release testing
- **Deployment management** Make each new release available in the new environment (including withdrawal from service)
  - Manage release transition
  - Validate.

6.2.4 Suggested Execute practices

- **Provisioning** Provides (or revokes) access to services (including self-help or manual requests)

  - Access management
  - Request management

- **Incident management** Classic incident management

  - Manage incident models
  - Execute incident model

- **Problem management** Classic, traditional problem management

  - Manage problem models
  - Execute problem model

- **Infrastructure/platform management** Primarily a monitoring and management function. Alteration to the infrastructure outside of tolerances goes through Change

  - Event monitoring
  - Event management.

6.2.5 Suggested Innovate practices

- **Continual innovation** There are multiple models for each type of innovation (incremental, sustaining, adaptive, and disruptive)

  - Innovation management
  - Model innovation types
  - Use innovation models

- **Performance measurement** Ensures that every practice (and the resulting processes) is appropriately instrumented to provide the necessary data to gauge performance, and recognize and determine performance gaps

  - Instrument practice outcomes
  - DVMS reporting

- **Gap analysis** An important practice area for recognizing and determining suitable responses to performance gaps and changes to the threat landscape

  - Determine the gap
  - Model and assess the gap.

6.3   Applying the DVMS FastTrack approach

We have provided a brief overview of the suggested practices in the DVMS to set the stage for integrating the DVMS and cybersecurity implementation. Table 6.1 establishes a predicate and potential "pre-work" before undertaking any cybersecurity initiatives. The approach is cybersecurity as part of the system, not a bolt-on. This approach may require adding or improving the practices and related processes necessary to "get ready."

6.3.1   Get ready

As previously noted, there is a family of cybersecurity controls for configuration management. The objective is to use and expand the existing capabilities to support cybersecurity, potentially requiring either expanding or maturing existing capabilities, or adding new ones.

Examine the cybersecurity control requirements for the selected cybersecurity informative reference to determine where to start. Start with Table 6.1 to determine the relationships between the cybersecurity control families and the DVMS capabilities. Suppose there is a "D" in the intersecting cell of the table. In that case, examining the DVMS capability and related practice areas is essential in light of the cybersecurity control requirements. Consider the following example:

- The first 800-53 control for the configuration management control family (CM-1) is "Policy and procedures." Read through the CM-1 requirements and ensure that the existing DVMS configuration management practice area supports the requirements

- The next configuration management control is "baseline configuration." If the organization already has and maintains conforming baselines, great; if not, start here

- Move through the rest of the relevant 800-53 controls in the configuration management family to determine the gaps in the DVMS capabilities, and improve those first.

If the intersecting cell has an "I," the process is similar to the one above. In this case, the issue is integrating the cybersecurity control requirements into the existing DVMS capabilities, unless the DVMS capability is either non-existent or not sufficiently mature to support the integration.

For either case ("D" or "I" in the intersecting cell), consult section 4.1.2 to review information about the Digital Value Capabilities Maturity Model.

Work on the DVMS equivalent first before starting the formal efforts to improve cybersecurity. As a generic agile approach (see section 5.1), if needed, DVMS FastTrack applies to "getting ready."

The following sections review the material about DVMS FastTrack phases presented in section 5.4, and provide additional details. Also, note that, in every cybersecurity control family in the NIST SP 800-53 publication, the first control requirements address policies and procedures. In every case, you should refer to the NIST publication (or other selected cybersecurity informative reference[59]) for more details about the referenced controls.

Each control family has several controls; each control documents one or more numbered requirements (e.g., a control in the system and communication protection family that addresses boundary protection [SC-7] lists 29 numbered requirements). We do not suggest implementing every numbered requirement corresponding to the first reference or mention of the control. As the numbers increase, control numbering and control requirements increase coverage and rigor. We recommend selecting the control requirements based on a strategy-risk-informed approach. This approach supports DVMS FastTrack phases and differences in organizational size and resources.

---

59   For a mapping from NIST SP 800-53 to ISO 27001, see NIST (n.d.). For mapping to the Center for Internet Security Controls v8, see CIS (n.d.). If the organization used NIST 800-171 (Controlled Unclassified Information), the names of the control families either match exactly or are easily recognizable.

As we go through the phases, notice there are occasionally controls from more than one control family listed, illustrating that the controls are related and not siloed. This approach is consistent with a "systems" view of cybersecurity.

Notes about the phase control listings:

- The list of associated controls is deliberately incomplete: it is a guide or initial set of recommendations in the absence of anything else the organization might already have. NIST SP 800-53 contains a complete list of related controls
- The "policy and procedures" control appears in every phase. As the organization adds more controls and associated phase rigor, it's essential to revisit the policies and procedures, making changes or tweaks to fit the organizational need.

6.3.2 Phase 0: Get started

Phase 0 initiates the activities necessary to implement and sustain cybersecurity initiatives. As noted in section 6.3.1, you should improve and/or mature existing DVMS capabilities before starting formal work on the cybersecurity initiative.

A quick summary of the material under "Phase 0: Initiate" in section 5.4.1.2:

- Planning
  - Objective alignment of business and cybersecurity
- Cybersecurity awareness and training
  - Literacy, role-based training, and training records
- Incident response
  - Planning
  - Developing additional cybersecurity incident models
  - Incident response training
- Contingency planning
  - Contingency plan, contingency training
- Program (and project) management
- Risk assessment (includes supply chain risk management).

Everything in Phase 0 is ongoing in every subsequent phase. Update the initiatives and activities associated with this phase concurrently with the development and implementation of the controls in each successive stage. Introduce a new control, and ensure there is synchronized updating or revision of the cybersecurity awareness and training curriculum. Similarly, ensure that incident models and associated incident response training are updated.

It is also essential to consider cybersecurity control requirements from two perspectives: implementor and auditor. The implementor and auditor work together to ensure both the appropriate implementation of each selected control requirement, and the existence of relevant, tangible evidence, ongoing monitoring, assessment, etc., to support the assurance side of the CPD Model.[60]

This revision and update cycle indicates the nonlinear nature of the DVMS FastTrack phases.

---

60   There is more on the topic of implementor and auditor in Chapter 7 as part of the discussion about GQM and QO–QM.

The suggested controls in Phase 0 are listed below (drawn from NIST SP 800-53, Revision 5 [61]). The idea is to get started. The organization may already have one or more of these controls as part of a "regular" organizational policy or to support a cybersecurity initiative. Every control (other than program management[62]) starts by ensuring appropriate policies and procedures to support the control family, integrated into the existing policies and procedures before creating a distinct set for cybersecurity.

The organization needs to ensure these policies and procedures address the creation *and* protection of digital business value. For example, in NIST SP 800-53, PL-2 a(1) requires that cybersecurity privacy plans are consistent with the organizational enterprise architecture, which suggests a link between the DVMS capabilities of Plan and Design. It also requires proof of this consistency – expressing the connection between creating and protecting value. Treat every control in every phase from this perspective.

In some cases, we recommend adding related controls from other NIST SP 800-53 control families. We've noted the source.

This book does not cover every control in NIST SP 800-53. That publication addresses requirements for organizations that handle government-classified information. Whether your organization does or does not have this requirement doesn't make a difference. These are recommendations, not an attempt to provide a single template for every organization. Adopt a cybersecurity informative reference and adapt it to fit the need.

- **Planning** (Table 6.2) Ensures the integration of cybersecurity with the Strategy/Governance loop in the CPD Model

  - PL-1 Policy and procedures
  - PL-2 System security and privacy plans
  - PL-4 Rules of behavior
  - PL-7 Concepts of operations

Table 6.2 Planning

Cybersecurity control families mapped to Z-X Model practice areas: Planning	Identify critical business systems	Establish digital business risk posture	Oversee DVMS performance	Establish assurance criteria	Assure strategic policy performance	Assure operational capability	Assure performance measurement accuracy	Governance	Assurance	Knowledge management	Portfolio, program, and project management	Strategy-risk management	Configuration management	System architecture	Change coordination	Solution adaptation	Release management	Deployment management	Provisioning	Incident management	Problem management	Infrastructure/platform management	Continual innovation	Performance measurement	Gap analysis
PL-1 Policy and procedures	D	D	D	D	D	D	D	D	D	D	D	D	D	D	D	D	D	D	D	D	D	D	D	D	D
PL-2 System security and privacy plans	D	D	D	D	D	D	D	D	D	D	D	D	D	D	D	D	D	D	D	D	D	D	D	D	D
PL-4 Rules of behavior	D	D	D	D	D	D	D	D	D	D	D	D	D	D	D	D	D	D	D	D	D	D	D	D	D
PL-7 Concepts of operations	D	D	D	D	D	D	D	D	D	D	D	D	D	D	D	D	D	D	D	D	D	D	D	D	D

Key to Z-X Model capabilities

Govern   Assure   Plan   Design   Change   Execute   Innovate

---

61   Refer to the NIST publication (NIST, 2020) for the specific control requirements.

62   Proper program and project management have their own sets of requirements to initiate a project, conduct a project, etc. The various approaches to project management are typically aligned with existing frameworks or methods (e.g., PMBOK, Praxis, or PRINCE2).

- **Awareness and training** (Table 6.3) Provides a means to ensure that the staff knows how to recognize, respond to, and report any cybersecurity-related events that extend to security and privacy. The training driver derives from the organizational strategic governance and policies, which define the bounds for the control-related management policies and procedures. The training is role-based and risk-based (including training for the implementor and auditor). In other words, develop the curriculum targeting responsibilities for each role. But it's more than just personal training: it's role-based to encourage appropriate collaboration across the organization that engenders the "see something, say something" approach combined with creating and protecting digital business value.

  - AT-1 Policy and procedures
  - AT-2 Literacy training and awareness
  - AT-4 Training records
  - PM-15 (from program management) Security and privacy group associations

Table 6.3 Awareness and training

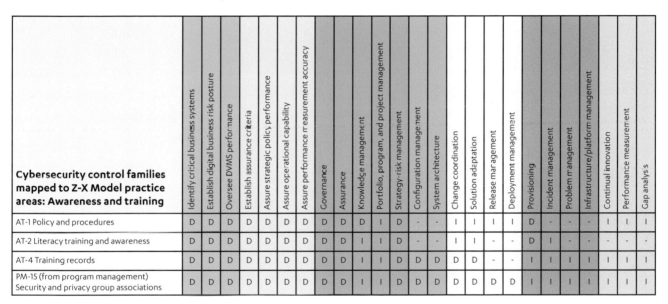

Cybersecurity control families mapped to Z-X Model practice areas: Awareness and training	Identify critical business systems	Establish digital business risk posture	Oversee DVMS performance	Establish assurance criteria	Assure strategic policy performance	Assure operational capability	Assure performance measurement accuracy	Governance	Assurance	Knowledge management	Portfolio, program, and project management	Strategy-risk management	Configuration management	System architecture	Change coordination	Solution adaptation	Release management	Deployment management	Provisioning	Incident management	Problem management	Infrastructure/platform management	Continual innovation	Performance measurement	Gap analysis
AT-1 Policy and procedures	D	D	D	D	D	D	D	D	D	D	I	D	-	-	I	I	I	I	D	-	-	-	I	I	I
AT-2 Literacy training and awareness	D	D	D	D	D	D	D	D	D	I	I	D	-	-	I	I	-	-	D	I	-	-	-	-	-
AT-4 Training records	D	D	D	D	D	D	D	D	D	I	I	D	D	D	D	D	-	-	I	I	I	I	I	I	I
PM-15 (from program management) Security and privacy group associations	D	D	D	D	D	D	D	D	D	I	I	D	D	D	D	D	D	D	I	I	I	I	I	I	I

Key to Z-X Model capabilities

Govern   Assure   Plan   Design   Change   Execute   Innovate

- **Incident response** (Table 6.4) Expands existing incident management capabilities to provide models for cybersecurity incidents, using information derived from the exercise suggested in section 2.1.

  - IR-1 Policy and procedures
  - IR-2 Incident response training
  - IR-4 Incident handling
  - IR-5 Incident monitoring
  - IR-8 Incident response plan.

Table 6.4 Incident response

Cybersecurity control families mapped to Z-X Model practice areas: Incident response	Identify critical business systems	Establish digital business risk posture	Oversee DVMS performance	Establish assurance criteria	Assure strategic policy performance	Assure operational capability	Assure performance measurement accuracy	Governance	Assurance	Knowledge management	Portfolio, program, and project management	Strategy-risk management	Configuration management	System architecture	Change coordination	Solution adaptation	Release management	Deployment management	Provisioning	Incident management	Problem management	Infrastructure/platform management	Continual innovation	Performance measurement	Gap analysis
IR-1 Policy and procedures	D	D	D	D	D	D	D	D	D	D	I	D	I	I	I	I	I	I	D	D	D	D	I	I	I
IR-2 Incident response training	D	D	D	D	D	D	D	D	D	I	I	D	-	-	I	-	-	-	-	I	-	-	-	-	-
IR-4 Incident handling	D	D	D	D	D	D	D	D	D	I	I	D	D	D	D	D	D	D	I	I	I	I	I	I	I
IR-5 Incident monitoring	D	D	D	D	D	D	D	D	D	I	I	D	D	D	D	D	D	D	I	I	I	I	I	I	I
IR-8 Incident response plan	D	D	D	D	D	D	D	D	D	I	I	D	D	D	D	D	D	D	D	D	D	D	D	D	D

Key to Z-X Model capabilities

Govern   Assure   Plan   Design   Change   Execute   Innovate

- **Contingency planning** (Table 6.5) Provides another example of extended existing capabilities, as opposed to creating something separate and distinct for cybersecurity

  - CP-1 Policy and procedures
  - CP-2 Contingency plan
  - CP-3 Contingency training
  - CP-4 Contingency plan testing

Table 6.5 Contingency planning

Cybersecurity control families mapped to Z-X Model practice areas: Contingency planning	Identify critical business systems	Establish digital business risk posture	Oversee DVMS performance	Establish assurance criteria	Assure strategic policy performance	Assure operational capability	Assure performance measurement accuracy	Governance	Assurance	Knowledge management	Portfolio, program, and project management	Strategy-risk management	Configuration management	System architecture	Change coordination	Solution adaptation	Release management	Deployment management	Provisioning	Incident management	Problem management	Infrastructure/platform management	Continual innovation	Performance measurement	Gap analysis
CP-1 Policy and procedures	D	D	D	D	D	D	D	D	D	D	I	D	I	I	I	I	I	I	I	I	I	I	I	I	I
CP-2 Contingency plan	D	D	D	D	D	D	D	D	D	I	I	D	D	D	I	I	I	I	I	I	I	I	I	I	I
CP-3 Contingency training	D	D	D	D	D	D	D	D	D	I	I	D	D	D	D	D	D	D	I	I	I	I	I	I	I
CP-4 Contingency plan testing	D	D	D	D	D	D	D	D	D	I	I	D	D	D	D	D	D	D	I	I	I	I	I	I	I

Key to Z-X Model capabilities

Govern   Assure   Plan   Design   Change   Execute   Innovate

- **Program management** (Table 6.6) Ensure the appropriate program- and project-level planning and support to create and protect digital business value, requiring integrating auditors into the project teams to ensure creating and protecting are concurrent project activities

  - PM-1 Information security program plan
  - PM-2 Information security program leadership role
  - PM-3 Information security and privacy resources
  - PM-4 Plan of action and milestones process
  - PM-5 System inventory
  - PM-6 Measures of performance

Table 6.6 Program management

Cybersecurity control families mapped to Z-X Model practice areas: Program management	Identify critical business systems	Establish digital business risk posture	Oversee DVMS performance	Establish assurance criteria	Assure strategic policy performance	Assure operational capability	Assure performance measurement accuracy	Governance	Assurance	Knowledge management	Portfolio, program, and project management	Strategy-risk management	Configuration management	System architecture	Change coordination	Solution adaptation	Release management	Deployment management	Provisioning	Incident management	Problem management	Infrastructure/platform management	Continual innovation	Performance measurement	Gap analysis
PM-1 Information security program plan	D	D	D	D	D	D	D	D	D	D	I	D	I	I	I	I	I	I	D	D	D	D	I	I	I
PM-2 Information security program leadership role	D	D	D	D	D	D	D	D	D	I	I	D	-	-	I	-	-	-	-	I	-	-	-	-	-
PM-3 Information security and privacy resources	D	D	D	D	D	D	D	D	D	I	I	D	I	I	I	I	I	I	I	I	I	I	I	I	I
PM-4 Plan of action and milestones process	D	D	D	D	D	D	D	D	D	I	I	D	I	I	I	I	I	I	I	I	I	I	I	I	I
PM-5 System inventory	D	D	D	D	D	D	D	D	D	I	I	D	D	D	I	I	I	I	D	D	D	D	D	D	D
PM-6 Measures of performance	D	D	D	D	D	D	D	D	D	I	I	D	D	D	D	D	D	D	D	D	D	D	D	D	D

Key to Z-X Model capabilities

Govern   Assure   Plan   Design   Change   Execute   Innovate

- **Risk assessment** (Table 6.7) Performed in the context of strategy-risk, not a separate risk department. This approach is consistent with the need to ensure the value created is appropriately protected

  - RA-1 Policy and procedures
  - RA-2 Security categorization
  - RA-3 Risk assessment
  - RA-7 Risk response
  - RA-8 Privacy impact assessments
  - SR-1 (from supply chain risk management) Policy and procedures
  - SR-2 (from supply chain risk management) Supply chain risk management plan
  - SR-5 (from supply chain risk management) Acquisition strategies, tools, and methods.

Table 6.7 Risk assessment

Cybersecurity control families mapped to Z-X Model practice areas: Risk assessment	Identify critical business systems	Establish digital business risk posture	Oversee DVMS performance	Establish assurance criteria	Assure strategic policy performance	Assure operational capability	Assure performance measurement accuracy	Governance	Assurance	Knowledge management	Portfolio, program, and project management	Strategy-risk management	Configuration management	System architecture	Change coordination	Solution adaptation	Release management	Deployment management	Provisioning	Incident management	Problem management	Infrastructure/platform management	Continual innovation	Performance measurement	Gap analysis
RA-1 Policy and procedures	D	D	D	D	D	D	D	D	D	D	I	D	I	D	I	I	I	I	D	D	D	D	I	I	I
RA-2 Security categorization	D	D	D	D	D	D	D	D	D	D	I	D	-	I	I	I	I	I	-	I	-	-	-	-	-
RA-3 Risk assessment	D	D	D	D	D	D	D	D	D	D	I	D	D	D	D	D	D	D	I	I	I	I	I	I	I
RA-7 Risk response	D	D	D	D	D	D	D	D	D	D	I	D	D	D	D	D	D	D	I	I	I	I	I	I	I
RA-8 Privacy impact assessments	D	D	D	D	D	D	D	D	D	D	I	D	D	D	D	D	D	D	D	D	D	D	D	D	D
SR-1 (from supply chain risk management) Policy and procedures	D	D	D	D	D	D	D	D	D	D	I	D	D	D	D	I	I	I	I	I	I	I	I	I	I
SR-2 (from supply chain risk management) Supply chain risk management plan	D	D	D	D	D	D	D	D	D	D	I	D	D	D	D	I	I	I	I	I	I	I	I	I	I
SR-5 (from supply chain risk management) Acquisition strategies, tools, and methods	D	D	D	D	D	D	D	D	D	D	I	D	D	D	D	I	I	I	D	D	D	D	-	-	-

Key to Z-X Model capabilities

Govern   Assure   Plan   Design   Change   Execute   Innovate

Note: The controls in Phase 0 are not limited to this phase. Implementing additional control requirements in subsequent phases requires revisiting and updating each control in this phase. This approach is consistent with systems thinking – consider the whole, not a hole.

6.3.3 Phase 1: The basics

A quick summary of the material under "Phase 1: Basic hygiene" in section 5.4.1.2:

- Configuration management

  - Baseline and control of hardware assets (do this first)
  - Baseline and control of software assets (follows hardware baseline)
  - Impact analysis
  - Secure configurations

- Access control

  - Account management
  - Controlled use of administrative privilege

- Assessment, authorization, and monitoring

  - Control assessments
  - Vulnerability management

- Audit and accountability

  - Event logging, the content of audit records, audit storage capacity, and time stamps

- System and information integrity

  - Maintain and monitor or audit logs
  - Malware defense

- Risk assessment

  - Maintain the risk assessment plan – started in this phase and ongoing in every phase
  - Criticality analysis[63]
  - Develop supply chain acquisition strategies.

We provided information about a Tier 1 research university in section 2.1.3 ("You can't protect what you don't know exists"). What we *didn't* say is relevant here.

The university performed the software scans before the hardware scans and used that as a baseline. This pattern was repeated: software before hardware. The Software Publishing Association (SPA) found additional trouble spots when they did their scans and examinations. The difference: the SPA did the hardware first, then software. As noted, you can't protect what you don't know exists.

In this and subsequent phases, many cybersecurity control requirements have dependencies and integration points with the practice areas for the Design and Execute capabilities. Don't stop there. Depending on the circumstances, investigate the relationships with the other capabilities (Plan, Change, and Innovate).

We do not suggest implementing every requirement for each control family in Phase 1. There is time and a plan for that as part of subsequent phases. Apply strategy-risk considerations to select the initial subset appropriate for the organization, knowing Phases 2 and 3 will add more.

---

63 Review the material in Chapter 2. The same proactive exercises to identify existing business systems and prioritize them are applications of criticality analysis.

Suggested controls in Phase 1:

- **Configuration management** Another case of integrating cybersecurity control requirements into existing organizational capabilities. The repetition of some controls between baseline hardware and baseline software is intentional; work on the hardware requirements first, then address the ones for software

  - Baseline hardware (first) (Table 6.8)

    - CM-1 Policy and procedures
    - CM-2 Baseline configuration
    - CM-3 Configuration change control
    - CM-4 Impact analysis
    - CM-6 Configuration settings
    - CM-7 Least functionality
    - CM-8 System component inventory
    - CM-9 Configuration management plan

Table 6.8 Baseline hardware

Cybersecurity control families mapped to Z-X Model practice areas: Configuration management – hardware	Identify critical business systems	Establish digital business risk posture	Oversee DVMS performance	Establish assurance criteria	Assure strategic policy performance	Assure operational capability	Assure performance measurement accuracy	Governance	Assurance	Knowledge management	Portfolio, program, and project management	Strategy-risk management	Configuration management	System architecture	Change coordination	Solution adaptation	Release management	Deployment management	Provisioning	Incident management	Problem management	Infrastructure/platform management	Continual innovation	Performance measurement	Gap analysis
CM-1 Policy and procedures	D	D	D	D	D	D	D	D	D	D	I	D	D	I	I	I	I	I	D	-	-	-	I	I	I
CM-2 Baseline configuration	D	D	D	D	D	D	D	D	D	I	I	D	D	I	I	I	-	-	D	I	-	-	-	-	-
CM-3 Configuration change control	D	D	D	D	D	D	D	D	D	I	I	D	D	D	D	D	-	-	I	I	I	I	I	I	I
CM-4 Impact analysis	D	D	D	D	D	D	D	D	D	I	I	D	D	D	D	D	D	D	I	I	I	I	I	I	I
CM-6 Configuration settings	D	D	D	D	D	D	D	D	D	I	I	D	D	D	I	I	I	I	D	-	-	-	I	I	I
CM-7 Least functionality	D	D	D	D	D	D	D	D	D	I	I	D	D	D	I	I	I	I	D	-	-	-	I	I	I
CM-8 System component inventory	D	D	D	D	D	D	D	D	D	I	I	D	D	I	I	I	I	I	D	-	-	-	I	I	I
CM-9 Configuration management plan	D	D	D	D	D	D	D	D	D	I	I	D	D	I	I	I	I	I	D	-	-	-	I	I	I

Key to Z-X Model capabilities

Govern   Assure   Plan   Design   Change   Execute   Innovate

- Baseline software (Table 6.9)
    - CM-1 Policy and procedures
    - AC-4 (from access control) Information flow enforcement
    - CM-2 Baseline configuration
    - CM-3 Configuration change control
    - CM-4 Impact analysis
    - CM-9 Configuration management plan
    - CM-11 User-installed software

Table 6.9 Baseline software

Cybersecurity control families mapped to Z-X Model practice areas: Configuration management – software	Identify critical business systems	Establish digital business risk posture	Oversee DVMS performance	Establish assurance criteria	Assure strategic policy performance	Assure operational capability	Assure performance measurement accuracy	Governance	Assurance	Knowledge management	Portfolio, program, and project management	Strategy-risk management	Configuration management	System architecture	Change coordination	Solution adaptation	Release management	Deployment management	Provisioning	Incident management	Problem management	Infrastructure/platform management	Continual innovation	Performance measurement	Gap analysis
CM-1 Policy and procedures	D	D	D	D	D	D	D	D	D	D	I	D	D	I	I	I	I	I	D	I	I	I	I	I	I
AC-4 (from access control) Information flow enforcement	D	D	D	D	D	D	D	D	D	I	I	D	D	D	I	I	I	I	D	I	I	I	I	I	I
CM-2 Baseline configuration	D	D	D	D	D	D	D	D	D	I	I	D	D	D	D	D	D	D	I	I	I	I	I	I	I
CM-3 Configuration change control	D	D	D	D	D	D	D	D	D	I	I	D	D	D	D	D	D	D	I	I	I	I	I	I	I
CM-4 Impact analysis	D	D	D	D	D	D	D	D	D	I	I	D	D	D	D	D	D	D	D	-	-	-	I	I	I
CM-9 Configuration management plan	D	D	D	D	D	D	D	D	D	I	I	D	D	I	I	I	I	I	D	-	-	-	I	I	I
CM-11 User-installed software	D	D	D	D	D	D	D	D	D	I	I	D	D	-	I	I	I	I	D	I	I	I	I	I	I

Key to Z-X Model capabilities

Govern   Assure   Plan   Design   Change   Execute   Innovate

- **Access control** (Table 6.10) It is likely the organization already has some means (either formal or ad hoc) to grant and revoke access to systems and services. Applying this control will either add rigor to organizations that perform the practice or require organizations to mature their ad-hoc approach

  - AC-1 Policy and procedures
  - AC-2 Account management
  - AC-3 Access enforcement
  - AC-6 Least privilege
  - AC-10 Concurrent session control
  - AC-11 Device lock
  - AC-12 Session termination
  - AC-24 Access control decisions
  - AU-6 (from audit and accountability) Audit record review, analysis, and reporting
  - MP-3 (from media protection) Media marking

Table 6.10 Access control

Cybersecurity control families mapped to Z-X Model practice areas: Access control	Identify critical business systems	Establish digital business risk posture	Oversee DVMS performance	Establish assurance criteria	Assure strategic policy performance	Assure operational capability	Assure performance measurement accuracy	Governance	Assurance	Knowledge management	Portfolio, program, and project management	Strategy-risk management	Configuration management	System architecture	Change coordination	Solution adaptation	Release management	Deployment management	Provisioning	Incident management	Problem management	Infrastructure/platform management	Continual innovation	Performance measurement	Gap analysis
AC-1 Policy and procedures	D	D	D	D	D	D	D	D	D	D	I	D	I	I	I	I	I	I	D	D	D	D	I	I	I
AC-2 Account management	D	D	D	D	D	D	D	D	D	I	I	D	-	-	D	-	-	-	D	I	I	I	I	I	I
AC-3 Access enforcement	D	D	D	D	D	D	D	D	D	I	I	D	D	D	D	D	D	D	D	I	I	I	I	I	I
AC-6 Least privilege	D	D	D	D	D	D	D	D	D	I	I	D	D	I	I	I	I	I	D	I	I	I	I	I	I
AC-10 Concurrent session control	D	D	D	D	D	D	D	D	D	I	I	D	D	I	I	I	I	I	D	I	D	D	I	I	I
AC-11 Device lock	D	D	D	D	D	D	D	D	D	I	I	D	D	I	I	I	I	I	D	I	D	D	I	I	I
AC-12 Session termination	D	D	D	D	D	D	D	D	D	I	I	D	D	I	I	I	I	I	D	I	D	D	I	I	I
AC-24 Access control decisions	D	D	D	D	D	D	D	D	D	I	I	D	D	I	I	I	I	I	D	I	D	D	I	I	I
AU-6 (from audit and accountability) Audit record review, analysis, and reporting	D	D	D	D	D	D	D	D	D	I	I	D	D	I	I	I	I	I	D	-	-	I	I	I	I
MP-3 (from media protection) Media marking	D	D	D	D	D	D	D	D	D	I	I	D	D	I	I	I	I	I	D	-	-	I	I	I	I

Key to Z-X Model capabilities

Govern   Assure   Plan   Design   Change   Execute   Innovate

- **Assessment, authorization, and monitoring** (Table 6.11) Once implemented, can it be appropriately monitored and assessed? Are there appropriate authorizations (and controls) to perform the related activities?

  · CA-1 Policy and procedures
  · CA-2 Control assessments
  · CA-5 Plan of action and milestones
  · CA-9 Internal system connections

Table 6.11 Assessment, authorization, and monitoring

Cybersecurity control families mapped to Z-X Model practice areas: Assessment, authorization, and monitoring	Identify critical business systems	Establish digital business risk posture	Oversee DVMS performance	Establish assurance criteria	Assure strategic policy performance	Assure operational capability	Assure performance measurement accuracy	Governance	Assurance	Knowledge management	Portfolio, program, and project management	Strategy-risk management	Configuration management	System architecture	Change coordination	Solution adaptation	Release management	Deployment management	Provisioning	Incident management	Problem management	Infrastructure/platform management	Continual innovation	Performance measurement	Gap analysis
CA-1 Policy and procedures	D	D	D	D	D	D	D	D	D	D	I	D	I	I	I	I	I	I	I	I	I	I	I	I	I
CA-2 Control assessments	D	D	D	D	D	D	D	D	D	I	I	D	D	D	I	I	I	I	I	I	I	I	I	I	I
CA-5 Plan of action and milestones	D	D	D	D	D	D	D	D	D	D	I	D	D	D	D	D	D	D	I	I	I	I	I	I	I
CA-9 Internal system connections	D	D	D	D	D	D	D	D	D	I	I	D	D	D	D	D	D	D	I	I	I	I	I	I	I

Key to Z-X Model capabilities

Govern   Assure   Plan   Design   Change   Execute   Innovate

- **Audit and accountability** (Table 6.12) The same comment above about assessment, authorization, and monitoring applies here
  - · AU-1 Policy and procedures
  - · AU-2 Event logging
  - · AU-3 Content of audit records
  - · AU-4 Audit storage capacity
  - · AU-6 Audit record review, analysis, and reporting
  - · AU-8 Timestamps
  - · AU-12 Audit record generation

Table 6.12 Audit and accountability

Cybersecurity control families mapped to Z-X Model practice areas: Audit and accountability	Identify critical business systems	Establish digital business risk posture	Oversee DVMS performance	Establish assurance criteria	Assure strategic policy performance	Assure operational capability	Assure performance measurement accuracy	Governance	Assurance	Knowledge management	Portfolio, program, and project management	Strategy-risk management	Configuration management	System architecture	Change coordination	Solution adaptation	Release management	Deployment management	Provisioning	Incident management	Problem management	Infrastructure/platform management	Continual innovation	Performance measurement	Gap analysis
AU-1 Policy and procedures	D	D	D	D	D	D	D	D	D	D	I	I	I	I	I	I	I	I	I	I	I	I	I	I	I
AU-2 Event logging	D	D	D	D	D	D	D	D	D	D	I	I	I	-	-	I	-	-	-	I	I	-	-	-	-
AU-3 Content of audit records	D	D	D	D	D	D	D	D	D	D	I	I	-	I	I	I	I	I	-	I	I	I	I	I	I
AU-4 Audit storage capacity	D	D	D	D	D	D	D	D	D	D	I	I	-	I	I	I	I	I	I	I	I	I	-	-	-
AU-6 Audit record review, analysis, and reporting	D	D	D	D	D	D	D	D	D	D	I	I	-	D	D	I	I	I	-	I	I	I	-	-	-
AU-8 Time stamps	D	D	D	D	D	D	D	D	D	D	I	I	-	D	I	-	-	-	-	I	I	I	-	-	-
AU-12 Audit record generation	D	D	D	D	D	D	D	D	D	D	I	I	I	D	I	I	I	I	I	I	I	I	-	-	-

Key to Z-X Model capabilities

Govern   Assure   Plan   Design   Change   Execute   Innovate

- **System and information integrity** (Table 6.13) The controls in this family should be part of system/enterprise architecture; they are essential to create and protect value

  - SI-1 Policy and procedures
  - SI-3 Malicious code protection
  - SI-4 System monitoring
  - SI-5 Security alerts, advisories, and directives
  - SI-6 Security and privacy function verification
  - SI-7 Software, firmware, and information protection
  - RA-2 (from risk assessment) Security categorization
  - RA-3 (from risk assessment) Risk assessment
  - RA-5 (from risk assessment) Vulnerability monitoring and scanning
  - RA-7 (from risk assessment) Risk response
  - RA-10 (from risk assessment) Threat hunting

Table 6.13 System and information integrity

Cybersecurity control families mapped to Z-X Model practice areas: System and information integrity	Identify critical business systems	Establish digital business risk posture	Oversee DVMS performance	Establish assurance criteria	Assure strategic policy performance	Assure operational capability	Assure performance measurement accuracy	Governance	Assurance	Knowledge management	Portfolio, program, and project management	Strategy-risk management	Configuration management	System architecture	Change coordination	Solution adaptation	Release management	Deployment management	Provisioning	Incident management	Problem management	Infrastructure/platform management	Continual innovation	Performance measurement	Gap analysis
SI-1 Policy and procedures	D	D	D	D	D	D	D	D	D	D	I	D	I	D	I	I	I	I	D	D	D	D	I	I	I
SI-3 Malicious code protection	D	D	D	D	D	D	D	D	D	D	I	D	-	I	I	I	I	I	-	I	-	-	-	-	-
SI-4 System monitoring	D	D	D	D	D	D	D	D	D	D	I	D	D	D	D	D	D	D	I	I	I	I	I	I	I
SI-5 Security alerts, advisories, and directives	D	D	D	D	D	D	D	D	D	D	I	D	D	D	D	D	D	D	I	I	I	I	I	I	I
SI-6 Security and privacy function verification	D	D	D	D	D	D	D	D	D	D	I	D	D	D	D	D	D	D	D	D	D	D	D	D	D
SI-7 Software, firmware, and information protection	D	D	D	D	D	D	D	D	D	D	I	D	D	D	D	D	I	I	I	I	I	I	I	I	I
RA-2 (from risk assessment) Security categorization	D	D	D	D	D	D	D	D	D	D	I	D	D	D	D	D	I	I	I	I	I	I	I	I	I
RA-3 (from risk assessment) Risk assessment	D	D	D	D	D	D	D	D	D	D	I	D	D	D	D	D	I	I	I	D	D	D	D	-	-	-
RA-5 (from risk assessment) Vulnerability monitoring and scanning	D	D	D	D	D	D	D	D	D	D	I	D	D	D	D	D	I	I	I	D	D	D	D	-	-	-
RA-7 (from risk assessment) Risk response	D	D	D	D	D	D	D	D	D	D	I	D	D	D	D	D	I	I	I	D	D	D	D	-	-	-
RA-10 (from risk assessment) Threat hunting	D	D	D	D	D	D	D	D	D	D	I	D	D	D	D	D	I	I	I	D	D	D	D	-	-	-

Key to Z-X Model capabilities

Govern   Assure   Plan   Design   Change   Execute   Innovate

Some controls (e.g., RA-3 Risk assessment) appear in more than one phase (and potentially in more than one control family). Recall we said in section 5.5.2: "We define a set of generic cybersecurity controls based on NIST SP 800-53." That's "based on," not precisely duplicating, the NIST publication. The reason is to facilitate mapping to DVMS FastTrack phases. It also requires the additional application of rigor to previous implementation efforts (with corresponding audit and assurance).

6.3.4 Phase 2: Expand

There are more controls in Phase 2 than in either of the first two phases.

You'll notice that some control requirements have the prefix "adds," which indicates adding more control requirements from a given control family. This approach is consistent with the phased approach, and supports improving the organizational maturity level in the Digital Value Capability Maturity Model (DVCMM) as described in sections 4.1.2 and 5.4.1.2 (under "Phase 3: Innovate").

- Access control
  - Adds access enforcement, least privilege, and unsuccessful login attempts
  - Adds controlled access based on the need to know
  - Adds monitor and control of accounts
- Audit and accountability
  - Adds response to audit logging failures; audit record review, analysis, and reporting
- Assessment, authorization, and monitoring
  - Adds continuous monitoring, penetration testing
- Configuration management
  - Adds control network ports, protocols, and services
  - Adds configuration change control, least functionality, system component inventory, configuration management plan, software restrictions, information location
  - Secure network (device) configurations
- Contingency planning
  - Adds contingency plan testing, contingency plan update, alternate storage site, and system backup
- Identification and authentication (uniquely identify and authenticate users)
  - Adds additional support for email
  - Adds additional support for browser
- Incident response
  - Adds incident response testing, incident handling, incident monitoring, and incident reporting
- Media and data protection
  - Media access
  - Media storage
  - Media use
  - Data protection
  - Data recovery
- System and information integrity
  - Adds boundary defense, wireless access
  - System and communication protection
    - Separation of system and user functionality, security, function, isolation
- Supply chain risk management (part of overall risk management)
  - System and services acquisition: allocation of resources, system development lifecycle, acquisition process, and system documentation.

The suggested controls in Phase 2 are listed below. In some cases, a control from Phase 1 appears here too, consistent with additional control requirements and rigor. Some organizations may elect to break this implementation phase into its own set of "sub-phases." That is not only perfectly acceptable – it's an essential part of adopt and adapt. The object is to proceed with pace, not at a pace reminiscent of a death march project (Wikipedia, 2022g).

- **Access control** (Table 6.14)
  - AC-1 Policy and procedures
  - AC-2 Account management
  - AC-3 Access enforcement
  - AC-6 Least privilege
  - AC-12 Session termination
  - AU-6 (from audit and accountability) Audit record review, analysis, and reporting
  - AU-10 (from audit and accountability) Non-repudiation
  - AU-13 Monitoring for information disclosure
  - IA-2 (from identification and authentication) Identification and authentication (organizational users)
  - IA-5 Authentication management
  - IA-8 Identification and authentication (non-organizational users)
  - PS-4 (from personnel security) Personnel termination

Table 6.14 Access control

Cybersecurity control families mapped to Z-X Model practice areas: Access control	Identify critical business systems	Establish digital business risk posture	Oversee DVMS performance	Establish assurance criteria	Assure strategic policy performance	Assure operational capability	Assure performance measurement accuracy	Governance	Assurance	Knowledge management	Portfolio, program, and project management	Strategy-risk management	Configuration management	System architecture	Change coordination	Solution adaptation	Release management	Deployment management	Provisioning	Incident management	Problem management	Infrastructure/platform management	Continual innovation	Performance measurement	Gap analysis
AC-1 Policy and procedures	D	D	D	D	D	D	D	D	D	D	I	D	D	I	D	I	I	I	D	I	I	I	I	I	I
AC-2 Account management	D	D	D	D	D	D	D	D	D	D	I	D	D	I	D	I	I	I	D	I	I	I	I	I	I
AC-3 Access enforcement	D	D	D	D	D	D	D	D	D	D	I	D	D	I	D	D	D	D	-	I	I	I	-	-	-
AC-6 Least privilege	D	D	D	D	D	D	D	D	D	I	I	D	D	D	D	D	D	D	D	I	I	I	I	I	I
AC-12 Session termination	D	D	D	D	D	D	D	D	D	I	I	D	D	D	D	D	D	D	D	I	I	I	I	I	I
AU-6 (from audit and accountability) Audit record review, analysis, and reporting	D	D	D	D	D	D	D	D	D	I	I	D	D	D	I	I	I	I	D	-	-	-	I	I	I
AU-10 (from audit and accountability) Non-repudiation	D	D	D	D	D	D	D	D	D	I	I	D	D	D	D	D	D	D	D	I	I	I	I	I	I
AU-13 Monitoring for information disclosure	D	D	D	D	D	D	D	D	D	D	I	D	D	D	D	D	D	D	D	D	D	D	D	I	I
IA-2 (from identification and authentication) Identification and authentication (organizational users)	D	D	D	D	D	D	D	D	D	D	I	D	D	D	D	D	D	D	D	D	D	D	D	I	I
IA-5 Authentication management	D	D	D	D	D	D	D	D	D	D	I	D	D	D	D	D	D	D	D	I	I	I	I	I	I
IA-8 Identification and authentication (non-organizational users)	D	D	D	D	D	D	D	D	D	D	I	D	D	D	D	D	D	D	D	D	D	D	D	I	I
PS-4 (from personnel security) Personnel termination	D	D	D	D	D	D	D	D	D	I	I	D	D	D	D	I	I	I	D	I	I	I	I	I	I

Key to Z-X Model capabilities

Govern Assure Plan Design Change Execute Innovate

- **Audit and accountability** (Table 6.15)
  - AU-1 Policy and procedures
  - AC-3 (from access control) Access enforcement
  - AC-6 (from access control) Least privilege
  - AU-2 Event logging
  - AU-3 Content of audit records
  - AU-4 Audit storage capacity
  - AU-5 Response to audit logging process failures
  - AU-6 Audit record review, analysis, and reporting
  - AU-7 Audit record reduction and report generation
  - AU-8 Time stamps
  - AU-9 Protection of audit information
  - AU-10 Non-repudiation
  - AU-11 Audit record retention
  - AU-12 Audit record generation
  - AU-13 Monitoring for information disclosure
  - MP-4 (from media protection) Media storage

Table 6.15 Audit and accountability

Cybersecurity control families mapped to Z-X Model practice areas: Audit and accountability	Identify critical business systems	Establish digital business risk posture	Oversee DVMS performance	Establish assurance criteria	Assure strategic policy performance	Assure operational capability	Assure performance measurement accuracy	Governance	Assurance	Knowledge management	Portfolio, program, and project management	Strategy-risk management	Configuration management	System architecture	Change coordination	Solution adaptation	Release management	Deployment management	Provisioning	Incident management	Problem management	Infrastructure/platform management	Continual innovation	Performance measurement	Gap analysis
AC-3 (from access control) Access enforcement	D	D	D	D	D	D	D	D	D	D	I	D	D	D	D	D	D	D	D	I	I	I	I	I	I
AC-6 (from access control) Least privilege	D	D	D	D	D	D	D	D	D	D	I	I	D	D	D	I	I	I	I	D	I	I	I	I	I
AU-2 Event logging	D	D	D	D	D	D	D	D	D	D	I	D	D	D	I	I	I	I	D	I	I	I	I	I	I
AU-3 Content of audit records	D	D	D	D	D	D	D	D	D	D	I	D	D	D	D	D	D	D	D	I	I	I	I	I	I
AU-4 Audit storage capacity	D	D	D	D	D	D	D	D	D	I	I	D	D	D	D	D	D	D	D	I	I	I	I	I	I
AU-5 Response to audit logging process failures	D	D	D	D	D	D	D	D	D	I	I	D	D	D	D	D	D	D	D	I	I	I	I	I	D
AU-6 Audit record review, analysis, and reporting	D	D	D	D	D	D	D	D	D	I	I	D	D	I	I	I	I	I	I	-	-	-	I	I	I
AU-7 Audit record reduction and report generation	D	D	D	D	D	D	D	D	D	D	I	D	D	I	I	I	I	I	I	I	I	I	I	I	I
AU-8 Time stamps	D	D	D	D	D	D	D	D	D	I	I	D	D	I	I	I	I	I	D	I	I	I	I	I	I
AU-9 Protection of audit information	D	D	D	D	D	D	D	D	D	D	I	D	D	I	I	I	I	I	D	I	I	I	I	I	I
AU-10 Non-repudiation	D	D	D	D	D	D	D	D	D	I	I	D	D	I	I	I	I	I	D	I	I	I	I	I	I
AU-11 Audit record retention	D	D	D	D	D	D	D	D	D	I	I	D	D	I	I	I	I	I	D	I	I	I	I	I	I
AU-12 Audit record generation	D	D	D	D	D	D	D	D	D	I	I	D	D	D	I	I	I	I	D	I	I	I	I	I	I
AU-13 Monitoring for information disclosure	D	D	D	D	D	D	D	D	D	I	I	D	D	I	I	I	I	I	D	I	I	I	I	I	D
MP-4 (from media protection) Media storage	D	D	D	D	D	D	D	D	D	I	I	D	D	I	I	I	I	I	D	I	I	I	I	I	I

Key to Z-X Model capabilities

Govern Assure Plan Design Change Execute Innovate

- **Assessment, authorization, and monitoring** (Table 6.16)
  - CA-1 Policy and procedures
  - CA-3 Information exchange
  - CA-7 Continuous monitoring
  - CA-8 Penetration testing
  - CA-9 Internal system connections

Table 6.16 Assessment, authorization, and monitoring

Cybersecurity control families mapped to Z-X Model practice areas: Assessment, authorization, and monitoring	Identify critical business systems	Establish digital business risk posture	Oversee DVMS performance	Establish assurance criteria	Assure strategic policy performance	Assure operational capability	Assure performance measurement accuracy	Governance	Assurance	Knowledge management	Portfolio, program, and project management	Strategy-risk management	Configuration management	System architecture	Change coordination	Solution adaptation	Release management	Deployment management	Provisioning	Incident management	Problem management	Infrastructure/platform management	Continual innovation	Performance measurement	Gap analysis
CA-3 Information exchange	D	D	D	D	D	D	D	D	D	D	I	D	I	I	I	I	I	I	I	I	I	I	I	I	I
CA-7 Continuous monitoring	D	D	D	D	D	D	D	D	D	I	I	D	-	I	D	D	I	I	I	-	-	I	I	I	D
CA-8 Penetration testing	D	D	D	D	D	D	D	D	D	I	I	D	D	D	D	D	D	D	-	-	-	I	I	I	I
CA-9 Internal system connections	D	D	D	D	D	D	D	D	D	I	I	D	D	I	I	D	I	I	D	-	-	I	I	I	I

Key to Z-X Model capabilities

Govern   Assure   Plan   Design   Change   Execute   Innovate

- **Configuration management** (Table 6.17)
  - CM-1 Policy and procedures
  - CM-2 Baseline configuration
  - CM-3 Configuration change control
  - CM-4 Impact analysis
  - CM-5 Access restrictions for change
  - CM-6 Configuration settings
  - CM-8 System component inventory
  - MA-2 (from maintenance) Controlled maintenance
  - MA-5 Maintenance personnel
  - RA-3 (from risk assessment) Risk assessment
  - RA-5 Vulnerability monitoring and scanning
  - SA-5 (from system and services acquisition) System documentation
  - SA-10 Developer configuration management
  - SA-11 Developer testing and evaluation
  - SR-3 (from supply chain risk management) Supply chain controls and processes
  - SR-4 (from supply chain risk management) Provenance

- SR-6 (from supply chain risk management) Supplier assessments and reviews
- SR-8 (from supply chain risk management) Notification agreements
- SR-12 (from supply chain risk management) Component disposal

Table 6.17 Configuration management

Cybersecurity control families mapped to Z-X Model practice areas: Configuration management	Identify critical business systems	Establish digital business risk posture	Oversee DVMS performance	Establish assurance criteria	Assure strategic policy performance	Assure operational capability	Assure performance measurement accuracy	Governance	Assurance	Knowledge management	Portfolio, program, and project management	Strategy-risk management	Configuration management	System architecture	Change coordination	Solution adaptation	Release management	Deployment management	Provisioning	Incident management	Problem management	Infrastructure/platform management	Continual innovation	Performance measurement	Gap analysis
CM-1 Policy and procedures	D	D	D	D	D	D	D	D	D	D	I	D	D	I	I	I	I	I	I	I	I	I	I	I	I
CM-2 Baseline configuration	D	D	D	D	D	D	D	D	D	I	I	D	D	D	I	I	I	I	I	I	I	I	I	I	I
CM-3 Configuration change control	D	D	D	D	D	D	D	D	D	D	I	D	D	D	D	D	D	D	I	I	I	I	I	I	I
CM-4 Impact analysis	D	D	D	D	D	D	D	D	D	I	I	D	D	D	D	D	D	D	I	I	I	I	I	I	I
CM-5 Access restrictions for change	D	D	D	D	D	D	D	D	D	D	I	D	D	D	D	D	D	D	-	-	-	-	I	D	D
CM-6 Configuration settings	D	D	D	D	D	D	D	D	D	D	I	-	D	I	D	D	D	D	D	D	D	D	I	I	D
CM-8 System component inventory	D	D	D	D	D	D	D	D	D	D	I	-	D	I	D	D	D	D	I	D	I	D	I	I	I
MA-2 (from maintenance) Controlled maintenance	D	D	D	D	D	D	D	D	D	I	I	I	D	I	D	D	D	D	I	-	I	D	I	I	I
MA-5 Maintenance personnel	D	D	D	D	D	D	D	D	D	I	I	-	D	I	I	I	D	D	I	I	I	D	I	I	I
RA-3 (from risk assessment) Risk assessment	D	D	D	D	D	D	D	D	D	D	I	D	D	D	D	D	D	D	-	-	-	-	I	I	I
RA-5 Vulnerability monitoring and scanning	D	D	D	D	D	D	D	D	D	D	I	-	D	I	-	D	D	D	-	-	-	D	I	I	I
SA-5 (from system and services acquisition) System documentation	D	D	D	D	D	D	D	D	D	D	I	-	D	I	I	I	D	D	D	I	I	D	D	D	D
SA-10 Developer configuration management	D	D	D	D	D	D	D	D	D	D	I	-	D	D	I	D	D	D	I	I	I	D	I	I	I
SA-11 Developer testing and evaluation	D	D	D	D	D	D	D	D	D	D	I	D	D	D	I	D	D	D	I	I	I	D	I	I	I
SR-3 (from supply chain risk management) Supply chain controls and processes	D	D	D	D	D	D	D	D	D	D	I	I	D	I	D	D	D	D	I	-	-	D	I	I	I
SR-4 (from supply chain risk management) Provenance	D	D	D	D	D	D	D	D	D	D	I	I	D	I	D	D	D	D	-	-	-	D	I	I	I
SR-6 (from supply chain risk management) Supplier assessments and reviews	D	D	D	D	D	D	D	D	D	D	I	-	D	-	D	D	D	D	-	I	I	D	I	I	I
SR-8 (from supply chain risk management) Notification agreements	D	D	D	D	D	D	D	D	D	D	I	-	D	I	D	D	D	D	-	I	I	D	I	I	I
SR-12 (from supply chain risk management) Component disposal	D	D	D	D	D	D	D	D	D	I	I	D	D	D	D	D	D	D	I	I	I	D	I	I	I

Key to Z-X Model capabilities

Govern   Assure   Plan   Design   Change   Execute   Innovate

- **Contingency planning** (Table 6.18)
  - · CP-1 Policy and procedures
  - · CP-2 Contingency plan (in Phase 2 to maintain the contingency plan in light of new circumstances and controls requirements)
  - · CP-3 Contingency training
  - · CP-4 Contingency plan testing
  - · CP-6 Alternate storage site
  - · CP-9 System backup

Table 6.18 Contingency planning

Cybersecurity control families mapped to Z-X Model practice areas: Contingency planning	Identify critical business systems	Establish digital business risk posture	Oversee DVMS performance	Establish assurance criteria	Assure strategic policy performance	Assure operational capability	Assure performance measurement accuracy	Governance	Assurance	Knowledge management	Portfolio, program, and project management	Strategy-risk management	Configuration management	System architecture	Change coordination	Solution adaptation	Release management	Deployment management	Provisioning	Incident management	Problem management	Infrastructure/platform management	Continual innovation	Performance measurement	Gap analysis
CP-1 Policy and procedures	D	D	D	D	D	D	D	D	D	D	I	D	D	D	D	D	D	D	D	D	D	D	D	D	D
CP-2 Contingency plan	D	D	D	D	D	D	D	D	D	D	I	D	D	D	D	D	D	D	D	D	D	D	D	D	D
CP-3 Contingency training	D	D	D	D	D	D	D	D	D	D	I	D	D	D	D	D	D	D	D	D	D	D	I	I	I
CP-4 Contingency plan testing	D	D	D	D	D	D	D	D	D	D	I	D	D	D	D	D	D	D	D	D	D	D	I	I	D
CP-6 Alternate storage site	D	D	D	D	D	D	D	D	D	D	I	I	D	D	D	D	D	D	D	I	I	D	-	I	-
CP-9 System backup	D	D	D	D	D	D	D	D	D	D	I	I	D	D	D	D	D	D	-	I	I	I	-	I	I

Key to Z-X Model capabilities

◼ Govern   ◻ Assure   ◼ Plan   ◼ Design   ◻ Change   ◼ Execute   ◻ Innovate

- **Identification and authentication** (uniquely identify and authenticate users) (Table 6.19)
  - · IA-1 Policy and procedures
  - · IA-2 Identification and authentication (organizational users)
  - · IA-3 Device identification and authentication
  - · IA-5 Authenticator management
  - · IA-6 Authentication feedback
  - · IA-8 Identification and authentication (non-organizational users)
  - · IA-9 Service identification and authentication
  - · AC-2 Account management
  - · AC-4 Information flow enforcement
  - · AC-12 Session termination
  - · AT-2 (from awareness and training) Awareness training
  - · AU-10 (from audit and accountability) Non-repudiation

- AU-13 Monitoring for information disclosure
- AU-14 Session audit
- CA-3 (from assessment, authorization, and monitoring) Information exchange
- CA-8 Penetration testing

Table 6.19 Identification and authentication

Cybersecurity control families mapped to Z-X Model practice areas: Identification and authentication	Identify critical business systems	Establish digital business risk posture	Oversee DVMS performance	Establish assurance criteria	Assure strategic policy performance	Assure operational capability	Assure performance measurement accuracy	Governance	Assurance	Knowledge management	Portfolio, program, and project management	Strategy-risk management	Configuration management	System architecture	Change coordination	Solution adaptation	Release management	Deployment management	Provisioning	Incident management	Problem management	Infrastructure/platform management	Continual innovation	Performance measurement	Gap analysis
IA-1 Policy and procedures	D	D	D	D	D	D	D	D	D	D	I	D	D	D	D	D	D	D	D	D	D	D	I	D	I
IA-2 Identification and authentication (organizational users)	D	D	D	D	D	D	D	D	D	D	I	D	D	D	D	D	D	D	D	I	I	I	I	I	I
IA-3 Device identification and authentication	D	D	D	D	D	D	D	D	D	D	I	D	D	D	D	D	D	D	I	I	I	I	I	I	I
IA-5 Authenticator management	D	D	D	D	D	D	D	D	D	D	I	I	D	D	D	D	D	D	D	I	I	D	I	D	D
IA-6 Authentication feedback	D	D	D	D	D	D	D	D	D	D	I	I	I	D	D	D	D	D	I			I	I	D	D
IA-8 Identification and authentication (non-organizational users)	D	D	D	D	D	D	D	D	D	D	I	D	D	D	D	D	D	D	D	I	I	I	I	D	D
IA-9 Service identification and authentication	D	D	D	D	D	D	D	D	D	D	I	I	D	D	D	D	D	D	-	I	I	I	I	D	D
AC-2 Account management	D	D	D	D	D	D	D	D	D	D	I	I	D	D	D	D	D	D	D	I	I	I	I	D	D
AC-4 Information flow enforcement	D	D	D	D	D	D	D	D	D	D	I	I	I	D	D	D	D	D	-	-	-	I	I	D	D
AC-12 Session termination	D	D	D	D	D	D	D	D	D	D	I	-	I	D	I	D	D	D	-	-	-	I	I	D	D
AT-2 (from awareness and training) Awareness training	D	D	D	D	D	D	D	D	D	D	I	I	I	D	I	I	I	I	I	I	I	I	I	D	D
AU-10 (from audit and accountability) Non-repudiation	D	D	D	D	D	D	D	D	D	D	I	D	I	D	I	I	I	I	I	I	I	I	I	D	D
AU-13 Monitoring for information disclosure	D	D	D	D	D	D	D	D	D	D	I	I	I	D	I	D	D	D	D	I	I	D	I	D	D
AU-14 Session audit	D	D	D	D	D	D	D	D	D	D	I	-	-	D	-	-	-	-	-	-	-	D	I	D	D
CA-3 (from assessment, authorization, and monitoring) Information exchange	D	D	D	D	D	D	D	D	D	D	I	-	I	D	I	I	I	I	-	-	-	-	I	D	D
CA-8 Penetration testing	D	D	D	D	D	D	D	D	D	D	I	I	D	D	I	I	I		-	-	-	-	I	D	D

Key to Z-X Model capabilities

 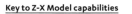

Govern   Assure   Plan   Design   Change   Execute   Innovate

- **Incident response** (Table 6.20)

  - IR-1 Policy and procedures
  - IR-2 Incident response training
  - IR-3 Incident response testing
  - IR-4 Incident handling
  - IR-5 Incident monitoring
  - IR-6 Incident reporting
  - CP-2 (from contingency planning) Contingency plan
  - CP-3 Contingency training
  - CP-4 Contingency plan testing
  - PM-12 (from program management) Insider threat program
  - PM-15 Testing, training, and monitoring

Table 6.20 Incident response

Cybersecurity control families mapped to Z-X Model practice areas: Incident response	Identify critical business systems	Establish digital business risk posture	Oversee DVMS performance	Establish assurance criteria	Assure strategic policy performance	Assure operational capability	Assure performance measurement accuracy	Governance	Assurance	Knowledge management	Portfolio, program, and project management	Strategy-risk management	Configuration management	System architecture	Change coordination	Solution adaptation	Release management	Deployment management	Provisioning	Incident management	Problem management	Infrastructure/platform management	Continual innovation	Performance measurement	Gap analysis
IR-1 Policy and procedures	D	D	D	D	D	D	D	D	D	D	D	D	D	D	D	D	D	D	D	D	D	D	D	D	D
IR-2 Incident response training	D	D	D	D	D	D	D	D	D	D	-	I	I	D	D	D	D	D	I	D	D	D	-	D	D
IR-3 Incident response testing	D	D	D	D	D	D	D	D	D	D	I	I	I	D	D	D	D	D	I	D	D	I	I	I	I
IR-4 Incident handling	D	D	D	D	D	D	D	D	D	D	I	I	I	D	D	D	D	D	I	D	D	I	I	I	I
IR-5 Incident monitoring	D	D	D	D	D	D	D	D	D	D	I	D	I	D	D	D	D	D	I	D	D	I	I	I	I
IR-6 Incident reporting	D	D	D	D	D	D	D	D	D	D	I	I	I	D	D	D	D	D	I	D	D	D	I	I	I
CP-2 (from contingency planning) Contingency plan	D	D	D	D	D	D	D	D	D	D	I	D	I	D	D	D	D	D	I	I	I	I	I	I	I
CP-3 Contingency training	D	D	D	D	D	D	D	D	D	D	I	I	I	D	D	D	D	D	-	-	-	I	I	I	I
CP-4 Contingency plan testing	D	D	D	D	D	D	D	D	D	D	I	I	I	I	D	D	D	D	I	-	-	I	I	I	I
PM-12 (from program management) Insider threat program	D	D	D	D	D	D	D	D	D	D	I	D	I	D	D	D	D	D	I	I	I	I	I	I	I
PM-15 Testing, training, and monitoring	D	D	D	D	D	D	D	D	D	D	I	I	I	D	D	D	D	D	-	-	-	I	I	I	I

Key to Z-X Model capabilities

Govern   Assure   Plan   Design   Change   Execute   Innovate

- **Media and data protection** (Table 6.21)

  - MP-1 Policy and procedures
  - MP-2 Media access
  - MP-3 Media marking
  - MP-4 Media storage
  - MP-5 Media transport
  - MP-7 Media use
  - CP-10 (from contingency planning) System recovery and reconstitution
  - RA-2 (from risk assessment) Security categorization

Table 6.21 Media and data protection

Cybersecurity control families mapped to Z-X Model practice areas: Media and data protection	Identify critical business systems	Establish digital business risk posture	Oversee DVMS performance	Establish assurance criteria	Assure strategic policy performance	Assure operational capability	Assure performance measurement accuracy	Governance	Assurance	Knowledge management	Portfolio, program, and project management	Strategy-risk management	Configuration management	System architecture	Change coordination	Solution adaptation	Release management	Deployment management	Provisioning	Incident management	Problem management	Infrastructure/platform management	Continual innovation	Performance measurement	Gap analysis
MP-1 Policy and procedures	D	D	D	D	D	D	D	D	D	D	D	D	D	D	D	D	D	D	D	D	D	D	D	D	D
MP-2 Media access	D	D	D	D	D	D	D	D	D	D	I	D	D	D	I	D	D	D	D	I	I	D	I	D	D
MP-3 Media marking	D	D	D	D	D	D	D	D	D	D	I	-	D	D	-	I	I	I	I	-	-	-	I	I	I
MP-4 Media storage	D	D	D	D	D	D	D	D	D	D	I	-	D	D	-	D	I	I	-	-	-	D	I	I	I
MP-5 Media transport	D	D	D	D	D	D	D	D	D	D	I	D	D	D	I	I	I	I	-	-	-	D	I	I	I
MP-7 Media use	D	D	D	D	D	D	D	D	D	D	I	I	D	D	I	D	I	I	D	-	-	D	I	I	I
CP-10 (from contingency planning) System recovery and reconstitution	D	D	D	D	D	D	D	D	D	D	I	D	D	D	D	D	I	I	-	I	-	-	D	I	I
RA-2 (from risk assessment) Security categorization	D	D	D	D	D	D	D	D	D	D	I	D	D	D	D	I	I	I	-	-	-	I	I	I	I

Key to Z-X Model capabilities

Govern   Assure   Plan   Design   Change   Execute   Innovate

- **System and information integrity** (Table 6.22)
  - SI-1 Policy and procedures
  - SI-2 Flaw remediation
  - SI-3 Malicious code protection
  - SI-4 System monitoring
  - SI-5 Security alerts, advisories, and directives (typically from recognized and approved external sources)
  - SI-6 Security and privacy function verification
  - SI-11 Error handling
  - SI-12 Information management and retention
  - AC-17 (from access control) Remote access
  - AC-20 (from access control) Use of external information systems
  - CA-3 (from assessment, authorization, and monitoring) Information system connections
  - IA-2 (from identification and authentication) Identification and authentication (organizational users)
  - IA-5 (from identification and authentication) Authenticator management
  - IA-8 (from identification and authentication) Identification and authentication (non-organizational users)
  - RA-5 (from risk assessment) Vulnerability scanning
  - SC-7 (from system and communication protection) Boundary protection
  - SC-18 Mobile code
  - SC-8 Transmission confidentiality and integrity
  - SR-9 (from supply chain risk management) Tamper resistance and detection
  - SR-10 (from supply chain risk management) Inspection of systems and components

Table 6.22 System and information integrity

Cybersecurity control families mapped to Z-X Model practice areas: System and information integrity	Identify critical business systems	Establish digital business risk posture	Oversee DVMS performance	Establish assurance criteria	Assure strategic policy performance	Assure operational capability	Assure performance measurement accuracy	Governance	Assurance	Knowledge management	Portfolio, program, and project management	Strategy-risk management	Configuration management	System architecture	Change coordination	Solution adaptation	Release management	Deployment management	Provisioning	Incident management	Problem management	Infrastructure/platform management	Continual innovation	Performance measurement	Gap analysis
SI-1 Policy and procedures	D	D	D	D	D	D	D	D	D	D	D	D	D	D	D	D	D	D	D	D	D	D	D	D	D
SI-2 Flaw remediation	D	D	D	D	D	D	D	D	D	D	I	I	D	D	D	D	D	D	-	I	D	D	I	I	I
SI-3 Malicious code protection	D	D	D	D	D	D	D	D	D	D	I	I	I	I	I	D	D	D	-	-	-	I	I	I	I
SI-4 System monitoring	D	D	D	D	D	D	D	D	D	D	I	I	I	D	i	D	D	D	-	I	I	D	I	I	I
SI-5 Security alerts, advisories, and directives	D	D	D	D	D	D	D	D	D	D	I	I	I	D	I	I	I	I	I	I	I	I	I	I	I
SI-6 Security and privacy function verification	D	D	D	D	D	D	D	D	D	D	I	I	I	D	D	D	D	D	I	-	-	I	I	I	I
SI-11 Error handling	D	D	D	D	D	D	D	D	D	D	I	I	-	D	I	D	D	D	I	-	-	I	I	I	I
SI-12 Information management and retention	D	D	D	D	D	D	D	D	D	D	I	I	D	D	I	D	D	D	I	I	I	D	I	I	I
AC-17 (from access control) Remote access	D	D	D	D	D	D	D	D	D	D	I	I	I	D	I	D	D	D	D	I	I	D	I	I	I
AC-20 (from access control) Use of external information systems	D	D	D	D	D	D	D	D	D	D	I	I	I	D	I	D	D	D	D	I	I	I	I	I	I
CA-3 (from assessment, authorization, and monitoring) Information system connections	D	D	D	D	D	D	D	D	D	D	I	I	D	D	I	D	D	D	-	-	-	D	I	I	I
IA-2 (from identification and authentication) Identification and authentication (organizational users)	D	D	D	D	D	D	D	D	D	D	I	I	D	D	I	D	D	D	D	I	I	I	I	I	I
IA-5 (from identification and authentication) Authenticator management	D	D	D	D	D	D	D	D	D	D	I	I	I	D	I	D	D	D	I	I	I	I	I	I	I
IA-8 (from identification and authentication) Identification and authentication (non-organizational users)	D	D	D	D	D	D	D	D	D	D	I	I	D	D	I	D	D	D	D	I	I	I	I	I	I
RA-5 (from risk assessment) Vulnerability scanning	D	D	D	D	D	D	D	D	D	D	I	I	D	D	-	D	D	D	-	-	-	D	I	I	I
SC-7 (from system and communication protection) Boundary protection	D	D	D	D	D	D	D	D	D	D	I	I	I	D	-	D	D	D	-	-	-	D	I	I	I
SC-18 Mobile code	D	D	D	D	D	D	D	D	D	D	I	I	I	D	-	D	D	D	D	-	-	I	I	I	I
SC-8 Transmission confidentiality and integrity	D	D	D	D	D	D	D	D	D	D	I	I	-	D	I	D	D	D	-	-	-	D	I	I	I
SR-9 (from supply chain risk management) Tamper resistance and detection	D	D	D	D	D	D	D	D	D	D	I	I	I	D	I	D	D	D	-	-	-	D	I	I	I
SR-10 (from supply chain risk management) Inspection of systems and components	D	D	D	D	D	D	D	D	D	D	I	I	I	D	I	D	D	D	-	-	-	D	I	I	I

Key to Z-X Model capabilities

Govern   Assure   Plan   Design   Change   Execute   Innovate

Don't let the number of controls overwhelm you; treat this as an adaptable to-do list – adapted to fit the strategy-risk-based business need. As noted previously in this section, do it with appropriate urgency to achieve a quality result rather than treating it as a checklist. Recall that every control requirement implementation requires a team member who can attest that it provides appropriate instrumentation to support audit and assessment – as a concurrent activity.

6.3.5   Phase 3: Sustain the momentum and innovate – an approach to Recover

In Phase 3, the organization updates and adds additional cybersecurity controls necessary to fit the evolving need. For example, it's vital to extend incident management support to new models for newly discovered cybersecurity incidents from MITRE ATT&CK. Similarly, the organization must expand its disaster recovery plan to include significant cybersecurity events. Stuff happens; that is why organizations have a disaster recovery plan. The organization should extend its major incident models to include cybersecurity events with the same elevated significance. However, that isn't enough: the enterprise must also expand its disaster recovery plan to include *digital* events that might have the same impact as a physical disaster. The same two aspects of a disaster recovery plan apply to a cybersecurity event: specifically mitigating the event's impact and then using it to learn and improve.

After integrating the cybersecurity recovery plan into the disaster recovery plan, treat it like a regular continuity plan: test it, update and improve it (in response to testing, changes to the threat landscape, reorganization, merger, acquisition, etc.), and test it again.

The NIST-CSF defines five functions: Identify, Protect, Detect, Respond, and Recover (NIST, 2018). NIST SP 800-53 does not provide explicit guidance for all aspects of recovery (e.g., public relations and reputation repair). If you think about it, this is not an omission: the specific audience for the publication is government entities and members of the defense-industrial base that handle classified information. The US government is not explicitly worried about the business aspects of public relations, reputation, etc.

Other NIST publications address recovery. We mentioned one: the NIST-CSF. The "Guide for cybersecurity event recovery" (NIST SP 800-184) addresses the function directly. Use 800-184 to plan for recovery; do not keep it on the shelf until you need to recover from a cyber event. Consider the following from that publication:

"This document is not an operational playbook; it provides guidance to help organizations plan and prepare [for] recovery from a cyber event and integrate the processes and procedures into their enterprise risk management plans. This document is not intended to be used by organizations responding to an active cyber event, but as a guide to develop recovery plans in the form of customized playbooks."
NIST (2016)

It is essential to assume that planning for a cyber event is an inherent part of the first stages of applying strategy-risk, making preparation for recovery an organizational imperative. There are two parts to cyber event recovery. The first is strategic and uses the information in NIST SP 800-184 to develop an organizational recovery operational guide or playbook. At the same time, it's essential to also focus on the ongoing innovation and improvement of every NIST-CSF function, to reduce the likelihood and mitigate the impact of future cyber incidents; specifically, the following controls from NIST SP 800-53 and references in the NIST-CSF (Table 6.23):

Table 6.23 Recover (from NIST SP 800-53 and NIST-CSF)

Cybersecurity control families mapped to Z-X Model practice areas: Recover	Identify critical business systems	Establish digital business risk posture	Oversee DVMS performance practice area	Establish assurance criteria practice area	Assure strategic policy performance practice area	Assure operational capability practice area	Assure performance measurement practice area	Governance	Assurance	Knowledge Management	Portfolio, program and project management	Strategy-Risk Management	Configuration management	System architecture	Coordination/orchestrate	Solution adaptation	Release management	Deployment	Provisioning	Incident management	Problem management	Infrastructure/platform management	Continual innovation	Performance measurement	Gap analysis
From NIST SP 800-53																									
CP-2 Contingency plan	D	D	D	D	D	D	D	D	D	D	I	D	D	D	D	D	D	D	D	D	D	D	I	D	D
CP-10 System recovery and reconstitution	D	D	D	D	D	D	D	D	D	D	I	D	D	D	D	D	D	D	D	D	D	D	I	D	D
IR-4 Incident handling	D	D	D	D	D	D	D	D	D	D	I	D	D	D	D	D	D	D	D	D	D	D	I	D	D
IR-8 Incident response plan	D	D	D	D	D	D	D	D	D	D	I	D	D	D	D	D	D	D	D	D	D	D	I	D	D
From NIST-CSF (Appendix A Subcategories)																									
RC.RP-1 Recovery plan executed during or after a cybersecurity incident	D	D	D	D	D	D	D	D	D	D	I	D	D	D	D	D	D	D	D	D	D	D	I	D	D
RC.IM-1 Include lessons learned	D	D	D	D	D	D	D	D	D	D	I	D	D	D	D	D	D	D	D	D	D	D	D	D	D
RC.IM-2 Update recovery strategies	D	D	D	D	D	D	D	D	D	D	I	D	D	D	D	D	D	D	D	D	D	D	D	D	D
RC.CO-1 Public relations managed	D	D	D	D	D	D	D	D	D	D	I	D	D	D	D	D	D	D	D	D	D	D	D	D	D
RC.CO-2 Reputation repair	D	D	D	D	D	D	D	D	D	D	I	D	D	D	D	D	D	D	D	D	D	D	D	D	D
RC.CO-3 Recovery actions communication transparency	D	D	D	D	D	D	D	D	D	D	I	D	D	D	D	D	D	D	D	D	D	D	D	D	D

Key to Z-X Model capabilities

Govern   Assure   Plan   Design   Change   Execute   Innovate

- From NIST SP 800-53 (NIST, 2020)
  - CP-2 Contingency plan
  - CP-10 System recovery and reconstitution
  - IR-4 Incident handling
  - IR-8 Incident response plan

- From NIST-CSF (NIST, 2018)
  - RC.RP-1 Recovery plan executed during or after a cybersecurity incident
  - RC.IM-1 Include lessons learned
  - RC.IM-2 Update recovery strategies
  - RC.CO-1 Public relations managed
  - RC.CO-2 Reputation repair
  - RC.CO-3 Recovery actions communication transparency

Everything discussed to this point represents a critical aspect of cyber resilience. Chapter 2 addressed being the menace. It discussed the role of questions, identifying business systems and associated data, and the IT systems that underpin and support the delivery of the business systems. Everything in that chapter provides potential input into creating the recovery contingency plan. Chapter 3 addressed the idea of thinking in systems terms:

seeing the *whole*. It also discussed the role of mentorship and preserving institutional knowledge. These are also critical aspects of cyber resilience.

Chapter 4 addressed cybersecurity in the context of the DVMS, providing a structured way to implement it and assure recovery goes according to plan. The same approach to implementing cybersecurity also applies to recovery from a cyber event.

6.3.6 Additional controls

As previously discussed, this book covers a subset of the controls in NIST SP 800-53. Consequently, a few control families that may be essential at some organizations have not yet been covered here. However, integrating their implementation with the DVMS FastTrack is straightforward. It is left to the organization to apply a strategy-risk-based approach to selecting and prioritizing the requirements and implementation. These control families are:

- Maintenance
- Physical and environmental protection
- Personnel security
- Personally identifiable information processing and transparency.

While we included two control requirements from the maintenance control family to expand coverage of configuration management in Phase 2, we did not cover the personally identifiable control family.

6.3.7 DVMS FastTrack and the Digital Value Management System

Section 4.2 began with the following:

"Our view of systems thinking is an approach that integrates the belief that the components of a system, when separated from the whole system, will behave differently. So, in complex systems, isolating parts of the system to 'fix' how the system behaves often results in unexpected system behavior."

Review Tables 5.1 and 6.1: these present a high-level view of the interconnections within the DVMS. Treating cybersecurity as a technical endeavor severs most of the links in these two tables – breaking the links ignores the principle of applying systems thinking. Look at the way the capabilities aggregate the practice areas. Then review Table 5.1 in the context of the material in section 6.2 to understand how the practices interact and relate across the capabilities. What this means is that the Z-X Model capabilities are not silos.

Think about the preceding in the context of the CPD Model (Figure 3.5). Each loop involves elements of the seven capabilities. Apply FastTrack in the context of the CPD Model, and recall that the first control requirement in every control family addresses policy and procedures. At some level, that touches every loop in the CPD Model, which means every cybersecurity control family has control requirements that involve multiple aspects of the model.

Don't stop there. Look at something more technical, such as the controls in Phase 1 (section 6.3.3) that are part of "assessment, authorization, and monitoring." When you get to vulnerability management, what do you protect and how? You can't do everything at once. Review the material in section 2.1. If you've prioritized the business systems, you start by adding the requirements for the most critical business systems. After you've addressed those systems, the next most critical get a promotion – they are now the most critical unprotected systems.

In other words, it's an organizational choice regarding how to approach the phases. However, we recommend "remaining" in a phase until the essential business systems have an appropriate strategy-risk-based level of protection.

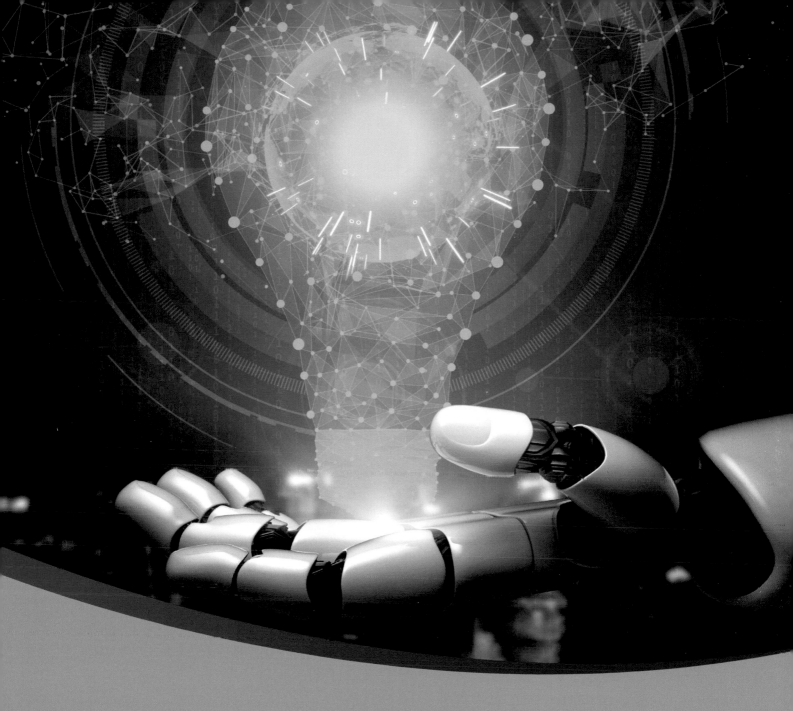

CHAPTER 7
Digital business risk management

7 Digital business risk management

This chapter discusses the mental models necessary to create (implement) and protect (including auditing for appropriate assurance of) digital value. It also provides a deeper dive into the practice areas associated with each Z-X Model capability.

7.1 Mental models and perspectives

In section 3.1, we said that a mental model is "a way of thinking about something." It provides a frame of reference (Merriam-Webster, n.d.-c): "a set of ideas, conditions, or assumptions that determine how something will be approached, perceived, or understood." Different perspectives (e.g., implementor and auditor) have diverse points of view regarding the focus of their efforts. The solution development teams create value with appropriate protection; the assessment teams verify and validate that the value created and protected conforms with the strategy-risk intent.

The solution development teams ask questions that focus on "how" (i.e., questions about a future state); the assessment teams ask questions focusing on accomplishments in the present state. The assessment teams focus on providing input to the solution development teams to assure that the value created meets the criteria for assessment, to assure it is appropriately protected. This perspective is akin to what good software developers do to ensure that their efforts are testable – either by applying test-driven development, which writes the test before the implementation code, or after the fact as part of QA.

Different mental models lead to different outcomes. Consider the all too true, and most likely familiar, contrast between the approaches at two different companies in the following example.

One of the authors developed a workshop for IBM to help developers convert their applications to OS/2. During the pilot workshop, because of the highly modular and structured approach to development, one company successfully converted almost 800,000 lines of code (out of 1.2 million)[64] and knew how to handle the rest. Another company sent a developer with a 5,000-line application. By the end of the week, the instructor and lab assistants removed all of the conditional compilation to produce a core application ready for conversion. After the workshop week, the instructor spent several hours on the phone for two weeks to continue to help the company with the conversion effort.

The difference between the two approaches was stark. One company planned and designed the code to be testable and easily convertible to another environment. The other company did not have a plan. Instead, the introduction of every "new thing" occurred through conditional compilation, making it nearly impossible to test the complete functionality. Conditional compilation replaced modularity, making every new enhancement or environment a bolt-on without testing the "whole" – the company tested each new addition to the code in isolation only.

---

64 Because of the modularity and structure of the code, only the parts that interacted directly with the operating system application programming interface (API) needed major rework. The modules that did not reference the OS/2 API required little to no rework. The 800,000 lines of code were compiled, and these modules executed a subset of the overall functionality in OS/2 on the last day of the workshop. The company completed the other 400,000 lines of code within two weeks of the workshop, and spent the next five weeks in rigorous beta testing and preparation of the marketing materials.

The first company planned to "create and protect" (outside of any explicit cybersecurity consideration). Every development team included the relevant viewpoints of stakeholders, leading to the launch of the OS/2 application within seven weeks following the workshop. The second company created unprotected value. Even though its application was about 0.4% of the size of that of the other application, it took nearly six months to launch the OS/2 version.

The first company's mental model exhibited a cohesive approach to creating and protecting value, which also suggests that *protect* is a much broader concept than cybersecurity. The approach to application development of the second company could only be called ad hoc.

Section 2.1.1 provided a template set of questions ending with this:

"How do we know? Are we sure? (Ask these last two questions in response to the answers [to other "operational" questions]. They also establish the predicate for assurance.)"

Including both perspectives in the development teams increases the likelihood of answering these two questions. Both the implementors and the auditors need a mental model supporting collaboration and cooperation toward the common goal of creating and protecting value.

7.2 Z-X Model capabilities, practice areas, and practices

The Z-X Model represents the minimum set of organizational capabilities necessary for an organization to create appropriately protected digital business value. By appropriately protected, we mean the level of protection is proportional to its value.

The Z-X Model (see Figure 4.1) has seven capabilities:[65]

- Governance
- Assurance
- Plan
- Design
- Change
- Execute
- Innovate.

Each capability provides practice areas that aggregate the practices necessary to achieve a minimum viable capability (MVC) to create, protect, and deliver digital business value.

The following describes the capabilities, practice areas, practices, and outcomes.[66] The description includes any internal DVMS relationships, a maturity capability model, and demonstrable artifacts for each outcome at each capability level.

---

65   The first two capabilities in this list are additional to the five core capabilities that follow it, as set out in section 4.1.1.1.
66   Processes execute the tasks and activities associated with each practice. Processes must be adapted to fit the organizational need and are, intentionally, out of scope for these publications.

7.2.1   Governance operating model

The Z-X Model capabilities operationalize organizational governance and assurance capabilities. The discussion of governance and assurance is limited to the context of the CPD Model's Governance/Assurance loop and reflects a subset of what the entirety of the governance operating model would include.

At a very high level, a typical governance operating model addresses the following:

- Structure

  - Organizational design and reporting structure
  - Organizational structure and charters

- Oversight responsibilities

  - Organizational oversight and responsibilities
  - Management accountability and authority
  - Committee accountability, authorities, and responsibilities

- Talent and culture

  - Performance management and incentives
  - Business and operating principles
  - Leadership development and talent programs

- Infrastructure

  - Policies and procedures
  - Transparency in reporting and communication
  - Digital business value.

The next two sections, 7.2.2 and 7.2.3, examine organizational capabilities abstracted from COSO ERM principles. It's essential to understand the scope of the organizational governance structure (the board of directors' job relative to management) and how the Z-X Model operationalizes governance and assurance capabilities.

7.2.2   Governance (GO)

The Z-X Model operationalizes the Governance capability; it is like bootstrapping governance. When we look at governance in the CPD Model Governance/Assurance loop, strategy-risk produces organizational objectives that result in cascading management policies as tools to create the organizational capabilities to create, protect, and deliver digital business value. In applying leverage within a system, the board sets the rules and goals for the system. Management establishes the business objectives to achieve the system goals. The policies provide the guidance that creates or improves the organizational capabilities to produce the desired system behaviors (recall that systems self-organize; see sections 3.2.3 and 3.4.2).

In the Z-X Model Governance capability, there are three practice areas:

- **Identify critical business systems** Determine what is valuable
- **Establish digital business risk posture** At what level to protect the value
- **Oversee DVMS performance** Instrument warranty and utility of the DVMS capabilities.

7.2.2.1 GO:1 – Identify critical business systems practice area

Senior leadership identifies critical business systems – not IT systems or applications, but business systems that create value for their stakeholders. The identified organizational capabilities that create business value and the enabling digital assets are part of that business system. Now the organization can assign and prioritize the business value enabled by its digital business assets (see PL:4-1 in section 7.2.4.4). As the organization becomes more adaptive, it must continually assess the value created for its stakeholders against the internal organizational needs, external requirements, and a dynamic threat landscape. New business systems will be created, and older ones improved or decommissioned.

7.2.2.2 GO:2 – Establish digital business risk posture practice area

The practices in this area seek to establish the optimal risk posture for the organization, which assesses organizational capabilities to protect digital business assets against internal needs, external requirements, and the threat landscape. The organization assesses its capabilities in detail but must look at its optimal risk posture. It must answer the question: "How much risk can we afford?"

While available resources constrain a risk-based approach to cybersecurity, it is not driven by costs. The organization makes informed decisions about its risk mitigation strategy. The organizational risk postures optimize the need to prioritize and protect critical business systems (see PL:4-1 in section 7.2.4.4).

7.2.2.3 GO:3 – Oversee DVMS performance practice area

This practice area is responsible for turning the organizational risk-informed business strategy (strategy-risk) into business objectives. The result is a cascading set of policies that provide management guidance for creating or improving the organizational capabilities to create, protect, and deliver digital business value for its stakeholders. This practice area includes the alignment of outcomes of the business objectives, and the subsequent expression of strategic and operational intent as measures and metrics used to identify performance gaps.

Review the system leverage points discussed in section 3.2.2. The board sets the rules and goals for the system (leverage point 4); management organizes to conform to the rules and works to see the established goals. An integral part of this requires ensuring the correct instrumentation of the organizational capabilities to produce the measures and metrics required to assure performance and tie the Governance/Assurance loop together at performance measurement.

7.2.3 Assurance (AS)

The Assurance capability of the Z-X Model provides the organization with confidence in executing its strategic policies. The resultant organizational capabilities give the appropriate level of warranty and utility (fitness for use and purpose) that the organization requires. The Assurance and Governance capabilities mesh at performance measurement in the Governance/Assurance loop. While the Governance capability establishes the "what and how" the organization achieves its objectives, Assurance "proves" the appropriate innovation authority addressed performance gaps.

In the Z-X Model assurance capability, there are four practice areas:

- **Establish assurance criteria** Instrument warranty and utility of the DVMS capabilities
- **Assure strategic policy performance** Identify performance gaps in execution of strategic policy
- **Assure operational capability** Identify performance gaps relative to fitness and use
- **Assure performance measurement accuracy** Identify gaps in the accuracy of the strategic and operational intent schema.

7.2.3.1   AS:1 – Establish assurance criteria practice area

This practice area is the counterpart to GO:3 (section 7.2.2.3): oversee DVMS performance practice area. The difference is that this practice area is concerned with establishing the "assurance point of view" for the instrumentation of the organizational capabilities. Both AS:1 and GO:3 combine to identify measurements and metrics used to determine that the organizational capabilities are fit for use and purpose. The Governance perspective seeks to confirm the capabilities we created or improved are as designed, and Assurance seeks to verify that they produce the desired outcomes and are effective and efficient. Both viewpoints result in different measures and metrics. Together, strategic and operational intent result as measures and metrics instrumented in the organizational capabilities. Performance measurement uses these measures and metrics to identify performance gaps.

7.2.3.2   AS:2 – Assure strategic policy performance practice area

Strategic policy performance measures gaps in organizational capabilities to follow the rules and goals established by strategy-risk. It measures the adaptation of the strategic policies to create or improve organizational capabilities to produce the desired business outcomes. The performance gaps generally reflect the residual capabilities achieved as the organization creates or improves existing capabilities. This is particularly important in an adaptive organization as it continually delivers incremental improvements to organizational capabilities. Even then, they are still tweaked within the design tolerance of the system established by policy. Do not think of a performance gap as a failure; instead, treat it as an indicator of progress toward a business objective.

7.2.3.3   AS:3 – Assure operational capability practice area

Like AS:2, this practice identifies performance gaps in organizational capabilities at the operational level. At this level, operational performance gaps determine whether organizational capabilities to produce the desired outcomes conform to the design, and are effective and efficient. The appropriate innovation authority acts to address performance gaps. However, all changes represent low-order leverage points within the system. An organization can tweak performance within its tolerances established by strategic and operational policies.

7.2.3.4   AS:4 – Assure performance measurement accuracy practice area

Performance measurement uses the measures and metrics that express the strategic and operational intent of the organization. This is "what we want to do and how." These measures and metrics are derived from the QO–QM (section 7.4) capability of the Governance/Assurance loop and instrumented within the organizational capabilities. If the measures and metrics are wrong, decisions made from that information may not be correct or effective.

7.2.4   Plan (PL)

The Plan capability enables the organization to govern; assure performance; create and execute a risk-informed business strategy; and manage its portfolio of programs, risks and projects, and organizational knowledge. The practice areas of the Plan capability subsequently enable the organization to create, protect, and deliver digital business value.

The purpose of the Plan capability subsumes two goals: to create and deliver digital business value, and to protect that delivered value at a level commensurate with its significance to the business.

There are five practice areas under the Plan capability:

- Governance
- Assurance
- Strategy-risk management
- Portfolio, program, and project management
- Knowledge management.

7.2.4.1 PL:1 – Governance practice area

Governance is "the act or process of governing or overseeing the control and direction of something (such as a country or an organization)" (Merriam-Webster, n.d.-d). The Z-X Model governance practice area defines the organizational structure (the who does what to whom, when, and why) and formulates the policies for the organization to work. The practice area has two practices.

PL:1-1 Create organizational structures

This practice area aims to develop an organizational structure to create, protect, and deliver digital business value. It's based on the principle that behavior and structure are inextricably linked. The resultant structure aligns with the organizational strategic and operational intent.

The associated practices that implement this practice result in the following outcomes:

- **Establish organizational roles** The DVMS is a "value management system." As such, everyone in the organization plays a role in creating, protecting, and delivering digital business value. Those roles are identified and described so that the incumbent understands the flow of communication, work, and improvement, and the context in which they add value
- **Defined organizational responsibilities** Responsibilities may be assigned to organizational units and individuals based on the context of the value produced. Responsibilities must be identified and described so that the responsible individual or organizational unit understands the flow of communication, work, and innovation, and the context in which it is responsible for the value added
- **Defined organizational accountability** Accountability is assigned to an individual. In the DVMS Model, it's "where the buck stops." Someone must ultimately be accountable for the performance of their part in creating, protecting, and delivering digital business value. The scope of accountability must be clearly defined, along with the rewards and consequences that accrue to the incumbent
- **Communicated strategic and operational intent** The Z-X Model operationalizes the CPD Model, and this practice communicates the expressed strategic and operational intent that is used throughout the Z-X Model practices to measure and report on their performance (value, fitness for use, and fitness for purpose).

PL:1-2 Sustain organizational structures

Every system or structure tends toward disorganization. This practice aims to examine and improve the organizational digital business risk culture and its resulting behaviors to sustain the organizational capability to create, protect, and deliver digital business value. It seeks to operationalize a structure that aligns with the organizational strategic and operational intent.

The associated practices result in the following outcomes:

- **Policy formation** This practice develops actionable policies that articulate the strategic and operational intent. This outcome enables identifying a family of measures to ensure the creation, protection, and delivery of digital business value
- **Organized work** The organization adapts its management structure to achieve an agile, outcome-oriented workforce. It accomplishes this in the context of evolved stakeholder needs and organizational complexity. This practice also maintains stakeholder communication channels, ensuring the proper communication to the

right group or individual at the right time. This outcome maintains an organizational approach to work and promotes organizational agility.

7.2.4.2 PL:2 – Assurance practice area

The Merriam-Webster dictionary defines *assurance* as "confidence of mind or manner: easy freedom from self-doubt or uncertainty" (Merriam-Webster, n.d.-a). The DVMS assurance practice area provides confidence that organizational strategic policies are executed efficiently and effectively; it also assures the DVMS capabilities are fit for use and purpose, and that the value created is protected at a level commensurate with its importance to the organization. Overall, this practice area seeks to identify performance gaps, assess them, and communicate them to stakeholders.

PL:2-1 Performance assurance

The performance practice seeks to identify the measures and metrics necessary to assure policies align with organizational strategic and operational intent. It aims to align organizational goals to create, protect, and deliver digital business value.

The associated practices result in the following outcome:

- **A family of measurements and metrics determines the degree of alignment or conformance with value delivered, and with strategic and operational intent** A family of measures categorizes metrics into logical groupings to produce a schema used to report performance. The schema scope includes measures and metrics for:
- Delivered value
- Operational intent
- Strategic intent.

PL:2-2 Review and revision

Continual innovation is a core organizational capability; this practice seeks to identify improvement opportunities for the DVMS capabilities and strategic policy realignment. It subsequently communicates validated improvement opportunities to the change coordination practice for assessment and action.

The associated practices result in the following outcomes:

- **Identified perceived gaps** Assurance provides confidence that digital business value is created, protected, and delivered. The DVMS operates in a dynamic environment, and some gaps will exist
- **Assessed change-related risks** Gaps in the performance of creation of value, the protection of value commensurate with its importance to the organization, or its delivery are assessed relative to changes intended to effect closure of the gap. The scope of this practice includes internal and external changes, and changes to the threat landscape.

PL:2-3 Information sharing and reporting

This practice creates a reporting framework that supports the CPD Model's capability to assure the stakeholders that strategic policies are executed efficiently and effectively, and that DVMS capabilities are fit for use and purpose. The reporting framework includes a stakeholder information sharing plan and provides a comprehensive report on the current state of the CPD Model.

The associated practices result in the following outcomes:

- **Reporting framework** This uses the schema produced by knowledge management and maps data to information and stakeholders. Since the schema is dynamic, the reporting framework reports in near real time on the current state of the CPD Model

- **Shared current CPD Model state** Because of the dynamic nature of the CPD Model and the operation of the DVMS capabilities, any snapshot of the state of the CPD Model represents just that one moment in time. The measures and metrics that express the strategic and operational intent are used to create the schema and describe performance tolerances. The CPD Model state reflects all in- and out-of-tolerance conditions. This capability enables rapid identification of out-of-tolerance conditions that require a response
- **Stakeholder information sharing plan** This plan provides the right information to the right stakeholder at the right frequency and the right time. It also enforces access rights among stakeholders and operates under the "least privilege" principle.

7.2.4.3   PL:3 – Strategy-risk management practice area

This practice area aggregates the practices that integrate the strategy-risk policies into the DVMS: strategy-risk policy execution, identifying improvement opportunities, planning, testing continuity plans, and oversight of the supply chain cybersecurity posture. These activities support creating resilience and accountability, and provide the basis for adaptive and disruptive innovation by defining performance tolerances – one result of making strategy-risk a single entity.

PL:3-1 Policy integration

The DVMS is how policies become actionable business objectives that create, protect, and deliver digital business value. The strategy-risk policies adapt the DVMS capabilities to effectively and efficiently execute policies.

The associated practices result in the following outcomes:

- **Integrated strategy-risk policies with DVMS capabilities** Policy integration with the DVMS shapes the behaviors and outcomes of the Z-X Model practices, executing the strategic and operational intent. The Z-X Model capabilities, practice areas, practices, processes, and activities are instrumented to provide the metrics necessary to assure policy execution
- **Improved capabilities based on changes to policy** Because the DVMS is instrumented, the measures are used to identify performance gaps. These gaps may lead to a realignment of policies that govern the DVMS capabilities and operation.

PL:3-2 Identify improvement opportunities

The dynamic nature of the CPD Model enables it to adapt to a changing organizational context, including the realignment of strategy-risk policies. Evaluate performance gaps for opportunities to improve (realign) strategy-risk policies.

The associated practices result in the following outcomes:

- **Identified risk relative to internal and external requirements and the threat landscape** This practice seeks to identify the risks associated with the constant changes to organizational internal and external requirements and a constantly changing threat landscape
- **Analyzed and evaluated strategy-risk relative to change and scope of DVMS improvements** All improvements are analyzed and evaluated in the context of strategy-risk and the scope and nature of the DVMS improvements
- **Improvement opportunities communicated to strategy-risk and stakeholders** Improvement transparency is communicated to all relevant stakeholders. This transparency enables stakeholder input and identifies potential issues or additional opportunities
- **Strategy-risk policy changes communicated to stakeholders** All changes to strategy-risk policies are communicated to all relevant stakeholders.

PL:3-3 Digital business continuity management

Businesses rely on digital assets to contribute to business value. The combination of strategy and risk into the single entity, strategy-risk, includes resilience in the form of digital business value continuity. This practice ensures the business has a tested plan that is verified and capable of supporting the recovery of the business in the event of a severe incident.

The associated practices result in the following outcomes:

- **Business continuity plans** The associated processes of this practice ensure the business develops continuity plans adapted to cover a range of incident types, including a serious cybersecurity incident. These plans support the necessary level of resilience to survive and recover from a serious incident
- **Tested plans that verify business continuity support** All business continuity plans must be tested initially and periodically to ensure they are effective. The plans are subject to continual improvement that must be considered and updated as part of any change to the digital business value proposition (including infrastructure changes).

PL:3-4 Supply chain risk management

No business in this interconnected business world stands alone. Digital business systems connect with suppliers and businesses to supply goods or services. Everyone is connected to everyone else. *This connectedness creates a complex problem for the organization: its cybersecurity posture is only as strong as the posture of its weakest supplier.* The associated processes of this practice seek to manage third-party provider risk and assure that those providers demonstrate a cybersecurity profile that supports achieving the desired organizational risk posture.

The associated practices result in the following outcomes:

- **Developed cybersecurity posture criteria for all third-party providers** The organization must establish criteria for all third-party providers in the supply chain. The diversity of these providers may require using different criteria for those in different categories based on organization size, business sector, and geography
- **Developed supply chain risk management plan** From strategy-risk management, a supply chain risk management plan applies to the entire organizational supply chain. This plan is subject to change with any change to the digital business infrastructure or a third-party provider's cybersecurity posture
- **Managed supply chain risk** Managing third-party risk is a continuous effort and requires adequate resources and the attention of the organizational management and executives. In particular, any change to the organizational digital business infrastructure must consider its potential impact on its up- and downstream providers.

7.2.4.4 PL:4 – Portfolio, program, and project management practice area

This practice area is involved in two aspects of the DVMS to provide the structural capacity to:

- Implement or improve the DVMS capabilities
- Manage the DVMS capabilities, practice areas, and practices to create, protect, and deliver digital business value.

The practice area focuses on the organizational values and protection needs. This focus gives the organization an objective measure to make critical resource decisions.

PL:4-1 Establish digital business value portfolio

This practice establishes and maintains a portfolio that provides visibility of the organizational offerings that create, protect, and deliver digital business value. It catalogs offerings and communicates value and risk performance. The objective information is used as a basis for everyday and critical business and resource decisions.

The associated practices result in the following outcomes:

- **Identified digital value offerings** An organization must identify all of its digital value offerings. This is important to understand its needs and requirements. Any list of value offerings is dynamic and subject to continual change by its very nature. The organization must understand this as "normal" and adapt
- **Maintained digital value offerings** Due to the dynamic nature of business and the pace of technological innovation, things that provide digital business value are continually in flux. This practice establishes mechanisms that maintain the up-to-date knowledge of the digital value offerings
- **Reporting on the creation, protection, and delivery of digital business value performance** The organizational stakeholder requires an understanding of the portfolio's performance and its creation, protection, and delivery of digital business value.

PL:4-2 Program and project management

This practice aggregates one or more related projects that apply the knowledge, skills, and tools to facilitate the introduction of change. It efficiently manages one or more projects, and effectively manages the activities that introduce change.

The associated practices result in the following outcomes:

- **Feasibility assessment** The practice establishes the project's feasibility and provides continual reassessment of this throughout the project lifecycle
- **Initiated project** The practice establishes the project's prerequisites and ensures compliance before proceeding
- **Managed project** Management of the project has an executive sponsor who is accountable for its performance. The executive sponsor provides project oversight, while a project manager is responsible for the daily management and project staff. Use any popular program or project management best-practice framework for guidance
- **Closed projects** All projects close, either successfully or as a failure. This outcome wraps up the project and releases its resources.

7.2.4.5   PL:5 – Knowledge management practice area

Knowledge management is the practice of creating, sharing, using, and managing organizational knowledge. It refers to a multidisciplinary approach to support decisions that achieve objectives using knowledge. The associated practices provide roles (included in the model discussed below) for authors, editors, and reviewers, in addition to rules for the retention and the expiry of data.

Let's look at the data, information, knowledge, and wisdom (DIKW) model and put that in context for the CPD Model and this DVMS practice area.

The DIKW model

The DIKW model is typically represented as a pyramid, with *data* forming its base. Data has no meaning until the application of a transform provides context; then, it becomes *information* that answers questions like "who," "what," "when," and "where." The application of additional transforms provides additional meaning; information becomes *knowledge*, answering the question of "how." Combined, data, information, and knowledge reveal questions and potential answers about relationships and patterns of behaviors over time that contribute to *wisdom*, resulting in better decisions – answering the question of "why." Purposely, "decisions" result in changes (adaptive or disruptive innovation).

Knowledge management model

Figure 7.1 depicts a high-level knowledge management model within the CPD Model.

The output of strategy-risk is risk-informed strategic policies. These policies are adapted to produce the DVMS control requirements necessary to create, protect, and deliver digital business value. The QO–QM method uses strategic policies and the desired DVMS capabilities to align strategic outcomes and produce the metrics and measures that express the organizational strategic and operational intent (SOI). QO–QM output metrics are used to instrument the DVMS practice and develop the SOI schema. The SOI schema maps the data collected in various data stores by operating the DVMS practices to determine performance gaps in the DVMS operation and execution of strategic policies.

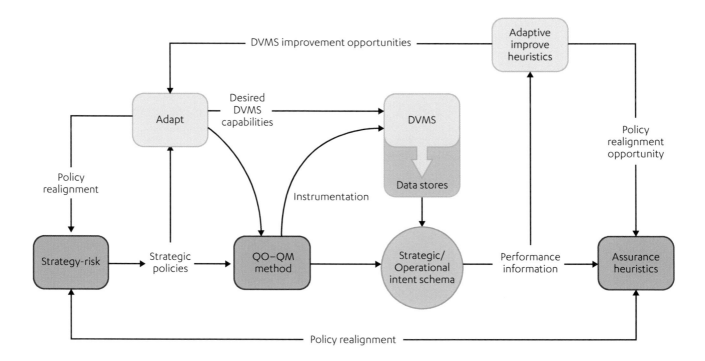

Figure 7.1 Knowledge management within the CPD Model

The information assures the DVMS capabilities are performing within tolerances and that policies are being executed effectively and efficiently. These two feedback loops allow the organization to improve continually relative to its environment. This method of innovation is considered to be adaptive.

Similarly, an innovation that results in a paradigm shift is assessed and actioned within the CPD Model's Strategy/ Governance loop, and in corresponding changes to strategy-risk and cascaded strategic policies.

PL:5-1 Manage the flow of information

One of the three "flows" fundamental to any organization is the flow of information. This practice aims to create, share, use, and manage organizational information and knowledge. It seeks to leverage information and knowledge to help achieve organizational objectives.

The associated practices result in the following outcomes:

● **Analyzed information creation, use, and flow** This practice seeks to provide information to the right stakeholders for daily operations, management, and strategic decisions. It aims to build vertical and horizontal organizational communication channels for the efficient and effective use of information

- **Optimized information creation, use, and flow to achieve organizational objectives** This practice seeks to optimize the organizational capability of providing the context for the efficient creation of information from numerous data stores across the organization and effectively disseminating that information.

PL:5-2 Audit and manage the information lifecycle

Information is only as good as the data it's based on and the understanding of its context. This practice aims to verify and validate information and knowledge to assure that organizational objectives are achieved. It aims to produce verifiable and validated information and knowledge to support organizational objectives.

The associated practices result in the following outcomes:

- **Use of verified and validated criteria throughout the information lifecycle** Criteria are established to verify and validate organizational information from creation to destruction
- **Verified data and resulting information** Both data and the information created from it are verified
- **Validated information and resulting knowledge** The information is given meaning, resulting in validated knowledge.

PL:5-3 Manage stakeholder information flow

This practice seeks to manage the flow of information used by stakeholders to achieve organizational goals. It provides the correct information to the right stakeholder in the right place and at the right time.

The associated practices result in the following outcomes:

- **Identified stakeholders** Stakeholders must be identified, and this information must be maintained
- **Maintained stakeholder information requirements** Produce a catalog of information the stakeholder requires, how often, and when
- **Verified and validated stakeholders' "need to know"** Similarly to the concept of "least privilege," each stakeholder identified must have a verified and validated "need to know."

7.2.5 Design (DE)

The Design capability enables the organization to create a straightforward, cohesive approach to creating, protecting, and delivering digital business value. It seeks to develop designs through the system architecture and configuration management practice areas that enable the organization to deliver and protect digital business value.

There are two practice areas under the Design capability:

- System architecture
- Configuration management.

7.2.5.1 DE:1 – System architecture

The system architecture practice area covers practices that support the organizational ability to create clear and cohesive designs to create, protect, and deliver digital business value.

DE:1-1 Performance management

The performance management practice develops and maintains the architectural plans that describe the organizational structure, relationships, interaction pattern, and environment to create, protect, and deliver digital business value. It delivers architectural plans that describe the creation, protection, and delivery of digital business value to assure conformance to architectural plans.

The associated practices result in the following outcomes:

- **Identified scope of business value** The scope of the business value created and protected is identified and documented in the digital business value portfolio. The portfolio represents the sum of the organizational digital business value
- **Maintained digital business value portfolio** Digital business value is dynamic and subject to change in internal needs, external factors, and the threat landscape. The digital business value must be continually assessed and updated to assure the organization has a complete picture of it and can make informed decisions
- **Identified architectural improvement opportunities** In any dynamic system, change is a constant, and improvement opportunities are identified, assessed, and actioned as necessary
- **Assessed performance against strategic and operational intent** The DVMS capabilities and business objectives flow from the policies formed from strategy-risk. These policies are also used to establish the measures and metrics that express the organizational strategic and operational intent. These measures and metrics are used to measure the performance of the DVMS in creating, protecting, and delivering digital business value. The organization can be assured that the DVMS is fit for use and purpose, and that the strategic policies are executed efficiently and effectively.

DE:1-2 Availability management

Availability management establishes the scope and tolerances of the operational availability of digital assets that create, protect, and deliver digital business value. The scope and tolerances include availability, reliability, maintainability, and continuity relative to the architectural performance management criteria.

The associated practices result in the following outcomes. In each case, the scope defines the digital asset or aggregated set of assets.

- **Scope and tolerance of availability** The scope establishes operational availability tolerances used to assess availability performance
- **Scope and tolerance of reliability** The scope establishes operational reliability tolerances used to assess availability performance
- **Scope and tolerance of maintainability** The scope establishes operational tolerances used to assess availability performance
- **Scope and tolerance of continuity** The scope defines the digital asset or establishes operational continuity tolerances used to assess availability performance.

DE:1-3 Capacity management

Capacity management establishes the scope and tolerances of the operational performance of digital assets that create, protect, and deliver digital business value. The scope and tolerances include operational performance relative to the architectural performance management criteria.

The associated practices result in the following outcomes. In each case, the scope defines the digital asset or aggregated set of assets.

- **Scope and tolerance of normal operation** The scope establishes the operational capacity tolerances used to assess capacity performance
- **Scope and tolerance of contingency operation** The scope establishes contingency capacity tolerances used to assess contingency capacity performance. There is an aspect of "contingency operation" that deals with normal fluctuation in the demand for digital assets (called demand management; capacity management and demand management are two sides of the same coin).

DE:1-4 Continuity management

Continuity management develops the architectural plans to ensure business continuity when responding to a serious incident. These plans are reviewed, verified, and validated to assure the organization that the plans support sufficient business recovery to respond to a serious incident.

The associated practices result in the following outcomes:

- **Reviewed, verified, and validated business continuity plans** that support sufficient business recovery to respond to a serious incident. Once the continuity plans have been produced, they are reviewed, verifying their accuracy and efficacy in recovering business sufficiently
- **Continuity plans are periodically reviewed** to test that they support sufficient business recovery to respond to a serious incident. Continuity plans are subject to improvement and may be impacted by changes in digital assets.

7.2.5.2 DE:2 – Configuration management

Configuration management plays an essential role in the organizational ability to associate digital assets with the systems that create, protect, and deliver digital business value. Configuration management defines the scope, including linkages to business value and assessment against strategic and operational intent.

DE:2-1 Configuration item management

Configuration item management establishes the scope and relationships of the configuration items managed in conformance with the system architecture. It logically represents the configuration item attributes and relationships contributing to digital business value creation, protection, and delivery.

The associated practices result in the following outcomes:

- **Defined scope of configuration item control** This scope defines the granularity at which the configuration items are tracked. Often, granularity is a function of the role of the infrastructure component within a digital asset
- **Identified configuration item attributes** Configuration attributes describe the configuration item and its relationship with other configuration items and digital assets.

DE:2-2 Configuration administration

Configuration administration establishes the scope of the administrative control over configuration items, and ensures conformance with the system architecture and digital business value. Conformance with the architecture ensures retention of the relationship and interaction patterns that are part of the architecture. The practice provides a representation of the configuration items to reflect their physical and virtual manifestation.

The associated practices result in the following outcomes:

- **Managed updates and editing of configuration representation** All changes to digital assets or their configuration are reflected via an update to the configuration database or repository
- **Audited, visible, and reported physical and virtual manifestations of the configurations are auditable** and either visibly confirmed or virtually verified within the digital asset
- **Assessed performance against the expected digital business value** Configuration administration plays an integral role in the assurance of digital asset performance relative to architectural performance management criteria and the measures and metrics of the expressed strategic and operational intent
- **Collaboration with change coordination** Configuration administration collaborates with change / change coordination practice. This close operational collaboration is essential to the effective operational performance of digital assets.

The final outcome listed above is one of many examples of how the seven minimum viable capabilities are part of a system, not silos. The resulting practice areas and practices interact. Consider what will happen if a configuration item recorded in the repository is changed without the analysis and coordination provided as part of the Change capability. The consequences to the organization include the potential to be unable to protect the created value, combined with elevated organizational risk.

7.2.6 Change (CH)

Change is a fundamental organizational capability that enables an organization to adapt to its environment. The Change capability is driven by internal and external needs and a dynamic threat environment. It affects digital solutions that meet the design requirements necessary to create, protect, and deliver digital business value. It establishes the governance structure essential to coordinate digital business value solutions.

There are four practice areas under the Change capability:

- Change coordination
- Solution adaptation
- Release management
- Deployment management.

7.2.6.1 CH:1 – Change coordination practice area

The change coordination practice area aggregates the organizational orchestration of how change impacts people, practice, technology, and risk. It provides overarching governance that involves the organizational authorized change authorities, stakeholders, and stakeholder relationships, and coordinates the selection, build, release, and deployment of changes to digital products, services, and systems.

CH:1-1 Change orchestration

The change orchestration practice ensures the coordination of the authorization to build, release, and deploy a change to digital products, services, and systems to create, protect, and deliver digital business value.

The associated practices result in the following outcomes:

- **Established scope of change** This practice establishes the scope of change to people, practice, technology, and risk that establishes activity or project boundaries
- **Identified change authorities** All changes must be authorized; therefore the individuals who are authorized to approve changes must be identified and this information maintained
- **Identified impacts on relationships** In complex systems, it is imperative that a change impacting stakeholders in digital products, systems, or services be surfaced and communicated to relevant stakeholders
- **Coordination** This practice coordinates the selection, build, release, and deployment of changed digital products, services, and systems.

CH:1-2 Performance assessment

The performance assessment practice ensures that each implementation of a change is assessed against the expected value expressed in the strategic and operational intent. It assures that each implemented change creates, protects, and delivers digital business value aligned with strategic and operational intent.

The associated practices result in the following outcomes:

- **Assessed changes against the expressed strategic and operational intent** Each change implemented is assessed against expressed strategic and operational intent. The assessment uses measures and metrics established from the expressed strategic and operational intent to assess operational performance
- **Evaluated changes that are fit for purpose and use** Once assessed, each change is assessed to determine whether the resultant change achieved its expected performance objective and is fit for use and purpose.

7.2.6.2   CH:2 – Solution adaptation practice area

The solution adaptation practice area is tightly integrated with change coordination, configuration management, and system architecture. These practices are core to the *creation* of digital business. They *must* be at DVCMM level 3 to provide the necessary capability for integration of dependent informative reference control requirements into the DVMS practices. The relationship between the DVMS capabilities and the informative reference control families (to the level of the individual control requirements) is critical and must not be overlooked or underestimated.

This practice area aggregates the adaptation of commercial solutions, digital hardware, software, XaaS, and performance assessment.

CH:2-1 Commercial solution acquisition

This practice ensures that the acquisition of hardware, software, and services aligns with the expressed strategic and operational intent to create, protect, and deliver digital business value by establishing the acquisition criteria.

The associated practices result in the following outcomes:

- **Acquisition criteria to create, protect, and deliver digital business value** This practice establishes the organizational acquisition criteria used for hardware, software, and services used in digital products, services, and systems
- **Hardware, software, and services meet the acquisition criteria** The organization uses the acquisition criteria for hardware, software, and services used in digital products, services, and systems.

CH:2-2 Digital hardware solution

The digital hardware solution practice ensures that the installation, integration, and removal of digital hardware align with the expressed strategic and operational intent to create, protect, and deliver digital business value.

The associated practices result in the following outcomes:

- **Installation, integration, and removal criteria** This practice establishes the criteria used by the organization for the installation, integration, and removal of digital hardware
- **Installation, integration, and removal that meet the appropriate criteria** The installation, integration, and removal of digital hardware meet the appropriate criteria.

CH:2-3 Software solution

The software solution practice ensures that the installation, integration, and removal of software align with the expressed strategic and operational intent to create, protect, and deliver digital business value.

The associated practices result in the following outcomes:

- **Installation, integration, and removal criteria** This practice establishes the criteria used by the organization for the installation, integration, and removal of software
- **Installation, integration, and removal meet the appropriate criteria** The installation, integration, and removal of software meet the appropriate criteria.

CH:2-4 XaaS solution

The XaaS solution practice ensures that the installation, integration, and removal of XaaS solutions align with the expressed strategic and operational intent to create, protect, and deliver digital business value.

The associated practices result in the following outcomes:

- **Installation, integration, and removal criteria** This practice establishes the criteria used by the organization for the installation, integration, and removal of an XaaS solution
- **Installation, integration, and removal that meet the appropriate criteria** The installation, integration, and removal of an XaaS solution meet the appropriate criteria.

CH:2-5 Performance assessment

The performance assessment practice looks at adapting solutions based on the expected value expressed in the strategic and operational intent. It ensures that the adapted solution creates, protects, and delivers digital business value aligned with the organizational expressed strategic and operational intent.

The associated practices result in the following outcomes:

- **Adapted solutions assessed against the expressed strategic and operational intent** The adapted and implemented solution is assessed against the organizational expressed strategic and operational intent behind the solution. Its operational performance is assessed using the measures and metrics derived from the expressed strategic and operational intent
- **Evaluated adapted solutions are fit for use and purpose** The operational performance of the adapted and implemented solution is evaluated using the measures and metrics established to determine whether the solution is fit for use and purpose.

7.2.6.3   CH:3 – Release management practice area

The release management practice area aggregates the planning of a release, monitoring its build and testing, and comprehensive testing of the entire release.

CH:3-1 Release planning

Release planning encompasses developing an actionable plan to release, independent of size, an identified set of components into the live environment to create, protect, and deliver digital business value. It identifies and sources the components to be released together.

The associated practices result in the following outcomes:

- **Identified release components** A release comprises one or more components to be released into the live environment. Once the components are identified, the release becomes an atomic entity throughout the release cycle
- **Identified responsible component resource** Components of the release are either built internally within the organization or acquired from a third-party resource. Each component has a source responsible for its delivery for inclusion in the release
- **Prepared release package** Once release components are identified and sourced, the release becomes a release package.

CH:3-2 Monitor component build and test

This practice ensures that all release components' build and testing are monitored throughout the build-and-test cycle. It provides the update of the release plan with the component build and testing results.

The associated practices result in the following outcomes:

- **Updated planned release** The release plan is updated with the current state of each component in the build-and-test cycle
- **Monitored and maintained test results** All component tests are monitored and maintained, assuring that each component is fit for use.

CH:3-3 Release testing

This practice develops and executes a release test plan to assure the release conforms with the strategic and operational intent. The executable test plan assures a release achieves the strategic and operational intent to create, protect, and deliver digital business value.

The associated practices result in the following outcomes:

- **Approved test plan** This practice approves a test plan that tests all release components and their interaction with other release package components and components of the test environment
- **Evaluated test results** The test results are evaluated to determine whether the release is fit for use.

7.2.6.4 CH:4 – Deployment management practice area

The deployment management practice area manages the deployment of the release package into the live environment and validates the result.

CH:4-1 Manage release transition

The manage release transition practice deals with the addition or decommissioning of functionality that aligns with the expressed strategic and operational intent. It adds approved release packages, or decommissions approved functionality that is no longer needed to create, protect, and deliver digital business value.

The associated practices result in the following outcomes:

- **Deployed approved release package** This practice manages the deployment of tested and approved release packages into a new environment. It coordinates all of the activities necessary to deploy the new release
- **Decommissioned approved obsolete functionality** When existing functionality is no longer needed, this practice is responsible for removing it from the environment and adequately decommissioning it. The scope is determined as part of pre-decommissioning and determines the resources necessary to decommission the functionality properly. This may occur coincidentally with the deployment of replacement functionality in one or more release packages.

CH:4-2 Validate

The validate practice assures that the addition or decommissioning of functionality is aligned with the expressed strategic and operational intent to create, protect, and deliver digital business value.

The associated practices result in the following outcomes:

- **Scoped validation plan** This practice spans the build and test of the release package and its subsequent deployment into a new environment. It ensures that the functionality added or decommissioned aligns with the expressed strategic and operational intent and can be validated against the digital business value creation, protection, and delivery
- **Validation results** Upon the execution of the validation plan, the results provide the organization with the assurance that the additional or decommissioned functionality is fit for use.

7.2.7   Execute (EX)

The Execute capability is where created and protected value is delivered. Its practice areas encompass providing access to digital products, services, and systems to authorized users; mitigating disruptions in the delivery of digital business value; identifying and resolving system disruption of digital business value; and the overarching management of the organizational infrastructure/platforms.

The Execute capability has four practice areas:

- Provisioning
- Incident management
- Problem management
- Infrastructure/platform management.

7.2.7.1   EX:1 – Provisioning practice area

The provisioning practice area aggregates the practices that manage the access to digital products, services, and systems. It also deals with access requests.

EX:1-1 Access management

The access management practice establishes and maintains the policies used to determine access to digital products, services, and systems. It executes the policies used to determine access to products, services, and systems in alignment with the expressed strategic and operational intent.

The associated practices result in the following outcomes:

- **Maintained access verification criteria, including least privilege** The access management executes the policies that establish access and verification criteria used in granting access to digital products, services, and systems under the concept of "least privileged access necessary"
- **Signal of approval or denial of access to the services** Each granting or denial of access is confirmed and communicated to the requestor and other stakeholders.

EX:1-2 Request management

The request management practice maintains authorized access to digital products, services, and systems in alignment with the expressed strategic and operational intent.

The associated practices result in the following outcomes:

- **Verified access request** This practice ensures that all access requests are verified. Upon verification, an authorized user's request is fulfilled. Upon rejection, the requestor and supporting stakeholders are notified
- **Fulfilled access request** Upon verification of a valid request by an authorized user, the access to a digital product, service, or system is granted, and the requestor and supporting stakeholder are notified.

7.2.7.2   EX:2 – Incident management practice area

The incident management practice develops and maintains incident models that support restoring business productivity in alignment with the expressed strategic and operational intent to create, protect, and deliver digital business value.

EX:2-1 Manage incident models

The manage incident models practice develops and maintains incident models to support the restoration of business productivity. The incident models enable the organization to restore business productivity in a timeframe aligned with the expressed strategic and operational intent.

The associated practices result in the following outcomes:

- **Defined incident models** Incident models describe actions taken for a given type of incident to restore business productivity in a timeframe aligned with the organizational expressed strategic and operational intent
- **Defined incident model categorization and selection criteria** Provides categorization and selection criteria for incident models.

EX:2-2 Execute incident model

The execute incident model practice applies and executes an appropriate incident model that restores business productivity in a timeframe aligned with the expressed strategic and operational intent.

The associated practices result in the following outcomes:

- **Selected incident model based on applied criteria** For each incident, an incident model is selected based on established selection criteria
- **Executed selected incident model** Once the appropriate incident model has been selected, the model is executed. The incident model provides the organization with a pre-planned course of action to deal with a specific type of incident. Incident models enable the organization to restore business productivity within the timeframes aligned with the organizational strategic and operational intent.

7.2.7.3   EX:3 – Problem management practice area

The problem management practice area defines problem models and their selection criteria, and executes them to remove systemic errors from digital products, services, and systems.

EX:3-1 Manage problem models

The problem management practice defines and executes an appropriate problem model that supports identifying and removing system errors in digital products, services, and systems in alignment with the organizational strategic and operational intent to create, protect, and deliver digital business value.

The associated practices result in the following outcomes:

- **Defined problem model based on applied criteria** Defines a problem model that provides a pre-planned set of actions to identify and remove a systemic error from a digital product, service, or system
- **Defined problem model selection criteria** Problem model selection criteria aid the organization in selecting and executing an appropriate problem model.

EX:3-2 Execute problem model

The execute problem model practice applies the model execution in identifying and removing systemic errors in digital product, services, and systems, or developing workarounds in alignment with the organizational expressed strategic and operational intent.

The associated practices result in the following outcomes:

- **Selected problem model** Use the appropriate criteria to select the problem model
- **Executed selected problem model** The execution of a problem model seeks to identify and remove a systemic error from a digital product, service, or system. If necessary, the model supports identifying a workaround until the system error can be removed.

7.2.7.4 EX:4 – Infrastructure/platform management practice area

This practice area aggregates practices that monitor and manage infrastructure events.

EX:4-1 Event monitoring

Event monitoring ensures the identification of events with the coordination, instrumentation, and monitoring provisions in alignment with the organizational expressed strategic and operational intent to create, protect, and deliver digital business value.

The associated practices result in the following outcomes:

- **Identified events monitored** This practice establishes selection criteria and selects events to be monitored. The selection criteria may change over time as digital products/services/systems mature and the overall understanding of critical events becomes well known (inclusive of events required for platform management)
- **Coordinated instrumentation** Instrumentation of the infrastructure components is coordinated to ensure that what needs to be monitored is adequately capable
- **Coordinated monitoring** This practice coordinates the monitoring of events across the entire digital infrastructure.

EX:4-2 Event management

The event management practice identifies, correlates, and responds to events in alignment with the expressed strategic and operational intent to create, protect, and deliver digital business value.

The associated practices result in the following outcomes:

- **Identified events** This practice identifies and maintains significant events across the entire digital infrastructure. As the digital infrastructure changes, events and their significance may change
- **Established event correlation** The practice is responsible for developing an event correlation scheme that identifies the root event and reduces the "noise" caused by superfluous cascading events
- **Coordinated event response** The practice coordinates event response, automatic response or human intervention, inspection, and response initiation.

7.2.8 Innovate (IN)

The DVMS Model is an overlay of organizational capabilities that represent a minimum viable capability necessary for an organization to create, protect, and deliver digital business value. It assumes the organization is at some unknown capability state when the DVMS Model is used, marking the beginning of the organizational journey.

The organization starts "where it is." That means anything the organization does is considered an innovation.[67] Innovation is the introduction of something new. The DVMS operationalizes the CPD Model. The CPD Model enables an organization to continually adapt to its current context through incremental or sustaining changes. The CPD Model also incorporates an organizational capability to operationalize changes that represent either a paradigm shift or disruption in the marketplace.

The Innovate capability seeks opportunities to innovate in creating, protecting, and delivering digital business value to achieve the organizational expressed strategic and operational intent. It measures the overall performance of the components and systems that create, protect, and deliver digital business value; analyzes performance gaps; and catalogs innovation opportunities.

---

67 Remember that the way we treat innovation subsumes improvement. The typical approach is "everything is an improvement" – that does not address every aspect we include in innovation.

Much like a flywheel in a car engine provides mass that keeps the engine turning, continual innovation keeps the DVMS capabilities adapting to the dynamic organizational environment.

The Innovate capability has three practice areas:

- Continual innovation
- Performance measurement
- Gap analysis.

7.2.8.1   IN:1 – Continual innovation practice area

The internal and external changes and the threat landscape provide the incremental impetus needed to improve continually. In this model, the Innovate capability identifies improvement types, recording, and the notification to a change authority. The change coordination practice area is responsible for effecting the change. The result reflects an update to capabilities, policies, or the strategic and operational intent.

IN:1-1 Innovation management

Innovation management promotes the systematic renewal and innovation of organizational capabilities that create, protect, and deliver digital business value. It creates and uses innovation models.

The associated practices result in the following outcomes:

- **Developed innovation models** The organization develops innovation models that are incremental (minor or small), sustaining (e.g., new version), adaptive (policy change), and disruptive (strategic change). Model selection is based on the organizational defined criteria
- **Documented categories of innovation** This practice identifies and categorizes different characteristics exhibited by the different types of innovation. This enables the organization to develop a limited number of models that can successfully innovate in its environmental context.

IN:1-2 Model innovation types

This practice develops and maintains improvement models that represent innovation opportunities, consistent with the strategic and operational intent to create, protect, and deliver digital business value. These models represent the types of innovation.

The associated practices result in the following outcomes:

- **Deterministic innovation model** Generally used in incremental or sustaining innovation. The model seeks a known (determined) outcome or state
- **Non-deterministic innovation model** Typically used in the context of paradigm shift or market disruption where the outcome is to be discovered and is not pre-determined
- **Heuristics-based innovation model** Used to apply the lessons learned by proactively innovating in similar contexts.

IN:1-3 Use innovation models

This practice applies the appropriate innovation model to assess, record, and notify a change authority of an innovation opportunity that conforms to the strategic and operational intent to create, protect, and deliver digital business value.

The associated practices result in the following outcomes:

- **Assessed innovation** The practice assesses an innovation opportunity that closes a performance gap
- **Recorded innovation opportunity** Each assessed innovation opportunity is recorded and made transparent for access by the appropriate change authority

- **Notification provided of an innovation opportunity to a change authority** The appropriate change authority is notified of all assessed and recorded innovation opportunities.

7.2.8.2 IN:2 – Performance measurement

The performance measurement practice area is responsible for the instrumentation of the DVMS practices, so their performance can be assessed against the organizational expressed strategic and operational intent and the delivery of expected digital business value. The measures and metrics derived from the strategic and operational intent are used to develop and maintain the DVMS reporting schema.

IN:2-1 Instrument practice outcomes

This practice ensures the DVMS practices are instrumented to support the determination of the alignment of the strategic and operational intent to create, protect, and deliver digital business value.

The associated practices result in the following outcome:

- **Instrumented DVMS practices** During design, DVMS practices are instrumented to produce metrics used to determine whether the practice is fit for use and purpose and capable of delivering the expected value.

IN:2-2 DVMS reporting

This practice develops and maintains a DVMS reporting schema for the instrumented practices in alignment with the strategic and operational intent to create, protect, and deliver digital business value. The DVMS reporting schema provides visibility into alignment with strategic and operational intent.

The associated practices result in the following outcome:

- **Developed and maintainable DVMS reporting schema** Maps the data collected and stored within the knowledge base to information used to make strategic and operational decisions. The entire DVMS operates in a dynamic environment that constantly changes, which requires constant maintenance of the schema.

7.2.8.3 IN:3 – Gap analysis practice area

This practice area develops and uses models to assess the gaps in the performance of the DVMS capabilities to create, protect, and deliver digital business value.

IN:3-1 Determine the gap

This practice determines whether there is an out-of-tolerance condition between the current state and the expressed strategic and operational intent to create, protect, and deliver digital business value. The activities related to this practice require teams working in the context of the 3D Knowledge Model – that's how they know what is *in* and *out* of tolerance, established by policies resulting in the strategic and operational intent.

The associated practices result in the following outcome:

- **Documented out-of-tolerance condition** The practice uses performance information to determine whether the operation of a DVMS practice is within its tolerance parameters to determine whether it is fit for use, fit for purpose, or delivering the expected value.

IN:3-2 Model and assess the gap

This practice develops and uses gap assessment models to determine the scope, urgency, and impact of out-of-tolerance conditions between the current state and expressed strategic and operational intent to create, protect, and deliver digital business value.

The associated practices result in the following outcomes:

- **Gap assessment models** These are developed to determine whether a DVMS practice is operating within its established tolerances. The models assess whether the practices are fit for use and fit for purpose, and create the expected digital business value
- **Scope, urgency, and impact determined** If there is a gap, its scope and urgency are determined.

7.3 Cybersecurity and Z-X Model capabilities

In section 6.3, we discussed the cybersecurity control families in detail. This section covers the relationship between the control families and the Z-X Model capabilities.

The Z-X Model capabilities represent the minimum viable capabilities (MVCs) an organization needs to create, protect, and deliver digital business value. The relationships described in the following tables are:

- "D": dependent
- "I": integrated
- "-": no relationship.

Dependent relationships occur when some or all of the controls in a control family require the existence of the Z-X Model capability at DVCMM level 3 (see section 4.1). It's like building a house: you can't install roof trusses without building the walls first.

Integrated relationships occur when some or all of the controls in the control family are integrated into the underlying Z-X Model capability. Consider installing the house plumbing fixtures, sinks, toilets, showers, and tubs, to the roughed-in plumbing connections.

7.3.1 Plan

The Plan capability (Table 7.1) has a dependent or integrated relationship with all cybersecurity control families.

Table 7.1 Z-X Model: Plan capability and cybersecurity control families

Plan capabilities mapped to cybersecurity control families	Access control	Awareness and training	Audit and accountability	Assessment, authorization, and monitoring	Configuration management	Contingency planning	Identification and authentication	Incident response	Maintenance	Media and data protection	Personally identifiable information processing	Personnel security	Physical and environmental protection	Planning	Program and project management	Risk assessment	System and communication protection	System and information integrity
PL: Governance	D	D	D	D	D	D	D	D	D	D	D	D	D	D	D	D	D	D
PL: Assurance	D	D	D	D	D	D	D	D	D	D	D	D	D	D	D	D	D	D
PL: Risk management	D	D	D	D	D	D	D	D	D	D	D	D	D	D	D	D	D	D
PL: Portfolio, program, and project management	I	I	I	I	I	I	I	I	I	I	I	I	I	I	I	I	I	I
PL: Knowledge management	I	I	I	I	I	I	I	I	I	I	I	I	I	I	I	I	I	I

The Plan capability's governance, assurance, and strategy-risk management practice areas are required for all control families. Governance establishes the DVMS controls, and assurance identifies performance gaps in the Z-X capabilities. Strategy-risk management sets strategic direction, objectives, and policies to create or improve Z-X capabilities.

Portfolio, program, and project management, and knowledge management, provide integration points for some or all of the controls of the control families. They become part of the organizational portfolio of capabilities and risks. Integrated controls have measures and metrics instrumented within the Z-X Model capabilities, and are used to determine whether they are fit for use and purpose. The aggregate performance capabilities of the Z-X Model are assessed against strategic intent to assure the execution of strategic policies.

7.3.2 Design

In the Design capability (Table 7.2), the system architecture practice area establishes four primary practices: performance, availability, capacity, and contingency. Most cybersecurity controls depend on the configuration management practice area, whose practices are configuration item management and configuration administration.

Table 7.2 Z-X Model: Design capability and cybersecurity control families

Design capabilities mapped to cybersecurity control families	Access control	Awareness and training	Audit and accountability	Assessment, authorization, and monitoring	Configuration management	Contingency planning	Identification and authentication	Incident response	Maintenance	Media and data protection	Personally identifiable information processing	Personnel security	Physical and environmental protection	Planning	Program and project management	Risk assessment	System and communication protection	System and information integrity
DE: System architecture	I	-	D	D	D	D	D	D	I	D	D	I	D	D	I	D	D	D
DE: Configuration management	I	-	D	D	D	D	D	D	D	D	D	I	D	D	I	D	D	D

The four practices in the system architecture practice area integrate with the access control, program and project management, and personnel security control families. The rest of the control families are dependent on these four practices.

Like system architecture, configuration management integrates with the same three control families and represents a dependent capability to the rest. Configuration management documents and maintains all the relationships among the digital assets. That makes it a core, mission-critical organizational capability. All the functions of the NIST-CSF rely on the ability to identify and manage the organizational digital assets.

7.3.3 Change

The scope of the Change capability (Table 7.3) includes coordinating changes to other capabilities and practices, and the underlying enabling hardware and software. This includes internally and externally sourced system components and their deployment.

Table 7.3 Z-X Model: Change capability and cybersecurity control families

Change capabilities mapped to cybersecurity control families	Access control	Awareness and training	Audit and accountability	Assessment, authorization, and monitoring	Configuration management	Contingency planning	Identification and authentication	Incident response	Maintenance	Media and data protection	Personally identifiable information processing	Personnel security	Physical and environmental protection	Planning	Program and project management	Risk assessment	System and communication protection	System and information integrity
CH: Change coordination	I	I	D	D	D	D	D	D	I	D	D	I	I	D	I	D	D	D
CH: Solution adaptation	I	-	D	D	D	D	I	I	I	I	I	I	I	I	I	D	D	I
CH: Release management	I	-	D	D	D	D	I	I	I	I	I	I	I	I	I	D	D	I
CH: Deployment management	I	-	D	D	D	D	I	I	I	I	I	I	I	I	I	D	D	I

Table 7.3 illustrates that many cybersecurity control families are integrated with the Change solution adaptation, release management, and deployment management practice areas. These three practice areas represent how the organization creates or improves its existing capability to create, protect, and deliver digital business value. It's essential to also look closely at the control families dependent on all of the practice areas of the Change capability. Think of this as where the existing organizational capability to create value gets updated DNA, enabling it to protect value.

7.3.4 Execute

The Execute capability (Table 7.4) is where value created and protected is delivered. The scope of the capability includes provisioning stakeholders with digital business services; and managing incidents, problems, and the underlying digital business services infrastructure.

Table 7.4 Z-X Model: Execute capability and cybersecurity control families

Execute capabilities mapped to cybersecurity control families	Access control	Awareness and training	Audit and accountability	Assessment, authorization, and monitoring	Configuration management	Contingency planning	Identification and authentication	Incident response	Maintenance	Media and data protection	Personally identifiable information processing	Personnel security	Physical and environmental protection	Planning	Program and project management	Risk assessment	System and communication protection	System and information integrity
EX: Provisioning	D	-	I	I	D	D	I	I	I	-	I	I	I	I	I	D	D	I
EX: Incident management	D	I	I	I	D	D	I	D	-	-	I	I	-	I	I	D	I	I
EX: Problem management	D	-	I	I	D	D	I	D	-	-	I	I	-	I	I	D	I	I
EX: Infrastructure/platform management	D	-	I	I	D	D	I	I	D	D	I	I	D	I	I	D	D	I

Notice that most control families that integrate with these practice areas are involved directly with the underlying execution of capabilities to deliver digital business services.

7.3.5   Innovate

The Innovate capability (Table 7.5) is where the organization actions feedback from its environment. Feedback from its performance in its environment, the performance of its capabilities, and its quality to its stakeholders all provide innovation opportunities to the organization.

Table 7.5 Z-X Model: Innovate capability and cybersecurity control families

Innovate capabilities mapped to cybersecurity control families	Access control	Awareness and training	Audit and accountability	Assessment, authorization, and monitoring	Configuration management	Contingency planning	Identification and authentication	Incident response	Maintenance	Media and data protection	Personally identifiable information processing	Personnel security	Physical and environmental protection	Planning	Program and project management	Risk assessment	System and communication protection	System and information integrity
IN: Continual innovation	I	-	I	I	D	D	I	-	-	-	I	I	-	D	I	D	I	I
IN: Performance measurement	I	-	I	I	D	D	I	-	-	-	I	I	-	D	I	D	D	I
IN: Gap analysis	I	-	I	I	D	D	I	-	-	-	I	I	-	D	I	D	I	I

As you can see in Table 7.5, all of the control families that have a relationship with the practice areas of the Innovate capability are in some way identifying or actioning innovation opportunities. Innovation opportunities actioned in the Governance/Execution loop aim to create or improve existing capabilities to ensure they are fit for use and purpose. The Strategy/Governance loop handles innovation opportunities involving policies or strategy-risk realignment.

7.4   Applied GQM and QO–QM: The role of performance measurement

QO–QM is an aspect of the CPD Model. The fundamental principle of the model is simple: the value delivered by the business must be created and protected at a level that corresponds to its importance to the organization. A value that is not protected has no value.

There are three aspects of value:

● Value requires a point of view (to whom is this valuable?)
● Merge the two activities (digital value creation and digital value protection) so that they are concurrent activities, not serial
● Value (to the consumer of the value) must be maintained and improved as part of the organizational core capability.

The CPD Model provides two primary loops: one is the Strategy/Governance loop, the other is the Governance/ Execution loop. QO–QM is an approach to demonstrate how outcomes contribute to value by developing metrics to gauge how organizational activities reflect strategic intent. It is our adaptation of GQM+Strategies (goal, question, metric plus strategy).[68] GQM+Strategies is itself an adaptation of GQM.

7.4.1   What is GQM?

As its name suggests, there are three parts to the GQM approach:

- **Goal** The conceptual level from a specific point of view
- **Question** The operational-level questions necessary to achieve the goal
- **Metrics** The quantitative level associated with each question.

The overall purpose of GQM is to ensure that you have the appropriate metrics to answer the questions that support the achievement of the goal. Using GQM applies a circular approach to refine all three parts (see Figure 2.1).

Define **goals** for products, practices, resources, and other areas. Anything that requires useful metrics is a candidate for GQM. Goals represent targets for achievement and define a gap. The best way to create goals for GQM is in a team, not individually. Why is this so? We've discussed the importance of cross-domain teams on more than one occasion. That also applies to working through GQM. Cross-domain knowledge makes it more likely that the GQM team will include (i.e., not overlook) relevant goal aspects. Cross-domain GQM teams also ensure that goals represent the gaps subject to measurement.

Questions address the operational level of GQM. Goals are not cast in concrete; the creation of questions may lead to goal revision (Figure 2.1). Questions have a quantifiable basis – you will create metrics to answer the questions. A quantifiable basis supports quantitative and qualitative questions, provided that a basis exists to quantify the answer (e.g., using Likert scales [Vinney, 2019]). Questions also serve to support buy-in for the goal, if appropriate.

Metrics answer quantitative questions that will support your understanding of how you will know whether you've achieved an aspect of the goal. Approach the creation of metrics from the systems thinking perspective, which we've reviewed many times. Avoid local optimizations, focusing on the part of the task instead of the product or outcomes.

Metrics come in two forms: quantitative/objective and qualitative/subjective. Objective metrics have a measurable value: e.g., hours spent on task X, or documentation exists to support a specific aspect of the goal (true/false). Subjective metrics require a point of view, expressed in the goal. In the same way that questions may lead to refining the goal, analyzing the questions may also lead to refining.

Any metric may apply to multiple questions without having to be rewritten.

7.4.1.1   General GQM template

If you're familiar with agile *stories*, you have one possible way to start the process of writing goals. An agile story takes the following form:

As a ____, I want to _____ so that ____ (as determined or measured by _____).

The first two parts of this statement represent the goal and the point of view. The third part addresses the issue or object. The last part addresses a start toward creating metrics.

---

68   GQM+Strategies is a registered trademark of the Fraunhofer Institute for Experimental Software Engineering, Germany and the Fraunhofer USA Center for Experimental Software Engineering, Maryland (Basili *et al.*, n.d.-a).

7.4.1.2 How to use GQM

The overall GQM flow starts with assembling the right people for the team with appropriate cross-domain knowledge. The next step is to create and agree on the goals. With the goals at hand, write the qualitative and quantitative questions. From the questions, derive the metrics. Review the whole set and revise it as needed. Then repeat for the next goal.

Record the metrics and establish an infrastructure to support the measurement program. It is essential to treat measurement as an integral part of project activities. As measurement data arrives, analyze it, focusing on the goals. Are things progressing within tolerances? If so, keep going; if not, take appropriate action.

Recall that goals should have a point of view. The point of view establishes the roles that interpret the result – this is essential for qualitative questions.

Use GQM metrics only to support the determination and achievement of the associated goals; using the resulting metrics outside of a GQM context is not the intent of the approach, and may lead to unintended consequences.

Figure 7.2 illustrates the relationship between the three parts of GQM. Notice the bottom two metrics relate to more than one question.

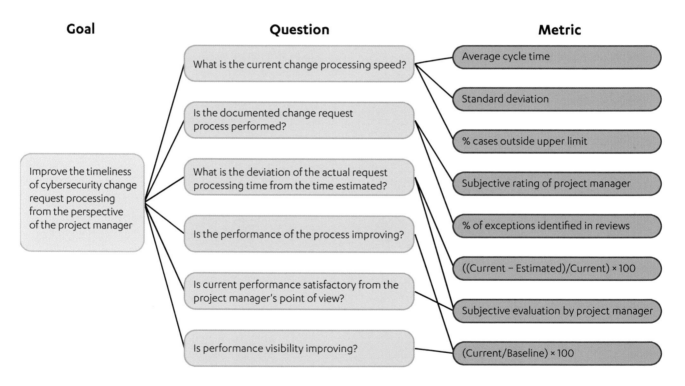

Figure 7.2 GQM example mapping of goals to questions to metrics

When does it make sense to use GQM? This question is answered by understanding the use cases[69] for GQM. While many people think use cases are for software development, they originated in the telecommunications industry. They apply to anything with interactions between entities (called *actors* or *systems*).

---

69   There is a special case of use cases called "misuse cases." A misuse case describes the process of executing a malicious act against the system, which would be useful for the exercises in section 2.2. You can find more information about misuse cases on Wikipedia (2021b).

7.4.2　What is QO–QM?

Before diving into QO–QM, we present a brief overview of GQM⁺Strategies. GQM⁺Strategies is an extension of GQM.

> *"The GQM+ Strategies approach ... makes the business goals, strategies, and corresponding software goals explicit. Strategies are formulated that deal with business goals such as improving customer satisfaction, garnering market share, reducing production costs, and more, taking into account the context and making explicit any assumptions."*
> Basili *et al.* (n.d.-a)[70]

One of the fundamental aims of GQM⁺Strategies is to ensure that the metrics reflect the relationship between development goals-related activities and the business-level strategy it supports. QO–QM provides the link at a strategy-risk level to support organizational resilience.

7.4.2.1　How it fits

Change is a constant. While this statement might seem like an oxymoron, it highlights that the organizational ability to change must be a core, mission-critical capability. QO–QM provides means to link strategy-risk intent with its operational execution. It supports creating new mental models[71] that form the basis for new responses to events.

Successful implementation depends on ensuring the alignment between strategy-risk and operational intent. QO–QM links strategy with appropriate operational measures and metrics. Input to QO–QM in the CPD Model includes the policies generated in the Strategy/Governance loop. The output of QO–QM provides an input to the alignment of strategic and operational intent that guides the measurement and metrics critical to the Governance/Execution loop.

From this perspective, QO–QM enables the auditor and implementor to develop appropriate metrics representative of their points of view. Integrating the 3D Knowledge Model allows combining the perspectives of working *on* the system and working *in* the system.

This approach provides clarity and focuses on what matters, the delivery and protection of digital business value. It seeks feedback to understand value gaps, operating on the assumption that there are two change-related issues: external change causing an organizational reaction, and the critical internal core mission capability to change.

7.4.2.2　Strategy-risk

The CPD Model treats risk as an intrinsic aspect of strategy – encapsulated in the concept of strategy-risk as a single entity. An organization *must* adopt an ERM framework so that the entirety of its business strategy is risk-informed. The basis for the CPD Model is simple: every aspect of strategy requires an understanding of risk. The model presents the idea as a single concept, "strategy-risk." Like "space-time," the two elements of strategy-risk exist together and cannot be separated.

QO–QM is fundamental for developing the link between strategic and operational intent. Later, in the Governance/Execution loop, we'll see how the measures and metrics identified here are used to instrument the DVMS to capture the desired metrics. The Governance/Execution and Strategy/Governance loops create the

---

70　Also see Mandic *et al.* (2010).
71　Think of mental models as internal simulations that frame actions in response to events.

dynamic capability of the CPD Model to continually seek to minimize gaps in strategy-risk, policies, DVMS, and the creation, protection, and delivery of digital business value.

QO–QM is an approach to ensure the alignment of strategic outcomes, and develops the measures and metrics used to assess the delivered digital business value against the expressed strategic and operational intent. Assess performance gaps to determine opportunities to improve (incremental) or innovate (disruptive) the delivery of digital business value. Remember that the 3D Knowledge Model is essential to the CPD Model and applying QO–QM.

Before we cover the details of QO–QM, we need to understand its origins. As stated previously, QO–QM is based on GQM[+]Strategies.

7.4.2.3   Systems thinking and mental models

We've covered systems thinking (Chapter 3) and the need to see the whole. This section addresses the role of the mental model in systems thinking as applied to QO–QM.

The first step in creating, fixing, or improving something is understanding the expected outcomes from the effort. Creating or improving value starts with understanding the solution and the appropriate degree of protection. Fixing or improving requires an understanding of what is broken and why.

We must understand what is required to resolve the issues raised by creating, fixing, or improving before embarking on the appropriate activities. We "think" solutions into existence that fit the appropriate aspects of the organizational history and our experience. This "thinking" results in either using an existing mental model or creating a new one.

Our mental models depend on three things:

● The content of our models
● The filters used to determine what fits a model and what doesn't
● The determinations applied to improve or adjust the model content and input filters.

A typical mental model combines factors contributing to successful outcomes, called *critical success factors* (CSFs). These factors are usually independent of each other. If there is a problem with an outcome, it is traced back to a linear cause, with the expectation that addressing the cause will have near-immediate results. One often-seen result from this approach is that a fix "here" has unintended consequences "there." CSFs don't work in the CPD Model (see Figure 7.3).

A mental model created from a systems thinking perspective incorporates a two-way dynamic that views factors as interdependent, not independent; causation can be bidirectional.[72] Further, in a system, impacts are both non-instantaneous and nonlinear.

QO–QM requires different thinking and mental models, leading to different questions that consider all three aspects of the 3D Knowledge Model. One of the reasons why a different way of thinking is required is that QO–QM is a team activity, not an individual effort. The team members reflect different perspectives, including implementor and auditor, working together to create, protect, and deliver digital business value.

---

72   This is consistent with earlier material about a system. Specifically: no part of a system, or collection of parts of a system, has an independent effect; and a system is not the sum of its parts; it is the product of their interactions. You cannot improve the parts of a system separately; performance of a system depends on how the parts fit and interact, not how they are taken separately. The structure of a system influences the behaviors within the system.

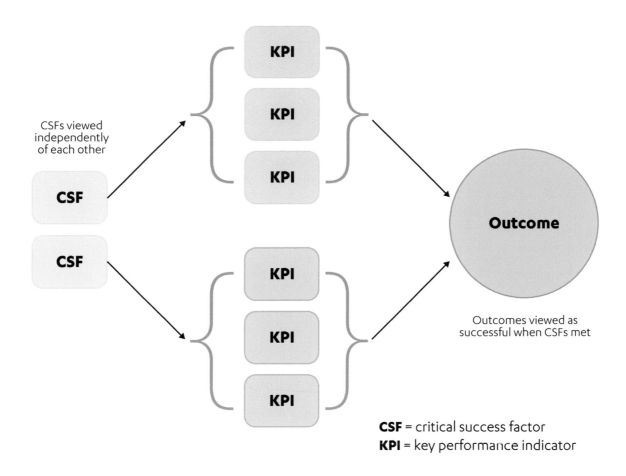

CSFs viewed
independently
of each other

CSF

CSF

KPI

KPI

KPI

KPI

KPI

KPI

Outcome

Outcomes viewed as
successful when CSFs met

CSF = critical success factor
KPI = key performance indicator

Figure 7.3 What's wrong with critical success factors?

7.4.2.4 Think differently: Learn to ask (different) questions

Applying this knowledge requires us to think differently about the questions we ask that lead us to the thing we measure. We need to ask different questions.

One of the fundamental principles of the CPD Model is to "adopt and apply systems thinking."

All systems tend toward disorganization. The behaviors within a system depend on its structure. Adopting systems thinking enables an organization to see the "whole" system and its behaviors. To make changes "sticky," the organization must work to change both the structure and the behaviors to bring the system's output within acceptable tolerances.

Fundamental to systems thinking is variable and sometimes indeterminate latency between cause[73] and the observation or detection of the related effect. Understanding latency enables better decision-making to effect change in a system.

---

73   Causation in any system is about behaviors within the system. It can be the behaviors of people, hardware, software, or other systems, or some combination of these.

7.4.2.5 Question Outcome–Question Metric (QO–QM) explained

During the height of the Covid-19 pandemic, one of the authors was asked to answer a question about the easiest skill to learn to do something in cybersecurity. The answer provided included the following:

> *"In response to the question, 'What's the best and easiest skill to learn in cybersecurity?', you've already started. You asked a question. Perhaps one of the most important skills everyone needs to learn is to ask better questions."*

As noted in section 2.1.1, you only get answers to the questions you ask. If you want better answers, you must ask better questions. In that section, we suggested a partial list of questions for different purposes:

- Opening doors
- Connecting and engaging with others
- Generating or improving ideas.

For QO–QM, we add another:

- Seeking to verify and validate an outcome that might include understanding or developing a different perspective to potentially get out of a rut.

This approach and additional thought led to the development of QO–QM. To see the whole, to operate within the context of the CPD Model requires that we avoid questions that lead to thinking along the lines of "Can we do X?" We need to ask different questions that enable us to focus on the whole.

- Questions that ask about an outcome in the context of the 3D Knowledge Model:
  - How does the outcome for team A impact (or how is it impacted by) team B?
  - How does the Z-axis impact the outcome?

- Questions that address strategy-risk. Not just what is the risk, but what are the thresholds:
  - When (not if) something happens, what is the organizational risk?
  - If the impact of the event exceeds the organizational tolerances, how do we respond? What can we learn?
    - If the event's impact was within tolerances, what can we learn? Do we need to adjust the tolerances? And so on

- How does "this" event impact the development teams?

From this perspective, QO–QM is a revised and simplified version of GQM⁺Strategies designed to work with the CPD Model. QO–QM is GQM with an added set of questions designed to link strategy-risk[74] with business outcomes. Start by asking questions about the strategy-risk objectives to clarify the outcome intent – the "O" in QO–QM represents the goal in GQM. The difference is in the initial questions that specifically address the goal in the broader strategic context as represented by the 3D Knowledge Model. Following the outcome refinement, QO–QM proceeds in the same way as GQM. While it is still possible that the quantifiable questions might cause outcome revision, the intent is to address the strategic fit first.

Figure 7.4 illustrates where QO–QM fits into a high-level overview of the CPD Model.

---

74 The practical application of QO–QM depends on the organization crafting unambiguous strategy-risk policies.

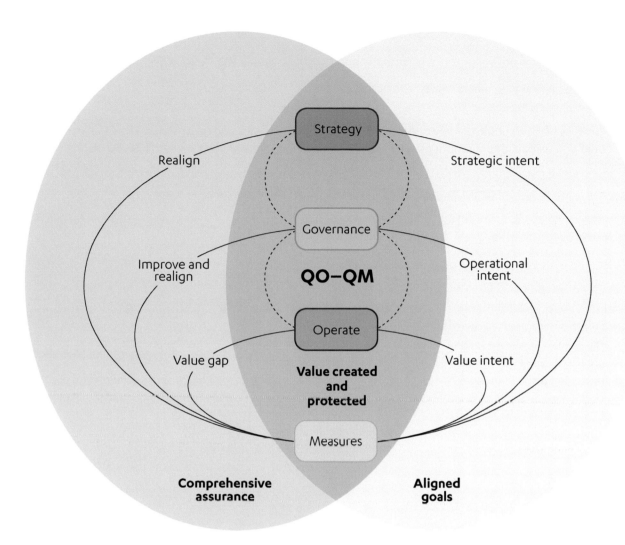

Figure 7.4 Where QO–QM fits

7.4.2.6   QO–QM implemented

As noted above, QO–QM is a team activity. Before explicitly starting down the first stage of questions in QO–QM, assemble the right team that covers the various stakeholders potentially affected by the selected goal. The team members represent the specific technical aspects of the goal and the 3D Knowledge Model. The team should also include people representing the implementor's and auditor's points of view.

7.4.2.7 Tell a story to generate questions

It is possible to borrow from agile stories to form the questions associated with metrics. For example:

As a____(POV)____I want to____(accomplish something)____so that____(outcome achieved) as determined by____(metric)____.

This type of story leads to point-of-view questions regarding the outcomes and the metrics. The associated metrics could be qualitative or quantitative. For example, from the users' perspective, is the performance improving?

If the point of view is not pertinent for this QO–QM (or GQM) outcome, change the story:

When____(N)____happens, we need to____(respond or accomplish something)____so that____(outcome achieved)__ as determined by____(metric)____.

In this case, the issue is not about a point of view; it addresses an event. When X happens, what is the response, what do we expect, and how will we know?

Implementors ask questions that result in metrics addressing "what" and "how"; auditors ask questions that result in metrics addressing, "How will we know?"

The organization can change the structure or behaviors to bring the system output within acceptable tolerances.

Fundamental to systems thinking is the idea that there is variable latency between cause (behaviors) and the observation or detection of the related effect. Understanding latency enables better decision-making in effecting change in a system.

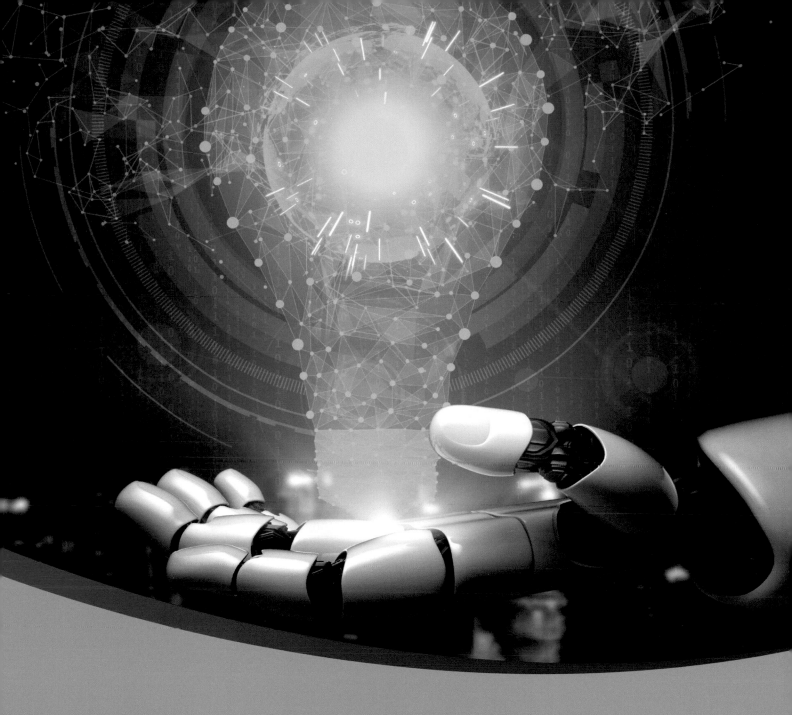

CHAPTER 8
The DVMS as a scalable overlay

8 The DVMS as a scalable overlay

The DVMS is a scalable overlay that enables any organization to treat value creation and value protection as aspects of quality, regardless of size. Earlier in this book, we have provided brief glimpses into the scalable nature of the DVMS; this chapter ties the pieces together.

8.1 Scalability? How?

Frameworks are descriptive: they describe what to do, not how to do it. Methods provide concrete guidelines to accomplish something without necessarily providing a way to adopt or adapt them. In addition, frameworks and methods don't always easily scale – or at least don't provide an approach to scalability other than adapting or tailoring.

The difference between a framework, method, and the DVMS is simple: it's not intended to be one-size-fits-all; as an overlay, it's adaptable by all, regardless of size. How is this possible?

8.1.1 DVMS overlay layers

The DVMS is a system. The best way to conceptualize this system is to think of the DVMS drawn on three sheets of very low-opacity tracing paper (Wikipedia, 2022q).

- The top sheet is an amoeba-like "blob" that represents any organization. Everything inside the organization is a black box to the outside world. This black box encapsulates every system, framework, method, or approach the organization currently uses
- The middle layer is the Z-X Model. It represents a set of minimum viable capabilities shared by all organizations. Every organization needs the following capabilities:

  - **Governance** Provide appropriate governance that forms the basis for the organizational rules. Governance defines "How we conduct business"
  - **Assurance** Provide appropriate assurance that the organization does the right things, the right way (e.g., conformance to the governance policies)
  - **Plan** Represents the (planning) effort that enables the organization to operationalize the governance and assurance of the Z-X Model core capabilities – what to do and the rules to do it
  - **Design** Enables the organization to create a cohesive approach to creating, protecting, and delivering digital business value – how to do it with available resources, etc.
  - **Change** Enables the organization to adapt to its environment
  - **Execute** Represents the practice areas that create, protect, and deliver digital business value
  - **Innovate** Seeks opportunities to improve the creation, protection, and delivery of digital business value

- The bottom layer is the CPD Model. Organization size is irrelevant to the model, which is an abstraction of what every organization must do to create and protect digital business value. Some organizations may apply a more formal approach than others – and that's not only acceptable, it must be that way for the three layers to be considered an overlay.

Each layer provides the means to operationalize the layer above. The Z-X Model represents the MVCs that must exist in the top layer. If any of the capabilities are missing or followed ad hoc by some business units, departments, groups, or other organizational units, then establish or improve these capabilities first.

Similarly, if any capability can't trace or identify how it fits into the CPD Model, then work to make appropriate adaptations. The likelihood is that what the organization does fits the model with some "mental retooling" and minor organizational adjustments.

The size of the organization does not matter. The purpose of the overlay is to expose gaps in organizational performance. Every organization can demonstrate some level of maturity for the MVCs that make up the Z-X Model.

8.1.2   How the DVMS scales

The DVMS is a scalable system that overlays any organization, from a small one-person business to a large multinational, including for-profit and not-for-profit, private and public entities. The DVMS is not limited to a particular sector.

How is this possible? The critical word here is "overlay." To visualize the DVMS, think of it as a system composed of three layers:

- **The DVMS layer** exposes the flows of communication, innovation, and work represented within the 3D Knowledge Model (intra-team, inter-team, and overall strategy, vision, and mission) (see Figure 3.7). At this level, it's essential to examine and understand the three flows – the first requirement is to understand the "system" that is "your" organization. Don't forget to include partners and suppliers when you examine the Y-axis

- **The Z-X Model** is composed of two parts. First, Governance and Assurance provide a wrapper around the operational aspect of the model. Second, the five core capabilities in the Z-X Model (Plan, Design, Change, Execute, Innovate) represent the active part of the model that brings together Governance and Assurance (see Figure 4.1). At this layer, it's essential to understand how the organization applies the seven capabilities within the Z-X Model

- **The CPD Model** represents a drill-down from the Z-X Model to provide the details that bring the Z-X Model to life (see Figure 3.5).

Moving through the layers requires more detailed knowledge and understanding of the organization. The approach we suggest is:

- **Stabilize** At the DVMS layer, strive to understand the flows in the context of the 3D Knowledge Model

- **Optimize** At the Z-X Model layer, work to improve the MVCs

- **Innovate** Start at the adapt aspect in the middle of the CPD Model. Use it to understand and close performance gaps with appropriate innovations (incremental, sustaining, adaptive, and disruptive) combined with system leverage points.

Notice that the preceding discussion does not mention cybersecurity. The DVMS addresses the creation and protection of digital business value; that's a statement we've made many times. The DVMS, combined with a principle-based ERM framework, represents a systems approach that addresses digital business risk management.

This last idea is essential. Cybersecurity should not be the goal; instead, the goal should be to create and protect digital business value by applying a strategy-risk approach to managing digital business risk, thereby achieving cyber resilience. The goal should be organizational resilience that includes cyber resilience – not just cybersecurity – you get cybersecurity as a by-product of the application of strategy-risk as part of digital business risk management and the integration of the selected cybersecurity IRs.

8.1.3   Identify and close performance gaps

Using the DVMS as an overlay requires a set of measurements to quantify and close performance gaps. We recommend starting with the Digital Value Capability Maturity Model (DVCMM).[75]

The DVCMM material describes characteristics of its four levels in the context of capability-related practice areas. This approach ties the Z-X Model to the CPD Model and the organization-created processes. The creation of processes is explicitly left to the organization. The desired outcomes for the practices form the basis for the organization to create processes to monitor, measure, and produce those outcomes.

It is critical to approach gap analysis, and the resulting activities to close a gap in a complex adaptive system, by considering the questions described as part of the iceberg model – remember, the application of leverage to a system has various latency factors.

It is also essential to recall the overarching goal of using digital business risk management in the organizational context as necessary to create, protect, and deliver digital business value.

8.2   Continual innovation

The DVMS operates an overlay system that supports digital business risk management by applying strategy-risk. By combining what might be separate organizational entities into one, the purpose is to ensure digital business risk is considered in everything the organization does.

The basis for the architecture of the DVMS layers was managing digital business risk – the essence of creating, protecting, and delivering digital business value. We also use continual innovation rather than continual improvement; it allows labeling multiple layers of changes to the organization: from incremental and sustaining, which impact the Governance/Execution loop of the CPD Model (Figure 8.1), to adaptive and disruptive, which impact the Strategy/Governance loop (Figure 8.2).

---

75   Discussed in sections 4.1.2 and 4.2.3.6. As noted in the former section, the DVCMM is an adaptation of the US Department of Energy's Cybersecurity Capability Maturity Model (C2M2) for use with the DVMS, the Z-X Model, and the CPD Model.

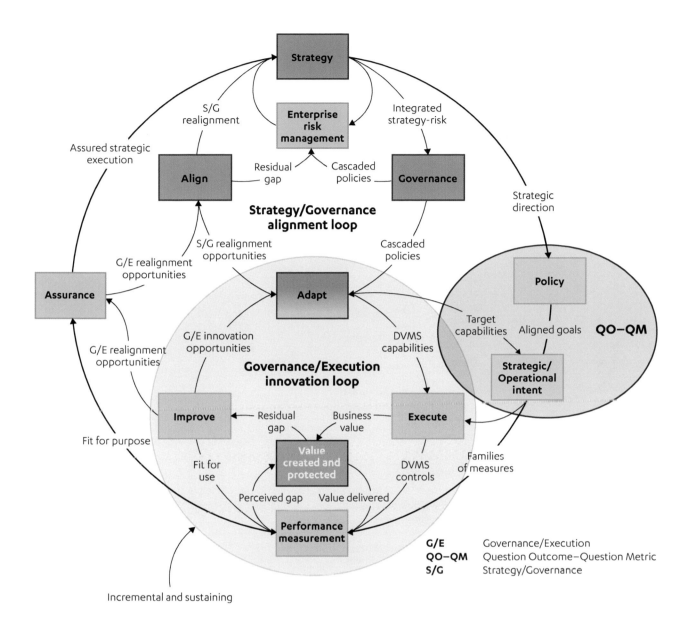

Figure 8.1 Incremental and sustaining innovation focuses on the Governance/Execution loop

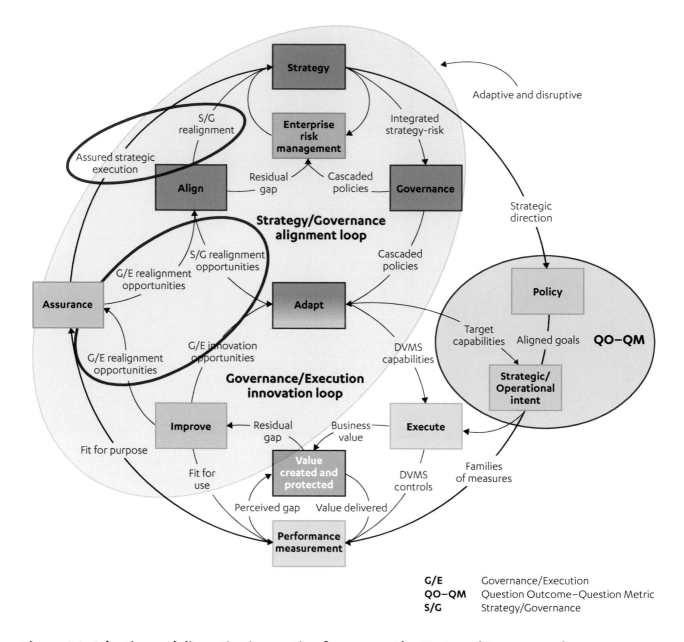

Figure 8.2 Adaptive and disruptive innovation focuses on the Strategy/Governance loop

8.2.1 Aspects of innovation

When we talk about innovation, we refer to introducing something new or changing something that already exists. We use it to categorize the introduction of new things within the CPD Model.

How are new things introduced in your organization? Does your organization understand the scope of the change? How small is small? How big is big? We use *innovation* to categorize introducing something new so that there is a clear understanding of what constitutes an improvement to system behavior (sections 3.1 and 3.2).

In the following section, we'll discuss the four aspects of innovation (see Figure 5.19).

8.2.2 Innovation and the CPD Model

Searching for "aspects of innovation" returns an interesting and eclectic collection of "innovation" approaches. Our approach is an abstraction of several product marketing approaches to dealing with innovation. Because the essence of the CPD Model is grounded in digital business risk, it forces ongoing evaluation of value created to ensure it is appropriately protected; this abstraction works best for three reasons:

- Value has stakeholders, and stakeholders have a point of view
- The CPD Model layer of the DVMS is an abstraction of a system that evaluates the scope of an improvement
- The four aspects of innovation fully support digital business risk management.

8.2.2.1 Incremental

Incremental innovations are gradual, continual improvements in organizational capability. The new things introduced are small. Each additional improvement builds on the previous modifications, progressively changing the organizational capabilities. These improvements are usually in response to minor changes in the operating environment. Performance gaps identify innovation opportunities necessary to stay within the tolerances of the organizational capabilities.

Imagine an organization needs to expand its customer-facing support services by introducing a consumer version of its business software product. The expansion of services includes adding three hours of support staff availability. These expanded hours of operation impact the system backup schedule, and the anticipated support volume requires additional storage space. Both changes represent small and measured changes to organizational capabilities, such as modifying the backup schedule, updating the runbook, and adding further volume sets.

8.2.2.2 Sustaining

Sustaining innovation is a significant improvement to sustain existing capabilities relative to the organizational context. This innovation opportunity represents a broader performance gap in an organizational capability. It deals with existing capabilities, not new ones. Its use applies when an organization needs to achieve a new level of competitive performance. Sustaining innovations, like incremental ones, identify necessary opportunities that stay within the tolerances of the organizational capabilities.

Example: Sales technology

An organization discovers that a competitor's sales force can use a mobile device to configure a product, take an order, and confirm product delivery dates. The organization identifies a significant performance gap that must be closed to retain parity in servicing its customer base. Consequently, it identifies several changes to its business systems to close the gap, including enabling technology, and adding or updating behavior patterns for its sales and administrative staff. Updates to the order-taking practices are needed, along with additional functionality being added to the server and mobile applications, increases in database storage, and training for the sales and administrative staff. You get the idea. However, the improvements needed fall within the tolerances established by strategic policies for this capability.

8.2.2.3 Adaptive

Adaptive innovation represents a change to how the organization does something; this change results from or causes a shift in policy. An adaptive innovation opportunity identifies performance gaps in organizational capabilities. However, in this case, the organizational capabilities are fit for use and purpose (operating efficiently and effectively as designed). In other words, they are operating within their design envelope. This type of innovation identifies changes needed to policies derived from business objectives in strategy-risk. Policies are the tools the organization uses to guide the creation or improvement of organizational capabilities.

Let's look at the example described above. Instead of matching the competitor's capability, the organization could realign its organizational policies to create a competitive advantage by adding the capability to use manufacturing resource planning information to plan, track, and publish delivery dates. The realigned policies bring the organizational capabilities into realignment with an existing business objective expressed in strategy-risk. The realignment of the policies occurs within the Strategy/Governance loop. The changes resulting from the changed policies occur in the Governance/Execution loop. The policy changes remain within the tolerances established by the objective within strategy-risk.

8.2.2.4 Disruptive

Disruptive innovation represents a strategic change that identifies unfulfilled gaps that disrupt the environment when closed. This type of innovation causes the organizational environment (other organizations, competitors, nations, etc.) to react. It raises the competitive bar, and it does so to disrupt its competitors. Every organization has core, mission-critical capabilities that differentiate it in its marketplace (competitive landscape: commercial, political, or military). These actions that impact these core, mission-critical capabilities occur within the Strategy/Governance loop and result in modified business objectives expressed in strategy-risk. Policies derived from the business objectives are subsequently adapted to provide management guidelines to create or improve organizational capabilities necessary to deliver business outcomes that achieve those goals.

Let's expand on the scenario above. The organization services a diverse business-to-business (B2B) community. It wants to use artificial intelligence (AI) to understand shifts in buying patterns, which enables it to anticipate orders, improve raw material acquisition, streamline its supply chain, and optimize manufacturing capabilities. The goal is to provide an optimized customer self-service capability, radically enhancing the customer experience.

Wow – none of this exists, and once it does, the organization will be the only competitor in its market space with this capability. The company anticipates it can reinvest cost savings realized through supply chain optimization in research and development (R&D) and lead the market in new product innovation. It must realign its strategy-risk objectives, align its strategic outcomes, and promulgate updated policies for management to follow and execute in the Governance/Execution loop.

8.2.2.5 A point of view

Anything of value has a stakeholder, and stakeholders have a point of view. The CPD Model subsumes the stakeholders' points of view by expressing strategic and operational intent and the measures and metrics necessary to ensure that the organizational capabilities are fit for use and purpose (Figure 8.3). When organizational capabilities are created or improved, the implementors and auditors ensure the capabilities are adequately "instrumented" so the appropriate measures and metrics are produced during execution.

The implementor's point of view is about building to the design specification, and operation as designed. The auditor's point of view seeks to assess the capabilities' warranty and utility, or fitness for use and purpose (covered in more detail in section 8.2.3). The resulting instrumentation of organizational capabilities is used by performance measurement to identify performance gaps or innovation opportunities.

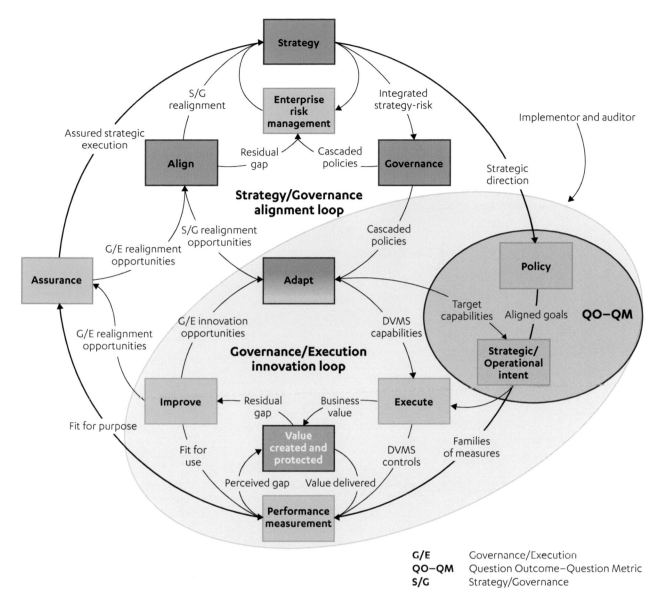

Figure 8.3 Innovation and a point of view

8.2.2.6 Applying leverage

The CPD Model is an abstraction of a system of systems that represents how an organization adapts and thrives in its environment. An understanding of innovation allows the organization to understand and innovate with knowledge and the ability to correctly identify and scope innovation opportunities to ensure the appropriate leverage points are used to effect the desired changes in organizational capabilities and performance. The reality of dealing with complex systems is that you don't try to change them, but coax them into behaving the way you want.

Coaxing a complex adaptive system does not happen in a vacuum. The mere application of leverage does not guarantee the results without putting the right things in place to achieve those results. Recall what we said about a system: it is not the sum of its parts; it's the product of their interactions. While the application of low-order leverage may be relatively simple, as the people impact of the leverage increases, and as the interaction ripple effect increases, the more it requires the application of the 3D Knowledge Model to ensure proper transparency, combined with organizational change management. To put this another way: applying leverage may be complicated.

8.2.3   The CPD Model and innovation

When we discuss innovation in the context of the CPD Model (Figure 8.4), we discuss how organizational capabilities change to adapt to its performance in its environment. The CPD Model uses the expressed strategic and operational intent (measures and metrics) to identify performance gaps in organizational capabilities. The organization seeks assurance of the organizational capabilities' warranty (fitness for use) and utility (fitness for purpose).

The concepts of utility and warranty can be challenging to understand. *Utility* refers to functionality, or what the organizational capability does. Questions around utility revolve around whether it is fit for its intended purpose – does it do the right things? We define *warranty* as how the organizational capability does what it does. Specifically, is it fit for use? Another way to think about it is to ask, "Is it free from defective materials or workmanship?" Utility asks, "Does it do the right things?"; warranty asks, "And does it do them the right way?"

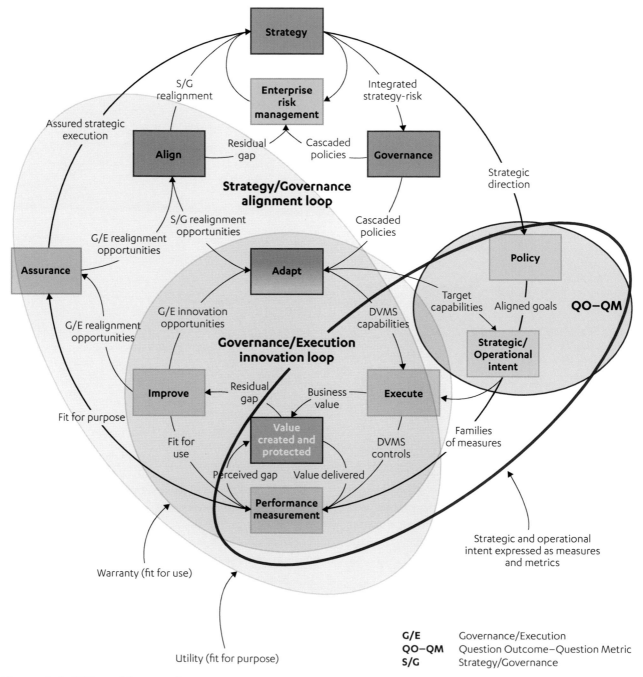

Figure 8.4   CPD and innovation

G/E	Governance/Execution
QO–QM	Question Outcome–Question Metric
S/G	Strategy/Governance

8.2.3.1 Utility

The concept of utility is based on the organizational need to assure the execution of its strategic policies. Management uses strategic policies as guidelines for creating and improving existing organizational capabilities, requiring assurance of four things:

- The organizational capabilities' fitness for use
- Their fitness for purpose
- That they produce the expected stakeholder value
- The execution of strategic policies.

Aspects of utility include:

- **Fitness for purpose** Fitness for purpose assures the organization that the organizational capabilities are efficient, effective, and fulfilling their intended purpose
- **Does the right things** It's good to be efficient and effective, but it's also great if the organizational capabilities are doing the right things in the right way. While there may be many ways to achieve the desired outcome, the "right way" is optimized, maximizing efficiency and effectiveness
- **Conforms to appropriate documentation (specifications, requirements, or design) that includes experience** The important part of this aspect of utility is that it includes the stakeholder's experience. Value is determined by the "customer" or, in our case, the stakeholders, which may consist of customers. Imagine calling an organization seeking to place an order only to go through nine levels of phone menu hell before being put in a queue with terrible music on hold
- **Experience of consumer and provider considered** The importance of the stakeholder experience within these two stakeholder groups cannot be understated. Strategic policies should be inclusive of guidelines on stakeholder experience. Such policies are used to create or improve existing organizational capabilities and express strategic and operational intent, which is used to identify appropriate measures and metrics for the expected stakeholder experience
- **Verifying requirements are met** This is circular to some extent, because it is measuring the measures and metrics used to identify performance gaps and assure execution of strategic policies. The organization must look at the data and determine the reliability and validity of the measures and metrics used to express strategic and operational intent. Knowledge management plays an integral role in this aspect of utility.

8.2.3.2 Warranty

Strategic policies establish the organizational guidelines to create or improve existing capabilities. The target capabilities are used to express operational intent: these are the capabilities we want, and this is how we're going to achieve them. Consider the "what we want" to be like specifications. The "how" becomes the requirements used to plan and design new or improved organizational capabilities.

Aspects of warranty include:

- **Fitness for use** We need a bridge to span a river that can carry trucks transporting raw materials and finished goods. So, we can determine its required span and load, assess the geological constraints, plan, design, and build the bridge. Does it span the river and carry the designed load?
- **Stakeholder experience** We now have a bridge that accommodates the free flow of goods across the river. The local stakeholders – government, industry, workers, etc. – experience benefit from the bridge. Expectations are met
- **Validating external stakeholder expectations** The external stakeholders' experience benefits from the bridge. Does the experience of the expanded benefits meet their expectations? Perhaps they expected the bridge to carry heavier loads, be less congested during working hours, or maybe be free of tolls.

It is essential to note that "value" depends on the combination of utility and warranty, not one or the other.

8.3 Digital business risk and resilience

> *"Resilience is all about being able to overcome the unexpected. Sustainability is about survival. The goal of resilience is to thrive."*
> Futurist Jamais Cascio

By creating a CPD program, an organization can stabilize its capabilities, assess its performance gaps, optimize its capabilities, and implement new or improved capabilities necessary to achieve the MVCs.

Figure 8.5 illustrates the knowledge domains for an organization to achieve the necessary MVCs to create, protect, and deliver digital business value. Digital business risk management includes cybersecurity, but it is not about cybersecurity.

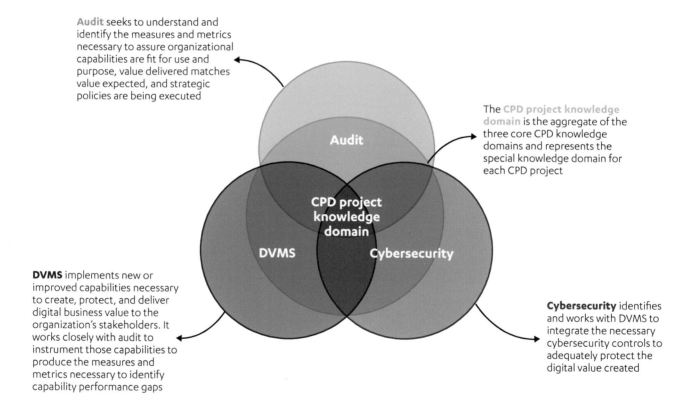

Audit seeks to understand and identify the measures and metrics necessary to assure organizational capabilities are fit for use and purpose, value delivered matches value expected, and strategic policies are being executed

The **CPD project knowledge domain** is the aggregate of the three core CPD knowledge domains and represents the special knowledge domain for each CPD project

DVMS implements new or improved capabilities necessary to create, protect, and deliver digital business value to the organization's stakeholders. It works closely with audit to instrument those capabilities to produce the measures and metrics necessary to identify capability performance gaps

Cybersecurity identifies and works with DVMS to integrate the necessary cybersecurity controls to adequately protect the digital value created

Figure 8.5 CPD project knowledge domain

Figure 8.6 illustrates how to implement what we've discussed in both *Fundamentals of Adopting the NIST Cybersecurity Framework* and this book. Start by using the Z-X Model practice area outcomes as an informative reference. When combined with cybersecurity informative reference control requirements and evaluated against the DVCMM, they provide an overlay that is usable by any organization to assess performance gaps and build out capabilities that will create, protect, and deliver digital business value.

Figure 8.6 Digital business risk praxis

8.3.1 And there is more!

There will always be more as we explore how to improve digital business risk management. We planned the DVMS books as a series. We plan to provide books exploring each capability in the DVMS Z-X Model, and a book about the DVMS that addresses digital business risk management. Our goal is to provide organizations with cohesive guidance to expand past the MVCs as the organizational maturity grows or the organizational needs change.

> *"In theory, there is no difference between theory and practice. In practice, there is."*
> The great American philosopher Yogi Berra

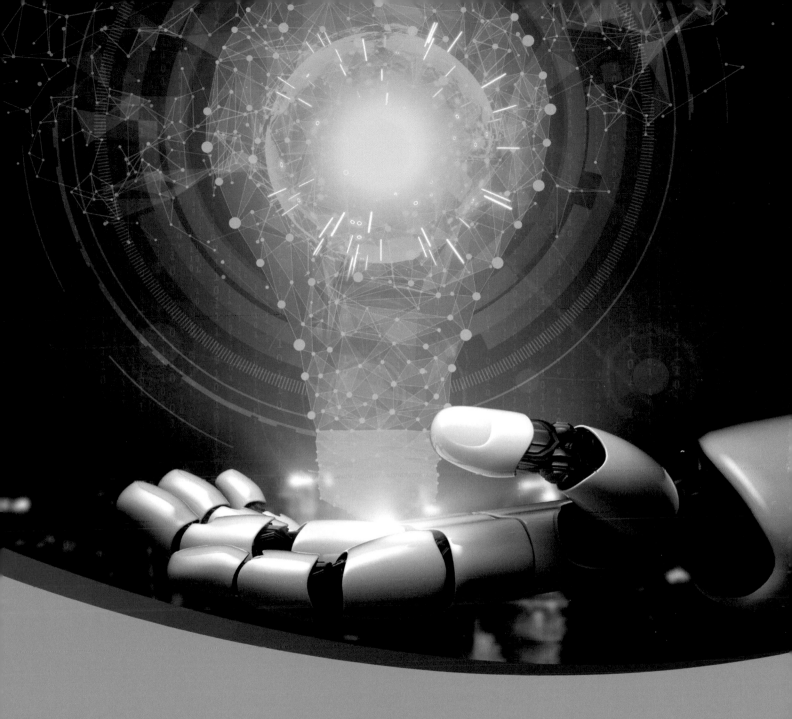

Glossary

Glossary

3D Knowledge Model™
A guide to handling knowledge management mentorship, based on three axes.

adapt
In the NCSP scheme, "adapt" refers to the management decisions that result from the strategic governance decisions to "adopt" a framework or cybersecurity informative reference.

adopt
In the NCSP scheme, "adopt" refers to the strategic governance decision to select and apply a framework or cybersecurity informative reference.

AICPA
American Institute of Certified Public Accountants

capability
In the systems engineering sense, "capability" is defined as the ability to execute a specified course of action. We also use it to aggregate one or more practice areas.
https://en.wikipedia.org/wiki/Capability_(systems_engineering)

COSO
Committee of Sponsoring Organizations of the Treadway Commission

CPD Model
Create, protect, and deliver digital business value is the bottom layer of the DVMS, an abstraction or conceptualization of an organizational operating system.

DVCMM
Digital Value Capability Maturity Model – an adaptation of the US Department of Energy's Cybersecurity Capability Maturity Model (C2M2) for use with the DVMS and the Z-X Model capabilities.

DVMS
The Digital Value Management System™ (DVMS) is the overarching system that delivers digital value to stakeholders. It is composed of three adaptable and scalable layers: the DVMS, the Z-X Model, and the CPD Model. The DVMS is a "black box" to the outside world. It overlays what the organization does and how it produces outcomes for stakeholders. The Z-X Model includes seven core organizational capabilities (Govern/Governance, Assure/Assurance, Plan, Design, Change, Execute, and Innovate). The CPD Model operationalizes the Z-X Model.

DVMS FastTrack™
A structured approach to adapt the NIST-CSF and one or more of its informative references. It provides rapid adaptation, implementation, operation, and improvement of the relevant cybersecurity control families. FastTrack™ addresses adaptation following the strategic decision to adopt the NIST-CSF.

ERM
Enterprise risk management (ERM) in business includes the methods and processes used by organizations to manage risks and seize opportunities related to achieving their objectives.

https://en.wikipedia.org/wiki/Enterprise_risk_management

ERM framework

A framework for risk management. In this context, a framework describes what to do, not how.

governance

The processes of interaction and decision-making among the actors involved in a collective problem that lead to the creation, reinforcement, or reproduction of social norms and institutions. https://arcticyearbook.com/arctic-yearbook/2015/2015-preface

Governance/Assurance loop

The outer loop of the CPD Model. The Governance side turns organizational strategy into policies that are executed to create, protect, and deliver digital business value. The Assurance side assesses the performance of the organizational capabilities that execute the strategic policies, and whether the value created is appropriately protected.

Governance/Execution loop

One of the two main inner loops of the CPD Model. It turns policies into organizational capabilities that create, protect, and deliver digital business value, and measures the organization's capability to execute its strategic and operational intent to produce this value.

GQM

Goal, question, metric (GQM) is an established goal-oriented approach to software metrics to improve and measure software quality. https://en.wikipedia.org/wiki/GQM

GQM⁺Strategies®

An adaptation of GQM, designed to ensure that the metrics reflect the relationship between development-goal-related activities and the business-level strategy.

informative reference (IR)

Informative references are citations of detailed cybersecurity documents to any combination of functions, categories, and subcategories within the NIST-CSF. Informative references demonstrate how a given cybersecurity document can be used in coordination with the framework for cybersecurity risk management. https://www.nist.gov/cyberframework/informative-references

misuse case

The term "misuse case" case is derived from and is the inverse of "use case". It describes executing a deliberate and malicious act against a system, while a use case describes any action taken by the system. https://en.wikipedia.org/wiki/Misuse_case

NIST

The National Institute of Standards and Technology (NIST) is part of the US Department of Commerce, and is one of the oldest physical science laboratories in the US. https://www.nist.gov/

NIST SP 800-53

The full title of this publication is NIST Special Publication 800-53 Revision 5, *Security and Privacy Controls for Information Systems and Organizations*. https://csrc.nist.gov/publications/detail/sp/800-53/rev-5/final

practice

Practices aggregate one or more processes that define or describe how an organization does things.

practice area

Groups of practices that describe what an organization does – not how.

QO–QM

Question Outcome–Question Metric (QO–QM) is an adaptation of the GQM⁺Strategies® approach to fit the CPD Model. It starts by asking about the outcome to assure it aligns with the strategy-risk. Once it is aligned, the outcome becomes the goal for GQM.

risk management

Risk management is the identification, evaluation, and prioritization of risks (defined in ISO 31000 as the effect of uncertainty on objectives) followed by the coordinated and economic application of resources to minimize, monitor, and control the probability or impact of unfortunate events or to maximize the realization of opportunities. https://en.wikipedia.org/wiki/Risk_management

Strategy/Governance loop

One of the two main inner loops of the CPD Model. It turns strategy into policies that are adapted and executed via organizational capabilities, actions, and feedback; these may cause a realignment of policy or strategy.

strategy-risk

A single-entity concept, based on the authors' experience. They found that treating strategy and risk as separate concepts didn't work.

systems thinking

An approach to examining and understanding complex systems by looking at the whole. The performance of a system depends on the interactions of the elements within the system. Each actor within a system has its own unique perspective of the system.

threat actor

In computer security, a threat is a potential adverse action or event that has been facilitated by a vulnerability, resulting in an unwanted impact on a computer system or application. A threat actor is an entity that carries out this action.

use case

A list of actions or event steps that defines the interactions between a role (or actor) and a system to achieve a goal. https://en.wikipedia.org/wiki/Use_case

XaaS (something as a service)

A general term for cloud-based services, such as software as a service and platform as a service.

Z-X Model

The Z-X Model is part of the DVMS. It represents the high-level aspect of the DVMS that executes a strategy. The objective is to recognize and action a value gap. The Z-X Model includes a common set of capability-flows across multiple DVMS adaptations. It defines seven organizational capabilities: Govern/Governance, Assure/Assurance, Plan, Design, Change, Execute, and Innovate. Governance addresses the oversight of organizational control and direction. Assurance addresses the confidence in the efficiency and effectiveness of execution.

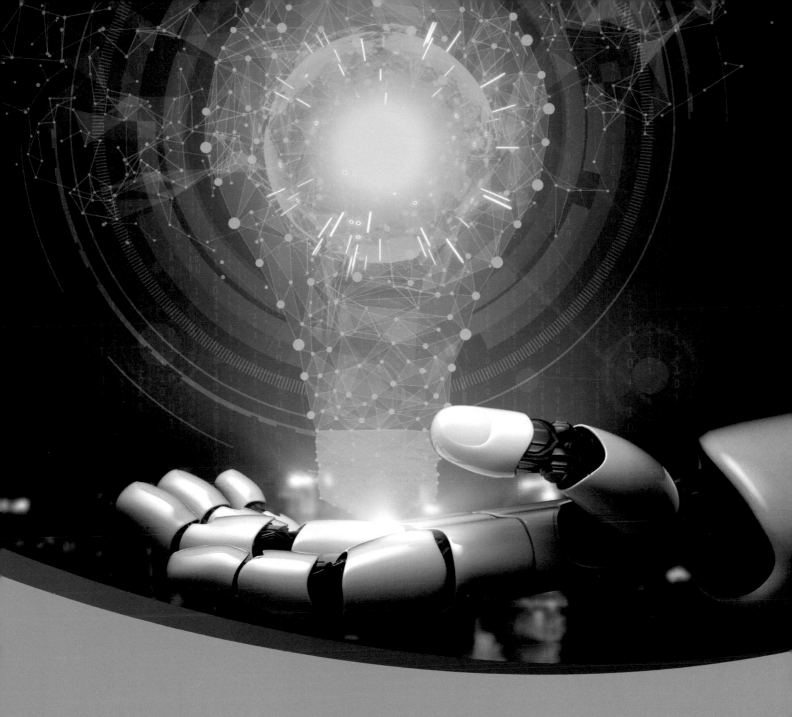

References

References

Ackoff, R. (1979). The future of operational research is past. *Journal of Operational Research Society* 30, 1.

Allen, W. (2016). Complicated or complex – knowing the difference is important. Learning for Sustainability. https://learningforsustainability.net/post/complicated-complex/.

Aronson, D., and Angelakis, D. (n.d.). Step-by-step stocks and flows: Improving the rigor of your thinking. Accessed Jul. 28, 2022. The Systems Thinker. https://thesystemsthinker.com/step-by-step-stocks-and-flows-improving-the-rigor-of-your-thinking/.

Basili, V., Heidrich, J., Lindvall, M., Münch, J., Regardie, M., and Trendowicz, A. (n.d.-a). GQM⁺Strategies – Aligning business strategies with software measurement. Accessed Aug. 6, 2022. Fraunhofer Institute for Experimental Software Engineering, Germany and Maryland; University of Maryland. https://www.cs.umd.edu/users/basili/publications/proceedings/P122.pdf.

Basili, V. R., Caldiera, G, and Rombach, H. D. (n.d.-b). The goal question metric approach. Accessed Aug. 6, 2022. University of Maryland; Universität Kaiserslautern. https://www.cs.umd.edu/~mvz/handouts/gqm.pdf.

Basili, V., Trendowicz, A., Kowalczyk, M., Heidrich, J., Seaman, C., Münch, J., and Rombach, D. (2014). *Aligning Organizations Through Measurement: The GQM⁺Strategies Approach*. Springer, New York.

Braun, W. (2002). The system archetypes. University at Albany, State University of New York. https://www.albany.edu/faculty/gpr/PAD724/724WebArticles/sys_archetypes.pdf.

CIS (n.d.). CIS critical security controls v8: Mapping to NIST 800-53 Rev. 5 (moderate and low baselines). Accessed Aug. 4, 2022. https://www.cisecurity.org/insights/white-papers/cis-controls-v8-mapping-to-nist-800-53-rev-5.

CISA (2022). Insider threat mitigation. Last modified Apr. 6, 2022. https://www.cisa.gov/insider-threat-mitigation.

CISA (n.d.). Free cybersecurity services and tools. Accessed Jul. 25, 2022. https://www.cisa.gov/free-cybersecurity-services-and-tools.

Cockburn, A. (2001). *Writing Effective Use Cases*. Addison-Wesley, Boston, Massachusetts.

COSO (2013). COSO internal control – integrated framework: Executive summary, framework and appendices, and illustrative tools for assessing effectiveness of a system of internal control (3 volume set). AICPA. https://www.aicpa.org/cpe-learning/publication/internal-control-integrated-framework-executive-summary-framework-and-appendices-and-illustrative-tools-for-assessing-effectiveness-of-a-system-of-internal-control-3-volume-set.

COSO (2017). Enterprise risk management: Integrating with strategy and performance – Executive summary. *https://www.coso.org/Shared%20Documents/2017-COSO-ERM-Integrating-with-Strategy-and-Performance-Executive-Summary.pdf.*

COSO (2019). Managing cyber risk in a digital age. https://www.coso.org/Shared%20Documents/COSO-Deloitte-Managing-Cyber-Risk-in-a-Digital-Age.pdf.

Covey, S. M. R. (2008). *The Speed of Trust: The One Thing that Changes Everything*. Free Press, New York.

Crosby, P. B. (1979). *Quality Is Free: The Art of Making Quality Certain*. McGraw-Hill, New York.

Deloitte (2013). Exploring strategic risk: 300 executives around the world say their view of strategic risk is changing. https://www2.deloitte.com/content/dam/Deloitte/global/Documents/Governance-Risk-Compliance/dttl-grc-exploring-strategic-risk.pdf.

Deming, W. E. (1982). *Out of the Crisis. MIT Press*, Cambridge, Massachusetts.

EarthSky (2022). Webb set to arrive at its final destination, L2. https://earthsky.org/space/james-webb-space-telescope-30-days-of-terror/.

Forbes Technology Council (2016). The benefits of using agile software development. https://www.forbes.com/sites/forbestechcouncil/2016/05/09/the-benefits-of-using-agile-software-development/?sh=721e2820b0f8.

Fowler, B. (2022). Average data breach costs hit a record $4.4 million, report says. https://www.cnet.com/tech/services-and-software/average-data-breach-costs-hit-a-record-4-4-million-report-says/.

Freund, J., and Jones, J. (2015). *Measuring and Managing Information Risk: A FAIR Approach*. Elsevier BH, Amsterdam.

Friedman, T. L. (2005). *The World is Flat: A Brief History of the Twenty-first Century*. Picador / Farrar, Straus and Giroux, New York.

Groysberg, B., Lee, J., Price, J., and Cheng, J. Y.-J. (2018). The leader's guide to corporate culture. *Harvard Business Review* (January–February). https://hbr.org/2018/01/the-leaders-guide-to-corporate-culture.

Heinlein, R. A. (1961). *Stranger in a Strange Land*. G.P. Putnam's Sons, New York.

ISO (2013). ISO/IEC 27001:2013: Information technology – Security techniques – Information security management systems – Requirements. https://www.iso.org/standard/54534.html.

Kim, D. (n.d.). Behavior over time diagrams: Seeing dynamic interrelationships. The Systems Thinker. https://thesystemsthinker.com/behavior-over-time-diagrams-seeing-dynamic-interrelationships/.

Kim, D. H. (1992). *Systems Archetypes I: Diagnosing Systemic Issues and Designing High-Leverage Interventions*. Pegasus Communications, Waltham, Massachusetts. https://thesystemsthinker.com/wp-content/uploads/2016/03/Systems-Archetypes-I-TRSA01_pk.pdf.

Kotter, J. P. (1995). Leading change: Why transformation efforts fail. *Harvard Business Review* (May–June). https://hbr.org/1995/05/leading-change-why-transformation-efforts-fail-2.

Kotter, J. P. (2012). *Leading Change*. Harvard Business Review Press, Boston, Massachusetts.

Lannon, C. (2018). Causal loop construction: the basics. The Systems Thinker. https://thesystemsthinker.com/causal-loop-construction-the-basics/.

Learning for Sustainability (n.d.). Systems thinking. Accessed Jul. 25, 2022. https://learningforsustainability.net/systems-thinking/.

Lungu, P. E. (2014). Organized chaos: The natural law of order. *HuffPost*. https://www.huffpost.com/entry/organized-chaos-the-natur_b_6282156.

Mandic, V., Basili, V., Oivo, M., Harjumaa, L., and Markkula, J. (2010). Utilizing GQM+Strategies for an organization-wide earned value analysis. University of Oulu, Finland; Fraunhofer Center for Experimental Software Engineering, Maryland. https://www.cs.umd.edu/users/basili/publications/proceedings/P131.pdf.

Meadows, D. H. (1997). Places to intervene in a system. Conservation Gateway (originally in *Whole Earth*, Winter 1997). https://www.conservationgateway.org/ConservationPlanning/cbd/guidance-document/key-advances/Documents/Meadows_Places_to_Intervene.pdf.

Merriam-Webster (n.d.-a). Assurance. Accessed Aug. 5, 2022. https://www.merriam-webster.com/dictionary/assurance.

Merriam-Webster (n.d.-b). Chaos. Accessed Jul. 28, 2022. https://www.merriam-webster.com/dictionary/chaos.

Merriam-Webster (n.d.-c). Frame of reference. Accessed Aug. 6, 2022. https://www.merriam-webster.com/dictionary/frame%20of%20reference.

Merriam-Webster (n.d.-d). Governance. Accessed Aug. 9, 2022. https://www.merriam-webster.com/dictionary/governance.

Merriam-Webster (n.d.-e). Resilience. Accessed Jul. 28, 2022. https://www.merriam-webster.com/dictionary/resilience.

Michels, D. and Murphy, K. (2021). How good is your company at change? *Harvard Business Review* (July–August). https://hbr.org/2021/07/how-good-is-your-company-at-change.

MITRE ATT&CK (n.d.-a). Getting started. Accessed Jul. 25, 2022. https://attack.mitre.org/resources/getting-started/.

MITRE ATT&CK (n.d.-b). Home page. Accessed Jul. 25, 2022. https://attack.mitre.org/.

Moskowitz, D. and Nichols, D. M. (2022). *Fundamentals of Adopting the NIST Cybersecurity Framework*. TSO, London.

Nadella, S. (2017). *Hit Refresh: The Quest to Rediscover Microsoft's Soul and Imagine a Better Future for Everyone*. HarperBusiness, New York.

NIST (2016). Guide for cybersecurity event recovery (NIST Special Publication 800-184). https://nvlpubs.nist.gov/nistpubs/SpecialPublications/NIST.SP.800-184.pdf.

NIST (2018). Framework for improving critical infrastructure cybersecurity. https://nvlpubs.nist.gov/nistpubs/CSWP/NIST.CSWP.04162018.pdf.

NIST (2020). Security and privacy controls for information systems and organizations (NIST Special Publication 800-53, Revision 5). https://csrc.nist.gov/publications/detail/sp/800-53/rev-5/final.

NIST (2021). Developing cyber-resilient systems: A systems security engineering approach (NIST Special Publication 800-160, Volume 2, Revision 1). https://nvlpubs.nist.gov/nistpubs/SpecialPublications/NIST.SP.800-160v2r1.pdf.

NIST (n.d.). NIST SP 800-53, Revision 5: Control mappings to ISO/IEC 27001. https://csrc.nist.gov/CSRC/media/Publications/sp/800-53/rev-5/final/documents/sp800-53r5-to-iso-27001-mapping.docx (note this is an automatic download).

North Carolina State University (2022). Report reveals risk management processes in U.S. organizations are not keeping pace with growing risks. https://poole.ncsu.edu/thought-leadership/article/report-reveals-risk-management-processes-in-u-s-organizations-are-not-keeping-pace-with-growing-risks/.

O'Neill, P. H. (2022). Inside the plan to fix America's never-ending cybersecurity failures. *MIT Technology Review*. https://www.technologyreview.com/2022/03/18/1047395/inside-the-plan-to-fix-americas-never-ending-cybersecurity-failures/.

Peters, T. (1988). *Thriving on Chaos: Handbook for a Management Revolution*. Harper Perennial, New York.

Pirsig, R. M. (1974). *Zen and the Art of Motorcycle Maintenance*. William Morrow, New York.

Readingraphics (n.d.). Understanding systems thinking – the beer game. Accessed Jul. 26, 2022. https://readingraphics.com/understanding-systems-thinking-the-beer-game/.

Senge, P. M. (1990). *The Fifth Discipline: The Art and Practice of the Learning Organization*. Doubleday Business, New York.

Smith, D. W., Stahler, D. R., Metz, M. C., Cassidy, K. A., Stahler, E. E., Almberg, E. S., and McIntyre, R. (2016). Wolf restoration in Yellowstone: Reintroduction to recovery. *Yellowstone Science* 24(1): 5–11.

US Department of Energy (2022). Cybersecurity Capability Maturity Model (C2M2), Version 2.1. https://c2m2.doe.gov/C2M2%20Version%202.1%20June%202022.pdf.

Vinney, C. (2019). Likert scale: What is it and how to use it? ThoughtCo. https://www.thoughtco.com/likert-scale-4685788

Westrum, R. (2004). A typology of organisational cultures. *Quality and Safety in Health Care* 13(Suppl II): ii22–ii27. https://www.ncbi.nlm.nih.gov/pmc/articles/PMC1765804/pdf/v013p0ii22.pdf.

Wikipedia (2021a). Beer distribution game. Last modified Nov. 29, 2021. https://en.wikipedia.org/wiki/Beer_distribution_game.

Wikipedia (2021b). Misuse case. Last modified Feb. 7, 2021. https://en.wikipedia.org/wiki/Misuse_case.

Wikipedia (2022a). All models are wrong. Last modified Jun. 7, 2022. https://en.wikipedia.org/wiki/All_models_are_wrong.

Wikipedia (2022b). Analysis. Last modified May 31, 2022. https://en.wikipedia.org/wiki/Analysis.

Wikipedia (2022c). Bullwhip effect. Last modified Jul. 14, 2022. https://en.wikipedia.org/wiki/Bullwhip_effect.

Wikipedia (2022d). Causal loop. Last modified Mar. 24, 2022. https://en.wikipedia.org/wiki/Causal_loop.

Wikipedia (2022e). Complex adaptive system. Last modified Jul. 26, 2022. https://en.wikipedia.org/wiki/Complex_adaptive_system.

Wikipedia (2022f). Configuration management. Last modified May 12, 2022. https://en.wikipedia.org/wiki/Configuration_management.

Wikipedia (2022g). Death march (project management). Last modified Jun. 8, 2022. https://en.wikipedia.org/wiki/Death_march_(project_management).

Wikipedia (2022h). Likert scale. Last modified Jul. 24, 2022. https://en.wikipedia.org/wiki/Likert_scale.

Wikipedia (2022i). MoSCoW method. Last modified Jun. 6, 2022. https://en.wikipedia.org/wiki/MoSCoW_method.

Wikipedia (2022j). Responsibility assignment matrix. Last modified Aug. 2, 2022. https://en.wikipedia.org/wiki/Responsibility_assignment_matrix.

Wikipedia (2022k). Sarbanes–Oxley Act. Last modified Jul. 13, 2022. https://en.wikipedia.org/wiki/Sarbanes%E2%80%93Oxley_Act.

Wikipedia (2022l). Self-organization. Last modified Jul. 22, 2022. https://en.wikipedia.org/wiki/Self-organization.

Wikipedia (2022m). Stock and flow. Last modified May 24, 2022. https://en.wikipedia.org/wiki/Stock_and_flow.

Wikipedia (2022n). Strategy. Last modified Jul. 21, 2022. https://en.wikipedia.org/wiki/Strategy.

Wikipedia (2022o). System dynamics. Last modified Jan. 22, 2022. https://en.wikipedia.org/wiki/System_dynamics.

Wikipedia (2022p). The Day the Universe Changed. Last modified Jun. 18, 2022. https://en.wikipedia.org/wiki/The_Day_the_Universe_Changed.

Wikipedia (2022q). Tracing paper. Last modified Apr. 21, 2022. https://en.wikipedia.org/wiki/Tracing_paper.

Wikipedia (2022r). Use case. Last modified Jun. 18, 2022. https://en.wikipedia.org/wiki/Use_case.

Wilkinson, P., and Schilt, J. (2008). *ABC of ICT: An Introduction to the Attitude, Behavior and Culture of ICT.* Van Haren Publishing, Zaltbommel, Netherlands.

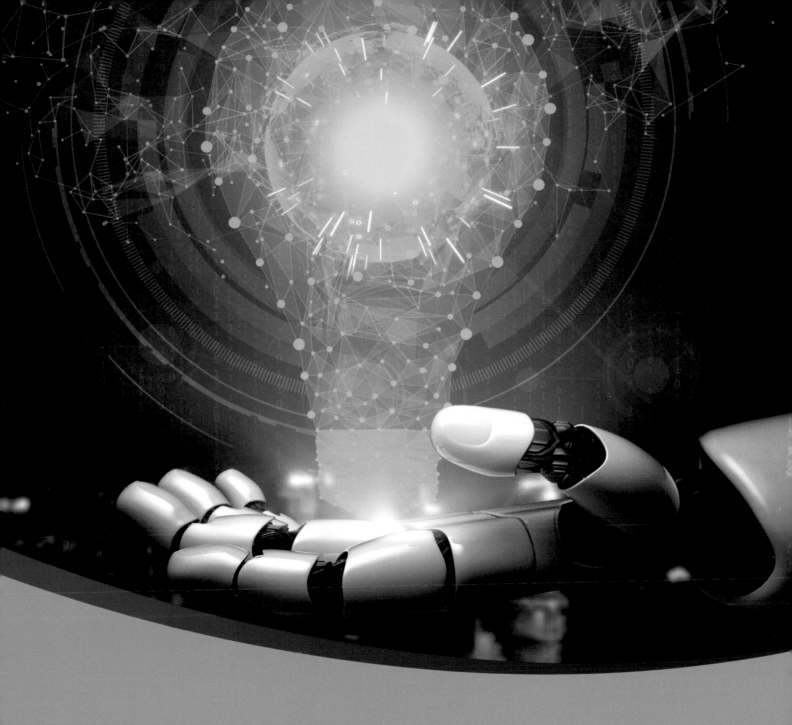

Index

Index

A Practitioner's Guide to Adapting the NIST Cybersecurity Framework is the second volume in the Create, Protect, and Deliver Digital Business Value series.

This publication provides practitioners with detailed guidance on creating a NIST Cybersecurity Framework risk management program using NIST Special Publication 800-53, the DVMS Institute's CPD Model, and existing digital business systems. The outcome is a cyber risk management program and culture fit for use, auditable for purpose, and aligned with global cybersecurity frameworks, standards, and regulations.

The key takeaway from this book is that securing digital business value is something every employee is responsible for doing every day. Cybersecurity is an intrinsic aspect of securing that value and must be factored into an organization's digital strategy and culture.

A culture of cybersecurity starts at the top of an organization and is translated into strategic policies and training programs which are designed to embed that culture across the whole enterprise and its supply chain.

ISBN 978-0-11-709395-9

9 780117 093959

a Williams Lea company

www.tso.co.uk